Dare to Change

Your Job and Your Life

Revised Edition

Carole Kan

JIST Works, Inc.

Dare to Change Your Job and Your Life
Second Edition
Copyright © 1987, 1991, 1996, Carole Kanchier

Published by JIST Works, Inc.
720 N. Park Aveune
Indianapolis, IN 46202-3431
Phone **317-264-3720**   Fax **317-264-3709**
E-mail JISTWorks@aol.com

Cover Design: Laura Nikiel, LGN Graphics

Library of Congress Cataloging-in-Publication Data

Kanchier, Carole,

    Dare to change your job and your life / Carole Kanchier.
— Rev. ed., 2nd ed.
      p.   cm.
    ISBN 1-56370-224-X
    1. Career changes. 2. Career development. I. Title.
HF5384.K35 1995
650. 14—dc20   95-50899
                                            CIP

00 99 98 97 96   2 3 4 5 6 7 8 9

Printed in the United States of America

Errors and Omissions: We have been careful to provide accurate information in this book but it is possible that errors and omissions have been introduced. Please consider this in making any career plans or other important decisions. Trust your own judgement above all else and in all things.

ISBN 1-56370-224-X

To my father

*Whose love, support, and encouragement
helped me to be myself*

Acknowledgments

I would like to express my deepest appreciation to the following individuals:

The Questers, who willingly gave their time and candidly shared their experiences. Although their names and, in a few cases some particulars, have been disguised to maintain their confidentiality, their stories have a factual basis.

The numerous students, clients, and individuals who participated in my research and taught me a great deal about adult and career development and offered valuable feedback on the questionnaires.

My friends and colleagues who took the time to read the entire manuscript and offered constructive suggestions and needed encouragement: Drs. Marnie Finstad, David Tiedeman, and Norman Feingold, as well as Kathleen Samphire, Sonja Eisler, Jean Yarwood, Sandra Mallett, Victoria Foster, and Hazel Sangster. Many other colleagues also shared information or assisted in numerous ways: Drs. Wally Unruh, John Krumboltz, Lorne Seaman, and Roman Odwazny, and Doug Jordan and Murray Axsmith Western Ltd.

Preface: Planning for Change

*I*f you are wondering what to do with the rest of your life because you are dissatisfied or bored with your job, reentering the work force, contemplating a career change, or unemployed, this book is for you. A major shift in the direction of your career creates important gains and losses. It forces you to step out of the well-worn groove of your life and confront yourself in very basic ways. It offers you the chance for either an expanded or diminished sense of self, growth or stagnation, hope or despair. *Dare to Change Your Job and Your Life* was written so that I could share my research and experience on the career quest with you.

A career really is a quest. As I look back over my life, I think my quest started when I was a teenager. As the physical and emotional tumults of adolescence raged on, I tried to make sense of who I was and what I wanted to do with my life. As the options floated in and out of my consciousness, I realized that what I wanted most was to enjoy every day to the utmost. Since a great part of my day would be devoted to work, I wanted to find a satisfying and rewarding career. I wanted to be involved, challenged, autonomous, and have a sense of meaning and purpose in my work. I wanted to thoroughly enjoy my work and life. I graduated from college and struck out into the world of work with high hopes. There, I made a discovery: When I no longer felt enthusiastic about a job, I felt lifeless and dull. My satisfaction and productivity nosedived. I left several jobs, never lasting more than seven years before my restless spirit guided me to another. Why did I, unlike my colleagues and friends, quit positions that I had initially loved and, according to society's yardstick, had been successful at? Was it because my life lacked balance? No matter how involved I became in hobbies and relationships, the old ache returned—and the jobs changed.

Then I began my doctoral research. Slowly the answers came. As I hunted through volume after volume of theory and research into developmental, personality, vocational, counseling, and industrial psychology, I began to find myself. Journeying across the country, I sought out the life stories of male and female executives to see how and why they made career changes. I was beginning to understand my own feelings and motivations better. Since then, I have conducted research on many other aspects of career and adult development as well as voluntary and involuntary career change and, as teacher, counselor, and psychologist, have worked with adults from many different occupations and educational backgrounds. The conclusions, based on research conducted with more than 5,000 adults, representing varied ages, occupations, and educational backgrounds, illustrate main themes that run through people's lives. They are presented in this book.

The life stories described here will give you a clearer picture of the contemporary career from the viewpoints of different branches of psychology. You will learn how your career development is intricately connected with your personality development and the transitions in other components of your life. You will discover the complex psychological dynamics that come into play when you dislike your work and are considering changing jobs. If you lost your job as a result of a plant closure, merger, downsizing, or reorganization, you will be encouraged to learn that you can turn this crisis into an opportunity for continuing growth and revitalization.

The questionnaires will allow you to examine your own personality and life situation. They will help you determine how satisfied you are with your career and life, how well you are coping with both, and whether you are a Quester—the new breed of creative risk taker.

The Questers' stories will teach you the process for making risky decisions so that you can sidestep some of the ruts and potholes they encountered when you are ready to make important changes in your life. Most importantly, *Dare to Change Your Job and Your Life* doesn't encourage you to take risks for which you are not ready or don't really need.

Trying to stop change is one of the riskiest steps you can take today. Your life—your growth and career development—is fueled by the dynamics of change. The energy you spend fighting to keep the status quo is energy that can be better used understanding the causes and nature of the changes occurring around you. The ability to take planned risks is just what's needed to manage your career in today's dynamic world. Without risk, there is no growth, no vitality, no true joy.

The ideas you will encounter in this book are not new. Many popular and informative books on career and adult development are only as far as your nearest library or bookstore. But none provide a complete picture of the contemporary career. Most explore career planning and job search. They look at how to put together the right resume, dress for success, or survive an interview. Little is said about emotions. None describe career growth and development throughout the life cycle. They can't provide a thorough understanding of the contemporary career. They don't explain what makes you like or dislike your job or show how these feelings are related to your personality development and your life's many transition periods. Nor do they describe the intricate dynamics of making risky decisions which come into play when you change jobs.

As you journey through the book—and through your life—do not hold back because of concerns about the economy or negative statements about the availability of jobs in your field. Whether the country is in an economic explosion or recession or whether you want to work in a broad or narrow field, attractive jobs *are* available. They are created by the mobility of the workforce—the deaths, retirements, and promotions of current job holders—and the growth of thriving companies. Regardless of prevailing economic conditions, good positions are out there. Somewhere, a company exists that can use your talents and experience and will pay you well for them. Finding that ideal job or becoming successfully self-employed is easier than you think.

Keep your options open. Focus on the opportunities available. By following the examples of the self-reliant Questers, who thrive on challenge and growth and turn crises into opportunities, you will gain the strength to take an active stance in your own career development. *Dare to Change Your Job and Your Life* will teach you to become the manager of your own life, in charge of your own destiny. You will have the knowledge and the courage to improve the quality of your life and work and make your innermost dreams come true. You will have the power to achieve a more meaningful, satisfying, and productive life in a changing, challenging, and exciting world.

Contents

Questers and the Contemporary Career

ould you know a Quester if you met one? Are you one? Could you become one? Who are Questers, anyway?

The answer comes first through jobs. Questers think of their work differently from most people. Like many of us, Questers will probably spend a third to half of their adult lives working, thinking about their work or commuting there. But, unlike most, at crucial points throughout their careers, they set off on a quest to find the missing links in their lives. Their life stories start out a lot like everyone's until one day when they begin a personal journey of discovery to find a better life and a better career. You, too, can take this journey.

Quester Qualities

- ❖ Self-reliant
- ❖ Flexible, resilient
- ❖ Sense of purpose
- ❖ Risk taker
- ❖ Androgynous
- ❖ Able to achieve intimacy
- ❖ Value internal rewards such as personal growth, autonomy, challenge, and achievement over external rewards such as prestige, security, and money
- ❖ Periodically assess values and goals
- ❖ Learn from experience
- ❖ Turn crises into opportunities
- ❖ Listen to feelings and other intuitive cues as well as intellect
- ❖ Confident
- ❖ Positive attitude
- ❖ Enjoy job and lifestyle
- ❖ Involved in work
- ❖ Committed to learning
- ❖ Energetic
- ❖ Self-aware

Questers are the new breed. They prevail during uncertain times by keeping their options open. Questers are not perfect. But, in varying degrees, they develop qualities most nonQuesters would envy.

Questers tend to be complex, individualistic, flexible, autonomous, and open to risk. They may have the best of male and female strengths. They tend to possess a high level of self-confidence and have a sense of purpose and meaning in their lives. Many hunger for more responsibility and more vital work, for tasks worthy of their talents and skills. They question authority and often desire socially responsible work. They tend to have a high need for job involvement and for other vital work rewards: challenge, self-fulfillment, a sense of achievement, and opportunity for growth. They take criticism and failure well, viewing defeat as a useful experience from which to grow. Their coping devices can include hard work, prayer, support from friends or spouses—and a sense of humor. When they experience life crises, such as divorce, the death of a relative or close friend, job loss or dissatisfaction, marriage or birth, they undergo intense critical self-analysis. Transition periods, like the age-thirty or the mid-life transitions, are times for taking another look into the mirror to find if they like what they see.

For many Questers, economic security and status come second to intrinsic satisfactions and the desire to have alternatives.

Questers can be found in a wide range of occupations, from law, management, education, the civil service, accounting and engineering, to construction, medicine, and health. They may change their occupations or status several times throughout their careers, sacrificing financial rewards and status for self-expression.

For many Questers, economic security and status come second to intrinsic satisfactions and the desire to have alternatives. They value flexibility and reshape their identities through self-determined career choices. They have a playful, task-centered approach to problem solving. They measure success by internal standards and value self-respect more than peer respect. Questers tend to be free from conventional restraints. They are independent and innovative spirits with a rich supply of inner resources. They strive to maintain some balance between work, love, and leisure. They love a challenge.

Questers tend to have a cheerful, optimistic outlook. Cheated or disappointed in life? Hardly ever! Going to work is usually a joy. Few are ever bored (unless they stay at one job too long). Questers generally arise with a smile, ready to meet the challenges before them.

Surely, Questers must be extraordinary, glamorous people. Not so. They are just ordinary individuals who faced career problems common to all. But they have learned to do something about their problems—to take control.

You probably know some Questers. They have been around in every age. Organizational behaviorist Douglas Hall called Questers "protean" persons. Searching for self-fulfillment through self-determined career choices, they tend to continuously reformulate their identities. Motivated by freedom, growth, achievement, job involvement, and job satisfaction, they measure success internally. They are unlike the Traditionalists who tend to be passively committed to an organizational career and who value advancement, power, position, salary, job satisfaction, and respect and esteem from others. The mobility of Traditionalists is low and their adaptability tied to organization-related flexibility and survival.

Many Traditionalists are concerned about how their careers measure up with the approved timetables for their professions. Failure to stay on track may leave a number of Traditionalists feeling panicky. Conforming rigidly to a single, narrow career track, they feel that they must travel systematically from section head to supervisor, to manager, to executive; from law clerk to junior, then senior, partner. Recognition, they hope, comes to those who are faithful, attentive, and loyal.

Although security is temporarily achieved, their future options are severely limited. The desire for security has its cost. Traditionalists worry too much about doing the right thing. They choose careers that conform to what is expected of them.

Self-seekers tend to be the opposite. Motivated by desire for personal fulfillment, Self-seekers refuse to work as hard as their parents and contemporaries. They want the perfectly balanced life with time for love, leisure, family, and personal expression. Their happiness formula is giving and getting love. Ambition and leadership are shunned in their search for the comfortable life. They want gratification now and responsibility later. These are the Self-seekers' rights: to work less and be self-fulfilled while enjoying life's genteel comforts.

Self-seekers have selected a lifestyle that suits them. They willingly pass up promotions or difficult business challenges that might threaten their comfortable lives. While satisfying work is important, Self-seekers aren't prepared to sacrifice for their careers or to have their jobs dominate their lives. Their greatest fears are not having enough money or being trapped by the constant pursuit of money. This is their dilemma. To pursue freedom at the sacrifice of a comfortable life is almost unthinkable.

You can become more purposeful, confident, loving, self reliant, and willing to risk.

Questers can be distinguished from Traditionalists and Self-seekers by their willingness to take control of their careers. Which are you? Traditionalist, Self-seeker, or Quester?

You probably are more like one than the others, but you may share traits from all three. Fortunately, you can be whichever you desire. Your personality is far from frozen. You can create and recreate it every day. You can become more purposeful, confident, loving, self-reliant, and willing to risk. Yes, researchers such as James Cattell, Hans Eysenck, Arnold Buss, and Robert Plomin have shown that certain aspects of personality, such as sociability and energy levels, are genetically based. But those, too, can be changed.

To achieve the transformations you want, look to the Questers.

Carl is an achiever, a winner, the kind of guy who thought life was a warm sea breeze. He is husky and handsome, with clear blue eyes. Carl grew up in an orphanage but, through hard work, won a scholarship to an Ivy League college. He taught for a while, then went on to graduate school for a master's degree in educational psychology. Eventually, he found himself in a government department where he rose with relative ease through several offices. But something was wrong.

"On paper I had it all," he explains. "Maybe more than I thought I should have had—a prestigious, secure, and well-paying job; a pretty wife and two kids; a house in the sub-urbs; club memberships; and a respectable backhand. But I had a persistent and nagging feeling that life wasn't working. It wasn't adding up. Something was missing. I should have talked to someone about it, but the last thing I wanted to show was my vulnerability. Search as I might, I seemed able to deal only with the symptoms. I got myself a raise, cut down on my drinking. I never looked at the big tapestry—what I really wanted—because that was too scary and, be-sides, didn't I already have the American dream?"

Then Carl started thinking of changing jobs. No single event started the process (that's rarely the case). Instead, a series of small jolts forced him out of his velvet-lined rut. First, he learned his wife was having an affair. What shocked him most was that he wasn't angry. He just didn't care. Soon they were on the road to divorce, and Carl was looking at life from a new angle. If his marriage had been a mistake, maybe his career was, too. In fact, marriage and career had something in common. He had gone into both because people expected him to. But now he began to question whether he should be devoting his energy to living up to other people's expecta-tions. He had traded off self-fulfillment and meaning for security. Not long after that, Carl quit his job. He stepped into the void. He had no idea what he was going to do.

Carl was a little frightened when he took that first step. He needed someone to talk to.

He found that person in the wife of a friend. "The first woman other than my wife I'd ever really confided in." His "overdone macho" had prevented him from revealing his vulnerability to any woman, Carl says now.

Carl began his search for a new job with a painful but neces-sary transition. He moved from his comfortable home to a bare room in a flat borrowed from a friend. He had a bed, a light bulb, and a stereo system. He missed his house and his children and felt especially guilty because, as an orphan himself, he'd vowed never to leave his children. For the first time in his adult life, he allowed himself to cry. Yet, despite his loneliness and guilt, Carl also felt what he calls "the exhilaration of trusting myself for the first time."

He now feels he was unhappier before he made the break than during the transition itself. "Earlier, I was using up more energy just justifying a life that wasn't working," he says. "But after the break, I was confronting myself for the first time. The fear and loneliness didn't begin to offset the feeling of integrity I had. The best way to describe it is to say that it was wonderfully terrifying."

Carl survived because he made the right decision. After leaving Washington, he started a management consulting firm in an eastern city. Carl and his ex-wife became friends again. These days, his young son lives with him. His daughter lives with her mother. He thinks that switching jobs made his divorce less bitter than it might have been. "I would have been unhappy with myself and have taken it out on others," he admits.

Evelynne understands what Carl went through. An attractive, petite woman with large, expressive brown eyes and dark brown hair, she looks 15 years younger than her 45 years. But Evelynne's early life in a large eastern city was far from happy. She was the second daughter in a family whose social standing never quite compared to their neighbors'. Her school years were tough. Treated shabbily by many of the "snobs," she determined to excel at everything she did. After high school, Evelynne joined a large clothing manufacturer as a secretary and a model. At 21, she married an athlete and continued working for several years until the birth of their first child. She had a second child and, with two babies at home, found time to take a part-time job writing fashion and food articles for a local newspaper. But as time went on, boredom set in. Evelynne turned 30 as her youngest entered kindergarten. Joining the newspaper full-time now, she soon graduated to a daily column. She had been on the job just over three years when a large department store asked her to manage an exclusive women's clothing department. The timing was perfect. Feeling stale and bored with her column, she eagerly accepted the new position. It proved to be challenging and full of variety. She was given enough freedom to develop a department, about which she was justifiably proud.

Evelynne's 38th birthday changed all that. Her marriage began to crumble and her freedom at work was drastically reduced by new management policies. With much of the decision making taken from her, the quality of her department's merchandise declined. After three years of soul searching, at 41, Evelynne decided to separate from her husband, leave the department store, and open her own boutique. Her parental responsibilities were decreasing as both her children entered their late teens and became increasingly independent.

Evelynne's first step was to thoroughly investigate the banks in her city. Then, preparing a well-researched proposal, she presented it to one of the city's more liberal bank managers. Her boutique took off. And Evelynne, then 45, began divorce proceedings as she contemplated marriage to a man she had known for the last five years. She feels her 50th birthday will bring new business projects. She looks to the future with excitement.

Kathy is looking forward to the future now, too. While she already had a B.A., what she didn't have was a clear career goal. Pretty, a good athlete, and with many interests and abilities, Kathy worked at a series of jobs until, at 22, she went to a state employment agency for career counseling. That led to a one-year managerial training program with a large insurance firm. Kathy enjoyed her training. The job seemed challenging enough. But within four years, her feelings had changed. Bored and suffering from extreme mood swings, she realized that she needed, even craved, challenge. Her father's death forced Kathy to take another look at her life. Again, she went for career counseling. This time she decided to leave her job, return to school, and retrain for another occupation—law. Three years passed from the onset of her dissatisfaction before Kathy decided on a new course of action. Then, at 31, after seven years in insurance, she embarked on an entirely new occupation and lifestyle. Today, she is excited about her new work in the legal field.

Luke, like Kathy, is also making a new start. For 30 years, Luke worked his way up from mechanic to middle manager for a trucking firm. Then, at 52, he bought a hardware store in a town 70 miles from the western city where he had lived his whole life. Was the decision spur-of-the-moment? No. "I planned my getaway. I saved my money and explored the communities within 100 miles of my hometown. I liked fixing things and the hardware business will let me expand the store into a repair shop later, if I feel like it."

Luke is talking like a Quester. He feels like one, too. This is how he describes his job now: "It provides me with a sense of accomplishment, the opportunity to use my skills, and the feeling that I have some control over my life. I now have more energy left over at the end of the day to do other things. I feel rather peaceful and content."

Verlynne has a different story to tell. As a 38-year-old home-maker, who enjoyed writing poetry and developing games, Verlynne felt pressured by peers to return to school to prepare for a job outside the home. It seemed to be the thing to do! So she enrolled in a journalism program at a local junior college with the idea that she would pursue a journalism career. She hated it and cried herself to sleep many evenings. But she stayed with it for a year because she wanted to show others that she could make and keep a commitment. Verlynne's husband, who supported her in all her ventures, suggested she seek professional counseling. By the third session, Verlynne realized that her real passion was to continue her creative pursuits at home. One of her most recent innovations, a doll that you can tell your problems to, is selling well at local stores.

Like these Questers, you, too, can journey along similar paths to take charge of your life and career. Career, family, relationships, and leisure will cross and intersect, clash and complement. The paths you choose will depend on your personality, goals, and life situation. To undertand how you can control the direction of your life and make well-informed choices, you need to understand your place in the modern work world.

Contemporary Life

Career as Movement

Career is the path you carve out for yourself. It also involves a continuing quest for a better fit between who you are and what you do. Your occupation is based on skills earned through education or training. But while you may have several occupations or several positions within an occupation during the course of your life, you will have only one career

To be fulfilled, you need a position that is compatible with many aspects of your personality.

because you have only one life. Your career is made up of a series of occupations or positions—yet, it is more. Your career is a lifelong process.

Like an obstacle course in which you climb, stretch, and swing to develop your muscles, your career spiral continues on—widening, everchanging, mutable, dynamic, ascending, expansive—throughout your life. So it may be that one occupation satisfies just one facet of your personality. Each stop suggests more challenges ahead. Moving on restlessly, using each job as an opportunity to grow, you plot your next move. What matters is not promotion on your job but advancement of your whole person. To be fulfilled, you need a position that is compatible with many aspects of your personality.

Howard discovered the difference when he reached 32. Throughout high school, Howard dreamed of becoming an executive with a large manufacturing company. He had worked part-time for the firm during high school and was excited about becoming a manager. It seemed prestigious. At 23, he was well on his way to middle management. During the first six years, Howard enjoyed his work. His first two supervisors were "fine people, supportive and helpful." But the next six years brought different supervisors and changing company policies. Howard's position became meaningless. The work was "monotonous" and the atmosphere "oppressive." The money and the prestige no longer seemed to matter.

Whatever his difficulties at work, Howard's marriage was in good shape and he enjoyed playing in a local band. As he became friendly with two of the band members, both policemen, they told him of the pros and cons of police work. He learned more by participating in several volunteer police programs. Then, just after his 31st birthday, his mother became unexpectedly ill and died. For Howard, this was a turning point. He realized that life is too short. If he was going to change, it would have to be now.

So, at 32, he decided to enter the police training program. He had discussed his disillusionment with his wife, and now found her willing to take a part-time job to help pay the bills. Today, Howard is a police captain. He has found a career that will let him grow, one that will provide meaning, variety, and an outlet for his desire to help others.

What happened to Howard? Like many, he simply outgrew his career. His needs, values, and priorities all shifted. He was no longer so interested in status. Money meant less to him. The decision to change jobs had not come easily; it was agonizing and took time. Moreover, Howard and his family had to give up many comforts. But, today, Howard is confident his decision was right. So is his family. His career grew and so did he.

Career as Job-Person Fit

Imagine the growth and development of your career as a spiral. If you could draw it, it would look like a track moving around a continuous curve toward a central point. That central point is you. You are the center of gravity and balance for your career spiral. If you look closely at the central point in your spiral, you will see a subtle, wonderful portrait of yourself. This portrait captures everything about you. It is a portrait of you as a whole person.

From this whole person, your energy radiates—your temperament, needs, values, interests, skills, aptitudes, and goals. Like a dynamo that fuels your spiral, your energy feeds into your career track. Building a successful career relies on evaluating the harmony among your portrait, your job satisfaction, and your goals.

Like your career, your personal characteristics and goals will change as you grow. As your portrait changes, so will the results of your evaluation.

Let's take a look at *Al's* career to see how it developed and changed over the years. Al was born and raised in a Midwestern town. After high school, he entered a computer science program at a nearby university because, in his words, "computers was the field to be in . . . the opportunities for employment and making good money were excellent." At 23, Al graduated with a master's in computer science, got married, and accepted a position as a systems analyst with a large firm 1,300 miles from his boyhood home.

At first, Al enjoyed his work. He felt it gave him challenge and autonomy. As his star continued to rise, he and his wife had their first child. But, seven years later, as he neared his 30th birthday, Al began to feel as if something, some sense of purpose or meaning, was missing. For three years, he searched his soul. Then Al left his job and returned with his family to the Midwestern town where he was raised. Using some of his savings to realize a lifelong dream, he bought a farm. Now he and his wife are devoted farmers. They enjoy their lifestyle and their work.

Al changed because his needs and values changed. But why and how? As in Howard's case, the changes Al made were caused by many different events. Al's job had lost its challenge. He felt stifled. The birth of his child and the joy of becoming a parent helped him realize that his family really was more important than his career. Al was also beginning to realize that time was passing. He was anxious to try something new—his longtime dream of becoming a farmer. The feelings and thoughts Al experienced were part of his age-thirty transition, a time of questioning and evaluating earlier decisions. He had to choose between either deepening or abandoning his earlier commitments.

Al abandoned them. But what if, at the very moment that Al looked into his life—his portrait—he had suddenly received a fabulous offer: a promotion to senior analyst and a fantastic raise? If Al had accepted, what would have happened to his career spiral? Would it have shot forward and upward? Unfortunately, no. It would have remained precisely where it was, in a state of suspended animation. Why? Because Al's development as a human being, as a whole person, would have come to a grinding halt.

Al's glance into the mirror of his dreams at 30 helped him to change. By moving back to a small town and buying a farm, Al created harmony between his portrait and the energy it was radiating for his career track. When he changed occupations, his career track leapt forward because Al, as a whole person, had advanced.

Marion's career also developed and changed over the years. Marion worked as a microbiology researcher for eight years while her husband went to medical school. Finally, she took time off to raise their two children. She filled her spare hours with volunteer work. Then, at 39, Marion made a decision that would radically change her life. "I wanted something to do—not just a job to earn grocery money—something that would excite me. But like most women, I had the feeling that I didn't have the right to please myself. After a great deal of thought, I decided what I really wanted to do was go back to college and get a master's degree in counseling psychology. So I did.

"At first, I was terrified. What if I failed? How could I compete with young people? Who would organize my family?" Today, Marion is a counselor at a women's resource center on the West Coast. She spends her time counseling women who are asking the same questions she once did. "I understand exactly where these women are because I was there myself. Like most women, they're asking a very important question: 'What should I do with the rest of my life?'"

Like Al, Marion decided what to do with her life by checking her image in the mirror. In her early twenties, she saw a young woman in a white lab coat. In real life, she worked hard for eight years to fit that image. When Marion looked at her portrait again, in her late twenties, she saw a young mother. She had changed and so had her life situation. After eight years as a lab researcher, she was getting bored. Her husband was now practicing medicine and could support them both. The biological clock was ticking. If Marion wanted children, the time was now. So Marion fused her portrait and her career by taking time out to have and raise two children.

The youngsters kept her busy for many years. But nine years later, when she looked into her portrait again, the image was blurred. Marion was confused. The children were in school and her husband was busily engaged in his career. Marion knew she wanted to go back to work, but could she and should she? All of her upbringing told her that a good wife and mother should stay home to cater to her family's needs. Marion didn't want to go back to research. That job no longer suited her. Nor did being a full-time homemaker. Marion's interests, needs, and values had changed. She wanted a job that suited her new personality. But what? Marion was perplexed. It took long deliberation, talks with her family, and career counseling before Marion concluded that what she really wanted to do was to become a counselor.

Now when Marion looks into her portrait, she sees a career woman. The picture is clear. Marion created harmony between her portrait and herself by moving forward when she became dissatisfied with her life. Making changes wasn't easy. But she did it.

Career as Purpose

Candice's purpose is helping others. She found this out by accident when, at 18, she worked as a salesclerk in a Midwestern city bakery. Candice said she really enjoyed helping the customers decide which bakery products they needed. After taking time out to raise two children, Candice, who completed grade six in Belgium, returned to work part-time as a salesclerk in a cosmetics shop because she liked to help customers enhance their appearance. Candice gained valuable experience and knowledge in this trade by attending seminars, workshops, and conferences, and reading. She saved her money and opened one, a second, and then a third cosmetics shop. Candice says, "I've always wanted to help people . . . . And despite all the frustration and debt I've experienced, I love my work. It makes me feel excited and gives meaning to what I do."

The women who work for Candice admire her as a boss because she cares about each one of them as individuals, and she listens to their private as well as work-related concerns. Candice's customers always return to her shop and bring new customers because her staff are extremely knowledgeable and helpful. In her spare time, Candice leads a young entrepreneurs' group at the local YWCA. Her children, now young adults, know that their mother is always available to listen and help, when necessary. Although their mother leads a busy life, she manages her time well.

Candice's life reflects a unity of purpose. Not only does her occupation reflect who she is and what is important to her, but all her activities are in harmony with her entrepreneurial position. Now 55 years young, Candice looks a radiant 40. She has never been ill and rarely feels tired despite the fact that she works 12 hours most days.

Career as purpose helps you express your inner self. It enables you to answer the universal questions: "Who am I?" "Whom do I want to become?" It helps you to select an occupation

Having a sense of

meaning and

purpose promotes

health, happiness,

a zest for life,

successful aging,

and maintenance

of morale in

difficult times.

and lifestyle that give your life meaning.

Purpose is the core around which many Questers' lives are organized and directed. Questers see all their activities (leisure, work, relationships) as reflecting a unity of purpose. But different themes run through the life of each Quester. The theme that runs through Candice's life is service to others. Other Quester themes include healing, fixing things, building, creating beauty, leading, being a change agent, learning, teaching, and creating family harmony.

The occupations Questers select help them express their life purpose and give their lives meaning. They are honest with themselves because they are living out who they believe they are. You may, for example, have a job as a teacher, but if your position does not allow you to express yourself and give your life meaning and satisfaction, then you don't have a teaching career. Teaching is just the work you do for pay.

Research shows that adults' most meaningful pursuits are related to work they enjoy and meaningful relationships and the least meaningful to material possessions. You must be committed to someone or something to experience a sense of purpose. Having a sense of meaning and purpose promotes health, happiness, a zest for life, successful aging, and maintenance of morale in difficult times.

Just as the course of your life is in constant movement, so, too, is your career. For both your career and your life to be truly satisfying, you must keep exploring the state of all your life components—occupation, family, relationships, and leisure—and then make the necessary changes to bring your inner and outer worlds into harmony.

Al, Howard, Kathy, Evelynne, Luke, Marion, Carl, Verlynne, and Candice are all Questers, people who dared to change so that they could be themselves. Their work gives them a livelihood, pleasure, and a sense of purpose.

Today, career development has become a continuing quest to create greater and greater harmony between your occupation and your personal characteristics. Surprisingly, studies show many people would continue to work even if they inherited a vast fortune or won a lottery. And amazing numbers of people nearing retirement fantasize about dying very soon after they stop working. But why is work so important?

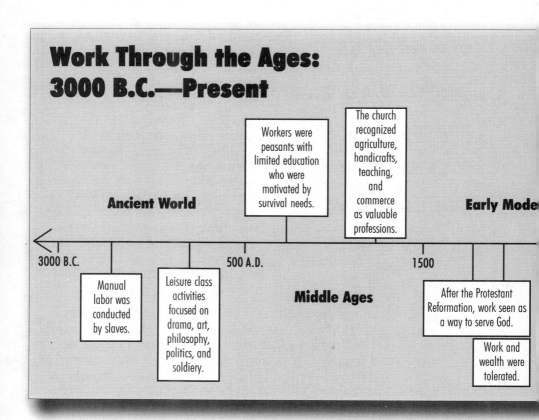

Work Through the Ages: 3000 B.C.—Present

Workers were peasants with limited education who were motivated by survival needs.

The church recognized agriculture, handicrafts, teaching, and commerce as valuable professions.

Ancient World

Early Mode

3000 B.C.   500 A.D.   1500

Manual labor was conducted by slaves.

Leisure class activities focused on drama, art, philosophy, politics, and soldiery.

Middle Ages

After the Protestant Reformation, work seen as a way to serve God.

Work and wealth were tolerated.

Most people will spend half to a third of their waking hours at work, commuting there, or thinking about their jobs. How ironic that work, once considered by the early Greeks and Romans to be punishment and drudgery, is now so important. Earlier societies considered manual labor tiring, vulgar, and degrading. Leisure, on the other hand, was exalted. Once, man's loftiest occupation was the exercise of the mind and spirit.

Early Christianity slowly changed the meaning of work. As the centuries passed, the now powerful church came to recognize agriculture, then handicrafts and commerce, as valuable professions. Work acquired "spiritual dignity." But not until the Renaissance was work recognized as a source of joy and creative fulfillment. The Reformation followed on its heels, shaping modern ideas about work and stimulating the development of capitalism.

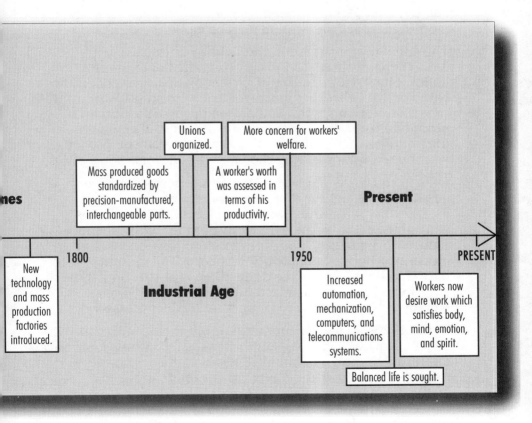

The Protestant Reformation elevated work to a new status. The search for excellence had begun. Yet another twist was added with the emergence of Calvinism. Work and wealth were okay, as long as they weren't enjoyed. To select a calling and follow it industriously was considered a religious duty.

Hard work, worldly achievements, high profits, and individualism were already entrenched in the work ethic when developments in scientific technology gave birth to the Industrial Revolution. The world was transformed. Entrepreneurs employing specialized labor and costly equipment were needed for efficient production lines. Since work was considered mindless and repetitive, workers could be subordinated to machines. Independent thinking, creativity, and personal ability were thrown to the wind.

Adam Smith believed money was the driving force behind capitalism and that if capitalism was to succeed, specialization and the division of labor were vital. Few people really enjoyed work, Smith pronounced. Most were lazy and only motivated by selfishness and lust for money.

The late nineteenth century brought a radical change to Smith's theory. Now Taylorism was grafted onto Smith's philosophy. Taylor's theory of "scientific management" was based on his belief that most workers were stupid. Inventing time-and-motion studies and a wide range of authoritarian procedures to increase productivity, he chained employees into systems that controlled their every movement. Money was the reward for getting the job done on time.

Even in today's workplace, that attitude persists. Some employers still believe that all employees need to be told exactly what to do and how, that independent thinking is dangerous, and that the only motivation for work is money. Industrial capitalism brought even more restrictions. The modern corporate bureaucracy was born. The evolution of the bureaucratic pyramid strengthened the idea that only those at the top had the intelligence to make decisions. Once again, employees were considered simply a mindless accessory.

In the 1920s, management began to question some of its own beliefs. How valuable was authoritarianism? Were people only interested in money? Should all decisions rest with the managerial talent at the top of the pyramid? In the late 1940s, the answers emerged. Elton Mayo discovered a clear connection between productivity and work satisfaction. It had little to do with money or even physical conditions. What people really wanted was a satisfying social milieu that offered involvement, attention, and recognition. The human relations school of management had been born. Job satisfaction and career development had become important issues.

Fastest Growing Occupations

Jobs that are predicted to grow in the next decade include all types of health-care, service, telecommunications, and computer-related occupations. Some of the hottest jobs in terms of growth and salary are listed below.

- Human services worker
- Computer engineer
- Computer systems analyst

- Physical therapist
- Paralegal personnel

- Electronic pagination
- Special education teacher

- Medical assistant

- Corrections officer
- Radiologic technician
- Medical records technologist
- Computer operations researcher
- Occupational therapist
- Subway operator
- EEG technologist
- Producer, director, entertainer
- Audiologist, speech pathologist
- Flight attendant
- Nuclear medicine technologist
- Insurance adjuster
- General manager and top executive
- Electronic and electrical engineer

- Respiratory therapist
- Psychologist
- Paving equipment operator
- Construction manager
- Data processing equipment repairer
- Bicycle repairer
- Food services/lodging manager
- Dental hygienist and assistant
- Management analyst
- Surgical technologist
- Registered nurse
- Loan officer, counselor

- Recreational therapist
- Social worker
- Insulation worker
- Licensed practical nurse

- Recreation worker

- Real estate appraiser
- Advertising clerk

- Podiatrist
- Accountant and auditor

- Sales personnel

The Information Age

Technological, social, and economic change also accelerated in the 1950s. Today, knowledge is power. The worldwide communications explosion means that if you don't or won't learn about computers, word processors, and telecommunications, a large number of doors will be closed to you. Many believe automation—the development of machines controlled by computers—may represent the greatest change in the history of mankind. As automation and information increase with lightening speed, so the jobs of millions of employees are altered drastically. Machines will soon relieve humans of almost all dirty, dangerous, strenuous, menial, and repetitive tasks. Factory jobs will dwindle and service positions will increase.

In factories of the future, the only humans employed will be those who install, program, monitor, and repair the robots that do the work. In offices of the future, word processors, intelligent copiers, and automated information systems will eliminate such drudgery as filing and stenography and will probably do away with the rote work of the typing pool.

To survive, you will need generalist skills such as the ability to manage information, design and plan, research and investigate, think critically, solve problems, and make decisions. You will also need to continuously upgrade your special professional skills and knowledge, such as those needed to keep current as an electrician, and think of yourself as a product to be marketed. Those who succeed will be resilient and will know how to take responsibility for their own careers.

The implications are enormous:

1. *How we define success is changing.* Some people are now using their own definitions of success to derive more meaning from work and leisure activities. They are not prepared to sacrifice their personal and family lives for the sake of their careers. The movement toward a more wholesome life, where career and other life components are balanced, is beginning. A growing number are becoming less willing to pay the high personal cost of health and family problems caused by excessive ambition.

2. *Dissatisfaction with authoritarian and impersonal work environments is leading to decreased loyalty.* Corporate control is break-

ing down as employees strive for freedom and decision-making power. Organizations will learn to earn the trust of people who work for them, whether these people are their own employees or not.

3. *The lifelong occupation is beginning to disappear.* New social attitudes toward personal liberation and occupational change are developing. Changing jobs is beginning to be seen as a desire for personal and professional growth rather than as a sign of personal instability. Some adults are learning that it's okay to periodically explore and change their values and goals. As middle-aged people realize they will continue to develop and grow throughout life, some are developing new attitudes about themselves. Some people are "retiring" early, then embarking on new occupations.

4. *Self-employment and part-time temporary work are escalating.* Increasingly, a great majority of educated people who work for organizations are not employees of the organizations. They are contractors, part-timers, temps, and consultants.

5. *Relations between organizations themselves are changing.* The most visible example is "outsourcing," in which a company, hospital, or government agency turns over an entire activity to an independendent firm specializing in that kind of work. Even more significant may be the trend toward alliances as the vehicle for business growth. Downsizing, divestitures, mergers, and aquisitions will continue to dominate headlines. But the greatest change in corporate structures and the way in which businesses are conducted may be the growth of relationships based on partnerships—joint ventures, minority investments cementing a joint-marketing agreement or an agreement to research, and semi-formal alliances.

6. *The basic unit of work is shifting from the job to a role.* Instead of being a business strategist, for example, an individual will assume a more blended task position such as "team member." The concept of being at a certain corporate "level" (clerical, professional, executive) is becoming less significant in pay considerations than performance and contributions. Instead of the traditional corporate ladder, career growth is being accomplished by expanding the abilities of a worker's current position. Assessments will increasingly be made by "work partners," such as coworkers, customers, and members of strategic alliances as everyone becomes more accountable for their own performance as well as that of others.

7. *The microchip is reducing the need for office towers in urban areas.* These buildings were created to house documents and numerous clerks who sorted, processed, and filed papers. Workers can now process infinitely more paper in a box smaller than a child's desk. Instead of secretaries, electrons are increasingly doing more work at a trace of the cost. Increasingly, thousands of workers are performing from home, which means they can relocate to places where they really want to live.

8. *Large corporations are defining and focusing on their own core capabilities, outsourcing jobs which they are less proficient in to smaller, specialized firms.* Inflexible corporate units, such as branches and divisions, are being replaced by integrated project teams and project clusters that draw on skill "pools" to accomplish a task, then dissolve as the members move on to other projects.

9. *Companies are increasingly turning toward contract workers on whom they can call for specific projects on an as-needed basis.* Many professionals will therefore choose to work for one or more companies on one or more projects, selecting when and where they will work according to their skills and desires.

10. *More companies are looking for multiskilled professionals who can adapt their skills to the job requirements.* These include astronauts with electrical engineering and business degrees and medical doctors with MBAs. Photographers transform images into digital formats for rapid retrieval and storage, and accountants program the databases of world-wide corporations. As companies shift to a "transnational" focus, technically trained specialists master at least one foreign language.

Other factors are contributing to change:

11. Surviving, to say nothing of thriving, is much more likely in this era of rapid and sweeping changes for those who keep their options open.

12. Well-educated adults with high expectations are insisting on opportunities to express themselves and to make a meaningful contribution to society.

13. The changing face of family life—divorce, death, and the empty nest—is forcing people to reexamine their relationships, to discover shifts in their goals and values, and to switch occupations more frequently.

14. Spouses are helping each other through the change cycle by shouldering financial and family obligations while their

partners study or search for more rewarding jobs. Couples are reversing roles and obligations.

15. People are living longer. Many different personal and environmental experiences will affect their occupations and how they feel about themselves throughout their lives.

The New Attitude Unfolds

As these changes take place, traditional career paths are being altered. Most people face tremendous pressures to readjust to the new demands of career development. To adapt, you will have to learn new attitudes and patterns of coping, new values, and new skills.

To be successful in the new type of work organization you will have to proactively leverage your skills by pursuing your specialty as you move from job to job. You will need flexibility and creativity, and you must be able to work on a team. If you want to work for a progressive company, you will have to be innovative, flexible, and willing to embrace evolving new technologies to discover new uses and applications. You must develop your curiosity, have an interest in leading technology, be a highly motivated self-starter, a leader rather than a follower. Other qualities you will need to exhibit include risk taking, energy, enthusiasm, positive attitudes, and environmental awareness. If you offer a package of capabilities, therefore, such as multiple academic degrees or fields of specialization as well as a foreign language combined with the right personal attributes, you will have an advantage over individuals with a single focus.

You will also need to find new ways of achieving a sense of belonging, personal identity, and self-fulfillment. You must know yourself, your deepest values, dreams, and beliefs and follow these with confidence and courage. In other words, there is a whole new set of attitudes toward career development that you will have to stay in tune with to get ahead.

You have the option of creating the kind of paid or unpaid work and lifestyle you want. You can design meaningful work by modifying your current position, convincing others to hire you, taking time out to study or travel, becoming a full-time homemaker, or establishing your own business. "Success" in the changing and evolving workplace means adapting to new

"Success" in the changing and evolving workplace means adapting to new rules and confronting both the risks and opportunities it provides.

rules and confronting both the risks and opportunities it provides.

The new attitudes are changing old theories about career development. To your parents and grandparents, the idea of career was a simple concept. The rewards of work usually centered on moving up the corporate ladder, achievement, individualism, and delayed gratification. Success meant being a good parent and sacrificing for your children, having money to buy the good things in life, as well as security and independence, and having social standing and respectability. No one agonized over self-fulfillment or even discussed it. No one thought of quitting a job. That was a sure sign of personal instability or irresponsibility. The future was as certain as the day was long.

Today, nothing is certain. The career ladder is a dead topic among a growing number. They speak instead about the altruistic and intrinsic—how to satisfy the body, mind, emotion, and spirit. The value of work is judged more by personal and job satisfaction and less by money and status.

Success has no one definition; it has many. Authenticity is making a comeback.

Tapping into Career Rewards

There are a number of rewards you can derive from your career: identity, self-confidence, status, stability, material comforts.

But if who you are is what you do, what happens when you don't find your work meaningful or satisfying? Like a steam cooker, life's pressures can build up until they explode. To resolve this pressure positively, you must discover who you are and what you want, then find a job setting that is compatible with your real self. By neglecting your needs and values, by "biting the bullet" and hanging in there (however great your excuses), you permit the malaise and lack of purpose to grow until they gnaw at every thread of your fiber.

Family life is tied into your work identity. No matter how hard you try, your family life and work life simply cannot be separated. You are a whole person. Your actions, feelings, and thoughts, your physical, psychological, and spiritual well-being, are one. Expressing yourself fully requires the careful meshing of all ingredients that go into making you who you are. Every experience in your life, not just those you wish, has an impact. As an adult, you must live with the experiences of childhood. As an employee, you must live with your role as husband or wife, as parent or child. How you feel about one is interwoven with how you feel about all the others.

Related to this is a growing reluctance to sacrifice personal and family gratifications for the sake of a job. Many are less willing to accept frequent transfers, even when promotions and raises accompany them. Desirable lifestyle and locale and personal fulfillment are heavily weighed before a job is selected or accepted. Expectations about work hours, advancement opportunities, status, salaries, and involvement are now judged as rewarding, demanding, or unreasonable. Always, there is the bottom line assumption that your occupation, or series of occupations and lifestyle, should fit your developing personality.

Your career may also function as a way to gain varied experiences. Frequent job changes no longer signal instability or indecision. A variety of work roles can be a hedge against obsolescence and can indicate personal drive, flexibility, and good generalist skills. Acquiring many different skills can also be good protection against unemployment. High unemployment, mergers, new technologies, even the move to overseas locations, have thrust the threat of job loss into our reluctant consciousness. Now, changing jobs is often a necessity. People who carefully attend to their careers allow their career paths to unfold in many new directions. Along the way, they increase their skills and sharpen their intellects, becoming better prepared for the future. Some monitor their careers and direct their energies to new opportunities to prepare for unemployment. They are careful not to stay too long in repetitive jobs that may rob them of their flexibility and their opportunities to grow. They know they can be easily replaced by younger and cheaper talent.

Abe understands that. From attorney to retail executive to administrator in the state college system, Abe has changed occupations several times. Currently, he is director of the human development department at a state university that offers career counseling and development programs. The key to an ever-evolving career is to monitor your own development and to be open to new opportunities. As Abe says, "You have to attend to what is happening to you personally, as well as to your economic value. Are you growing or are you just hanging on? Ask yourself: If you had to move, could you move? And where to?"

Issues related to career are being debated in the public forum. Today, career is viewed as an area for achieving social equality and humane working conditions. The movement toward civil rights in the workplace promises fair hiring and promotion practices. Organizations face increased pressure to eliminate unsafe working conditions that threaten the physical or emotional well-being of their employees. As people become increasingly aware of their rights and responsibilities in the contemporary work world, job quality and employment practices have become issues for political drum beating. Studies in vocational, industrial, and social psychology are showing how career satisfaction and adjustment, including job involvement, organizational commitment, and burnout, affect your life.

And all these many reasons, causes, and effects, influence a number of Questers to change the direction of their careers. They are the people who view their jobs as vehicles for self-expression and growth. They value movement—the right to grow and to maintain their usefulness. Their career goals are often open-ended. Questers find challenge in a wide variety of occupations and environments. Taking the initiative in their own career development, when they no longer derive desired rewards, they look for new ventures. So they proceed through several occupational cycles of entry, mastery, and disengagement throughout their careers.

At the same time, Questers are not simply job hoppers. Questers tend to make appropriate choices. They usually initially like their work and are committed to and involved in it. But after three or more years, if they can no longer grow, they leave. They are willing to take prepared risks. They are not irresponsible. They don't forget the family, say "to hell" with their obligations, or decide they couldn't care less about money, status, or respectability. They usually do want some degree of financial, marital, family, and material well-being. But they also struggle to make room for greater personal choice against what they consider to be institutional encroachments.

Some Famous Questers

You may suspect by now that many Questers are either highly successful in their careers or complete failures. The truth is that success is measured differently by Questers than by most Traditionalists, as we have already seen. Yet many famous successes are indeed among the ranks of the Questers. Most of them also found purpose in their work.

You are

your work.

Pablo Picasso had this to say about his work: "What is always there is your work. It is the extension of you, not your child, but you. You are your work. The passions that motivate you may change, but it is your work in life that is the ultimate seduction." Picasso was one of many creative people who learned to express hidden emotions through work. "Painting and making love were very much the same for me. At the greatest moment for each, painting and sex were the same. But painting you can do alone."

Eminent French designer *Coco Chanel* was indomitable at work. But in private she was totally vulnerable. Everything worried her. "I believe that every little girl should be taught as early as possible something she can do to take her through her whole life. I shall always be grateful to my work because it taught me independence. Even more important, it saved me from boredom. Boredom is a terrible thing."

Lee Iacocca suffered a devastating emotional blow before masterminding Chrysler's remarkable financial turnaround. Iacocca had spent 34 years working his way up to president of Ford Motor Company when he was fired in 1978. A generous separation agreement guaranteed him $1 million a year until 1980 if he remained unemployed. By joining Chrysler, he would trade $2 million for the helm of a faltering auto giant teetering on the brink of bankruptcy. To fail would add hundreds of thousands of Chrysler employees to Detroit's unemployment rolls. The future of Detroit was on the line. To take the job would be to jeopardize his reputation. He did. By December 1984, Iacocca's marketing genius had turned a dying company into a $2.3 billion financial giant. All for the love of a challenge and through concern for humankind.

The Questers you have already met have found both the courage and the means to take command of their lives. Why did they do it? What personality trait or traits gave them the courage to risk and to persevere? Could you do the same? Are there characteristics you already possess or could develop that would turn you into a Quester?

Questers Are Made

ome Traditionalists and Self-seekers may possess certain Quester qualities such as self-confidence, the desire for challenge, and a sense of achievement. However, most Questers have strengthened these and developed other Quester qualities necessary to prevail in a changing world. They have learned to risk, to learn from experience, to turn crises into opportunities, and to maintain career flexibility and positive attitudes.

You could say no two Questers are alike. Yet, they share many of the same personality traits. A very few have them all. The willingness to take control of their careers, to periodically assess their values and goals, and to listen to their inner voices is what distinguishes Questers from Traditionalists and Self-seekers.

In order to make the changes you want, let's take a closer look at the Questers. Some started taking charge of their careers quite early. Others were near retirement. By reading about the courage and imagination Questers relied on to find career happiness and growth, you may discover ways you can take better control of your career and life. Maybe you share some of the personality characteristics Questers tend to have: a sense of purpose, a desire for autonomy, the capacity for intimacy, confidence, the ability to combine the best of male and female strengths, the desire to achieve, and the need to grow. Where do you fit in?

Finding a Purpose

Questers give their lives purpose by pursuing activities they enjoy and that give their lives meaning.

Questers give their lives purpose by pursuing activities they enjoy and that give their lives meaning. Work, an idea, other people, a social goal—it can be anything. For many, much of that purpose comes from their careers. It satisfies their need to believe in something or someone. Making a commitment to a project (or another person) helps them move outside themselves. They feel good because they are achieving something or helping someone. By selecting occupations that help them fulfill their life goals, Questers are being honest with themselves. The congruence of inner and outer worlds gives Questers a sense of inner peace and joy.

Candice, whom you met in chapter 1, fulfills her purpose of helping others by owning and managing cosmetics shops. Her leisure and family activities also reflect this purpose. Some Questers, such as Pablo Picasso and Coco Chanel, have become famous pursuing their purposes. Other Questers accomplished their goals through homemaking or volunteer activities. They know they are accomplishing something worthwhile.

Brenda finds meaning in writing and raising five children. She has yet to create the great novel, but she loves to write short stories and poetry. As a young mother, Brenda knew that she could pursue both her love of writing and her desire to be at home with her children. A few night courses led to short stories in magazines. Brenda squeezed in a bachelor's and then a master's in English while the children were growing up, graduating from college with her eldest son. Now in her sixties, Brenda does public relations and writes in her spare time. She also finds time for her growing family. Brenda has even won some writing competitions. She is truly content with her life.

Fred is pursuing his passion in a different way. As a young boy, Fred always liked fixing things—toys, bicycles, household gadgets. At the urging of his parents, he earned a mechanical engineering degree and subsequently worked his way up to a senior management position with a large manufacturing organization. His career and life seemed relatively happy until he was laid off at 52. After Fred addressed his initial shock and anger, he turned the crisis into an opportunity. Fred pursued his boyhood passion of fixing things by becoming a maintenance man in a large apartment complex. "If you're doing something you like, then it's not really work and you're making money . . . . Your best work goes into it because you like it." Fred is obviously happily engaged in pursuing his purpose. Not only is he cheerful, but he also makes everyone who comes in contact with him happy. He radiates joy.

Byron's passion is to be an "agent of change . . . to influence public policy." Byron's dissatisfaction with the education his children were receiving influenced his decision, at 33, to run for the school board. As chairman of the school board, he was responsible for implementing many progressive educational policies. Byron subsequently held a number of public service positions (including broadcaster and member of the state legislature) in which he influenced change. Now in his fifties, Byron continues his mission to be an agent of change in his position of director of programming for a national television company.

Some jobs, such as those in education, health, or social services, naturally have social benefits. A dedicated principal who saves a dying school, a nurse or physician who helps the sick, the therapist who aids a troubled family—all these professionals derive a sense of purpose from their work. But Questers go beyond the ordinary. Debra and Gerald are Questers.

Debra is petite, attractive, and fragile-looking. Who would guess she was 50? She began her career as a physical education teacher who wanted to make gym fun for all her students, not just the few truly gifted. So Debra did what she could to change the system. She made sure more time, space, and effort were devoted to programs just for girls. She started a keep-trim club to teach her students how to eat a balanced diet and keep their bodies healthy. She offered classes in dance, badminton, and golf, activities her girls could use in later life. Debra's students went on to become top contenders in city and state competitions. But, more than that, Debra let her ideas be known to her peers and superiors. She pioneered a program girls of every level of ability could enjoy.

The challenge was over. Debra needed a new cause now. She took a job as vice-principal and was quickly promoted to principal. Debra believed she could have more influence as an administrator. Her first administrative task was to help deprived children and underprivileged minorities. And, as the years went on, Debra did it—building up teacher morale, reducing dropouts, improving the behavior of her often-difficult students.

Debra's next project was setting up a school for unwed mothers. It was a radical idea for the Midwest of the late 1960s. But Debra's persistence won out. The project is now part of the Midwest school division's services. Her next achievement was starting a training program in a nearby penitentiary.

In her late forties, Debra went back to school to pick up some courses in geriatrics. Helping seniors has become her new goal. Debra's mission was, and still is, to provide educational services for the deprived. Like most Questers, Debra had to keep changing to keep the challenge alive. The sense of purpose she gets from her work gives her life more meaning and fulfillment than "just a job" ever could.

Gerald feels the same way. An eye specialist in his late forties, he started off as a general practitioner, but soon became interested in the eye problems of his patients. So, in his early thirties, he returned to school to specialize. On first impression, Gerald seems nondescript, a colorless man. But when he talks about his work, he shines. His eyes light up and the sympathetic, warm, caring doctor emerges. Gerald likes finding new and better ways to help his patients. Research is a big part of his life. Gerald has pioneered many projects, such as the use of laser eye surgery and radial keratotomy, which help the severely shortsighted to see better (sometimes without glasses). Many of the operations are performed in his office because Gerald believes the trauma of a hospital stay prolongs recovery. Those who can't pay, don't. His holidays are spent in Third World communities performing eye surgery for free. Gerald's life really is his work, though he also enjoys his family, friends, and peers, plus regular workouts in the pool and on the racquetball court.

Research indicates that, in addition to giving meaning and direction to life, having a sense of purpose is related to good physical and psychological health, high levels of energy, high levels of confidence, a sense of security, involvement and enthusiasm for life, and better than average ability to manage stress and cope with tragedy. The more clear, focused, and concrete a sense of purpose one has, the greater his or her attainment of the foregoing qualities will be.

A number of prominant scholars in the fields of psychology, religion, and medicine explain the importance of purpose in different ways. Victor Frankl, a reknowned psychotherapist who overcame extreme difficulties as a Nazi prisoner during World War II, contends that a major illness of contemporary society is the failure of people to find meaning in their lives. He refers to this phenomenon as "existential vacuum." Frankl stresses that meaning in life—derived from commitment, optimism, and transcendence of self-interests—enables a person to maintain sanity and integrity under the most adverse conditions. Abraham Maslow, the father of Humanistic psychology, emphasizes that a person must follow his or her calling to be ultimately at peace with one's self. He refers to to this as the need for self-actualization—to become everything that one is capable of becoming. Bernie Siegal, physician and author of *Love, Medicine and Miracles*, also advocates the importance of purpose. He advises readers to follow their bliss and warns them ". . . not to climb the ladder of success only to find it leaning against the wrong wall." He suggests that pursuing one's purpose may even help one regain health.

Louise shows us that this is possible. A nun for 31 years, she initially enjoyed teaching in the convent but as she approached 50, she began to feel empty, helpless, and alone because she was trapped in a setting she had outgrown. She became a compulsive eater and drinker, had difficulty sleeping, and was diagnosed with cancer. Part of Louise's treatment for the disease included counseling which enabled her to develop the courage to take charge of her life. She left the convent and moved into a tiny apartment. Continued counseling helped Louise understand that her purpose was still to learn and teach, but at this period in her life, it was more appropriate to continue with her teaching in another setting and develop other aspects of her personality and life. Louise soon began to feel alive, she smiled, she stopped eating and drinking compulsively. Now 56, Louise is teaching in a junior college and feels great! Her cancer is in remission.

Becoming Autonomous

Questers tend to motivate themselves. They make their own decisions, do and say what they want. They're not afraid to swim against the tide. Questers tend to avoid situations in which they have to blindly conform. The binding ties of custom and habit do not hold them back. They move forward at their own speed, doing what they know is right for them.

Those who take charge of their own lives have higher expectations of getting what they want.

Questers enjoy freedom. But their freedom is not bought by rebellion or by using someone. Nor are they unconventional in everything they do. They usually behave in socially acceptable ways and within legal and ethical structures. Questers know how to transcend their environment.

Being inner-directed is part of being autonomous. Questers know they control their lives. They take responsibility for their successes *and failures*. They say, "I was successful because I worked hard." Or, "I succeeded because I'm bright." Or, "I failed because I didn't try." Because Questers know they can control their lives, they don't depend on others to reach their goals. Those who take charge of their own lives have higher expectations of getting what they want. Moreover, they have the marvelous, exuberant feeling of personal power that comes with believing anything is possible and what happens depends on you.

Jay understands the importance of taking charge of his own career. A stocky man with an honest face, Jay quit school during the Depression to support his family. He was lucky to find a job as a construction worker. A go-getter, Jay worked hard to learn his trade. By 30, he was a successful contractor. At 36, Jay decided to satisfy a longtime dream. He entered municipal politics. For the next seven years, he ran unsuccessfully for city council. Some laughed at this simple workingman. Friends and advisers told him to change his home and his lifestyle. Jay and his wife lived in a modest two-bedroom bungalow in a lower-middle-class part of the city, dressed plainly, and refused to "show off" their new-found wealth. Although a prosperous businessman, Jay didn't forget the people who were kind to him in his hungry days. He remained loyal to his basic principles and values.

Jay was an optimist. He persevered. He knew he would win. And he did! At 43, Jay became mayor and continued to be reelected for 20 years. He was a kind, honest, and caring administrator, who increased tourist trade, renovated the core, restored historical buildings, and expanded the city's park land. Social climbers who earlier had laughed at Jay now begged him to join their circles. A perceptive and forgiving man, Jay did. But he also remained loyal to his friends and supporters.

Jay had the courage to be himself and the conviction to follow his goals. He also learned from his mistakes. Jay is individualistic, self-directed, self-reliant, and independent. This persistent man didn't complain about being "unlucky." He listened carefully to what others said, but made his own decisions. Jay isn't afraid of social disapproval or societal pressure.

Many other Quester qualities tend to fortify and are fortified by their sense of autonomy. Let's look at a few.

Winners See Themselves as Winners

Many Questers know they can make things happen. So they do. Questers accept defeat. They understand some rotten breaks are an unavoidable part of the game. But they don't let them rule their lives.

Erika didn't let bad experiences hamper her career. Her first venture into the work world was a disaster. Fired from her first job for chronic lateness and laziness, Erika didn't realize a rare, easily treatable blood disease was causing her lassitude. "I wasn't able to get a second job because of the unfavorable reference from my first employer," Erika remembers, "and it was a whole year before I was diagnosed. After I found out what was wrong, I went back to my former boss and explained. I got my old position back and within six months I was promoted. I don't deny that I had an awful piece of bad luck, but I think you have to expect some undeserved blows sooner or later. You just have to cope with them as best as you can."

Vanessa is a beautiful, vibrant woman who lived through a disastrous marriage to a man who beat her. Hounded by an obsessive, frightening man, she came through both a divorce and the failure of her career as a professional dancer. Her unfailing aura of hope and good cheer managed to attract and keep a faithful circle of friends. "I've got nowhere to go but up," she would say, undaunted by yet another unsuccessful audition or a midnight phone call from her unbalanced ex-husband. Vanessa critically evaluated each audition and set herself a time frame to make it on Broadway. Then she gave up on elusive stardom and opened a dance school. "I just admitted I didn't have what it takes to be a star. But I did have the makings of a good teacher. I faced the realities of my own talents and limitations." And at about the same time, Vanessa's ex remarried and dropped out of her life.

Questers tend to win because they know their own limitations.

But most Questers also know when to quit. They have no hesitation about abandoning unrealistic goals or ill-conceived projects.

Knowing your own limitations is important. You don't have to settle for second best. You just have to find out what your best really is. Vanessa, the aspiring Broadway star who finally opened a dance school, could have ended up a loser if she had single-mindedly pursued her goal without reassessing her true talents. Instead, Vanessa is now a real winner. She makes a good living from the art she loves because she shook off the chains of an unattainable dream. Questers tend to win because they know their own limitations. They don't beat their heads against a brick wall or blame others for their failures.

Learning How to Be Autonomous

Positive thinking goes a long way toward improving your sense of control. Getting new and better coping skills is the first step. You can become more autonomous just by learning how to set and achieve goals.

Setting goals puts you in control. You feel better when you are in charge and so you do better. Adults who are in control are better able to cope with the few problems they do have. Biological researchers have discovered people who are taught coping strategies have low levels of cortisol. Cortisol is a stress hormone produced by the adrenal glands to help the body cope with stress. Too much cortisol, caused by chronic stress, can deplete vitamins we take into the body, particularly C and the B complexes.

They are healthier, develop fewer illnesses, and are less likely to suffer setbacks in chronic conditions. Your mind and body interact. Stress-related illnesses and behavioral disorders are really created by your body's chemistry interacting with psychological and sociocultural stressors. Because most Questers have learned to be in control of their environment, they are happier and healthier. You can be, too.

Developing Intimacy

Real Questers tend to understand the importance of intimacy. They can tell their deepest dreams and fears to others. They can also accept others' needs for intimacy.

Developing the capacity for intimacy is the first step to developing supportive relationships. Neither marriage nor sexual relationships can buy intimacy. Even the most active sexual partners can feel isolated if they lack mature, caring attitudes.

Real intimacy demands that you commit yourself to relationships that require sacrifice and compromise. It's the ability to share empathy, to give and receive pleasure without exploitation, to regulate your own needs to another's. It's the ability to say, "I don't want to use you. I want to love you. I want to experience you. I want to know you. I want to smell you. I want to feel you. I want to grow with you." Those who share real intimacy know it takes energy, risk, and adjustment. The only way you can ever grow is to experience intimacy.

The Intimate Marriage

Tom and *Elva* share real intimacy. They married when both were 26. Tom is tall, blond, athletic. Elva is a bookkeeper, tall, willowy, and blond. "We are good friends as well as lovers," they both said at the same time. They have an open, supportive, tender relationship. As they grow closer, neither fears losing his or her own identity. They can make independent judgments. But they can also achieve intimacy because both saw themselves as valuable, competent, meaningful individuals, with needs of their own, before they married.

As Tom approached 30, his management position became restricting and frustrating. Elva knew he was disturbed and encouraged him to talk. Tom didn't really know what he wanted to do, besides step off the bureaucratic treadmill. He needed time out—an extended trip, somewhere, anywhere—to rethink his goals. And he wanted Elva to go with him. She was hesitant. Elva liked her job. Leaving it for the unknown was scary and risky. But she also saw Tom's apathy and depression. Tom, on the other hand, saw what his request was doing to Elva. So he didn't push. After a year of talking over their feelings and hopes for the future, they decided on a moratorium—time from responsibilities and future commitments. They sold most of their belongings and bought a van. "But you're giving up everything—good positions, losing money on your belongings. What will you do when you come back?" their baffled, concerned friends and relatives cried.

For a year and a half, they drove up and down North America, from Alaska to Central America, up the East Coast and into

Labrador, through northern Quebec and Ontario, and down into the Central states. They had no plans, no schedules to meet, no phones to answer. They had no one to answer to except each other. They stopped in little agricultural towns, big cities, fishing villages, mountain parks, and mobile home parks. Finally, they settled in a scenic Oregon town. Tom wanted to work with his hands, to do carpentry, an old hobby, and odd jobs. He set himself up as a jack-of-all-trades. Elva got a bookkeeping job in a local motel.

Two years later, both are healthy and happy. Each has made new friends and found activities they enjoy alone. They also have plenty of time for one another. Tom and Elva are thinking of starting a family. This combination of autonomy and shared interests not only strengthens their marriage, but also reinforces their independent strengths. Still young, they have achieved the empathy and commitment that makes a good marriage a sanctuary. "Your relationship becomes much more precious and intimate when you commit yourself to doing something like this together," Tom says.

Not all Questers have been happily married all their adult lives. About a third (as with the general population) have been divorced. But by the time most reach their forties, fifties, and sixties they may be happily involved with another mate.

Finding Intimacy with Others

Intimacy is the ability to commit yourself to genuine love. But it's more. Intimacy is the ability to communicate at a sharing level with friends of both sexes. It means having close friends to share your dreams, sorrows, and experiences. Close friends can be just as intimate as married lovers. Many Questers are more intimate with their friends than a great many married couples are with each other.

To Questers, intimacy also means nurturing humankind. It means helping people in trouble, assisting the less fortunate, treating others with kindness and sympathy, doing small favors, being generous, listening to confidences with empathy and understanding.

You need intimacy to grow and be healthy.

You need intimacy to grow and be healthy. When you are cared about, that person (your "caregiver") helps you grow and develop by giving you positive feedback and constructive criticism about your strengths and weaknesses. This honest and caring feedback helps you see yourself more objectively. It helps you understand yourself better so you can learn to capitalize on your strengths and minimize your weaknesses.

Achieving Intimacy

Having successful relationships requires several qualities. You can develop them. Many Questers have them. As you become more confident and independent, your capacity for loving will expand, too. Rather than fearing that an independent spouse might leave, Questers understand that it is their individuality and belief in themselves that allow men and women to accept the emotional risks of intimacy. A popular quotation from John Donne sums up how many Questers feel about those they love: "If you love something, set it free. If it comes back, it is yours. If not, it never was." So it is with Questers. They can accept the need for intimacy without losing their individuality.

Questers know the secret of maintaining balance between love and work. Even though many are achievers and work hard, they don't let work take precedence over the people they care about. Many try to spend some time each day with their partners. They have freed themselves from the tyranny of trying to please. Rather than looking to one man to confirm their worth, most female Questers develop multiple sources of identity. Questers tend to be comfortable revealing their innermost thoughts and feelings to their mates as well as their closest friends.

Questers remember they have needs, too. They can be loving and, at the same time, love themselves. Many of us forget to look after our own needs. We take care of our physical needs, such as food, shelter, and health. But we forget to look after our psychological needs to achieve, to be accepted, recognized, creative, and autonomous, to enjoy the world and to grow. Unless we love and respect ourselves, we cannot love and respect others. Questers have learned this. Liking ourselves and doing things to please ourselves is not being selfish and does not stop us from achieving successful intimacy.

Everyone Needs Intimacy

The overwhelming desire for intimacy is reflected in the high percentage of divorced people who remarry. The happiest men in the world are married, the unhappiest single and childless. By their own account, young, unmarried men are lost. They have little motivation, no emotional nourishment, and suffer from loneliness and dissatisfaction. In contrast, survey after survey shows the happiest men are married men with young children who were planned. Looking back, many successful men in their fifties and sixties regret not giving more energy to "this human thing." For many women, too, the happiest years are the married years.

Acquiring Self-Confidence

How Questers feel about themselves colors their dealings with the world. Self-confidence gives them the courage to set higher and higher expectations, to change jobs, to risk, to dare to grow. Self-confidence is a vital component of Questers' personalities. Earl and June possess self-confidence.

Earl is self-confident and self-accepting. In his mid-sixties, Earl is rather short, five feet four, and average-looking. Earl is kind, caring, warm, friendly, and has a sense of inner calm. Currently, he heads a research and development department at a university on the West Coast and teaches a few courses to undergraduates. Because his field is research methods and statistics, he has taught at several universities and worked on a variety of research projects in many disciplines.

Earl began his career at an Ivy League college where he was a full professor at 34. He then spent six years on the West Coast doing research for industry. In the late 1960s, he moved back East to teach and set up a computer services program at a large university. Then it was the Midwest to head a university research department.

Earl is a brilliant man, very much in demand. He has many books and articles to his credit. But he doesn't flaunt his intelligence. Earl works hard to accomplish things. This gives him a humility that is neither self-depreciation nor diffidence, but one that promotes self-acceptance and self-respect. Earl isn't embarrassed to say he doesn't know the answer to a student's question. He has learned how to be wrong. In fact, he rather enjoys having students challenge his views. Earl says this about criticism: "You need constructive criticism and feedback from other people. That's how you learn. I know I'm not infallible. I often get good advice from the criticism of others. I decided early that I would learn how to take criticism in a positive way. I had to, to grow as a professional and a person.

Unlike Earl, many people fear criticism. They avoid experiences where they might be criticized. They take jobs that are too easy or lovers who won't ask for too much. What they don't realize is that they are losing out on opportunities for growth.

Earl wasn't a self-confident young boy. He acquired his self-confidence through friendships with other people. Success in his work also enhanced his level of self-confidence Earl said: "As a child, I lacked for nothing but confidence. I was a small, skinny boy and I had few friends. I spent most of my time in the library. Most of the boys my age were into sports and I wasn't. But, gradually, as I became successful at work, it came. I was a success and suddenly I had more confidence in me."

What Are Your Limitations?

June has the look of self-confidence. Forty-six, a youthful woman with auburn hair and aqua eyes, June operates her own gift shop. She married right out of high school and had four children. Because money was tight, June went to work as a telephone operator, then as a salesclerk and finally, a restaurant hostess. When the children were in school, June signed up for a real estate course and sold houses. Her husband was transferred to the West Coast when she was in her late thirties. By then, June was ready for something different. She wanted to open a gift shop. Her husband didn't mind her working and, by now, the children were independent.

June loves her work. She feels good about her accomplishments. Because she believes she will do well, she does. Like Earl, June can take criticism and learns from her mistakes.

Looking at June, you would never guess she once lacked self-confidence. Her carriage, her well-modulated voice, her private smile, all exude confidence. Surprisingly, June says, "For a long time, I thought of myself as an ugly duckling . . . . My nose was too long, my eyes were too close together, I was fat. So I played up to it . . . making jokes about my looks and putting myself down. I know now that was a mistake. If you look at yourself in a negative way, everybody's going to look at you that way. I finally realized I could improve the looks I had. I became involved in an exercise program, styled my hair so it emphasized my good points. But, more important, I placed more emphasis on internal qualities. I learned to be more accepting and tolerant of others, to see the good in them, to see what each person had to give. I learned not to dwell on mistakes I made, but to use these as learning experiences. I learned how to stop feeling sorry for myself, how to take advantage of growing older, and how to accept myself and become more independent."

June has learned to accept herself for who she is, independent of other people's standards. Instead of being indecisive and afraid of criticism and change, she's learned to accept that some people will like her and some won't. She's no longer in the business of pleasing everybody. June knows you have to love yourself first.

Trying too hard to make others like you makes you dependent. June tried so hard to be all things to all people that she made herself feel wishy-washy and insignificant. June has learned to cultivate qualities she likes in herself, and now others like her, too. The qualities she developed had nothing to do with good looks, status, or contacts. She learned how to enjoy her own company, to have fun with her family and friends. And they, in turn, enjoy being with her.

Liking yourself and doing things to please yourself does not mean you are selfish. June is not selfish. She explains, "I'm not self-centered . . . I'm happiest when I'm not absorbed in my problems. When I'm nice to others, I get that back. And that makes me feel good about myself. Much of what we do in life is motivated by selfishness. When you give money to charity, it makes you feel good. Givers get!"

Even though June is content, she keeps working on herself. "I'm trying to get rid of my silly inhibitions . . . I want to be more spontaneous. Spontaneity is freeing the child in you. Not being childish, but childlike."

Energizing Yourself

June and Earl have a lot of energy because self-confidence is energizing. They don't waste time and effort trying to impress other people or worrying what others will think. They search for and accept situations that relate to their own self-images rather than those that are socially desirable. They don't waste time and effort deciding what's right. They do it!

Self-confidence and self-acceptance are qualities June and Earl acquired and developed as they grew older and more experienced. Many things contributed to their newfound self-confidence. Past experiences—triumphs, the way they handled humiliations, the way parents, teachers, friends, and other people have reacted to them—all contributed to their self-confidence. Much of their self-confidence is also the result of their successes at work. The positive feedback they receive from performing a difficult job well feeds their self-confidence. Their self-confidence gives them courage to contact new employers, to tackle difficult assignments, and to solicit the support of others when they need help.

Similarly, the way Earl and June behave with their spouses and other people affects their self-confidence. Because they give and receive love, June and Earl feel good. They get positive feelings and acts that tell them they are worthy, too.

June and Earl carry with them positive pictures of themselves and then proceed to act on these. In short, they behave like the sort of people they believe they are.

You can learn from people like Earl and June. You are never too young or too old to start developing self-confidence and accepting yourself. Appreciating your own worth is not egotistical. Nor are you ruined or worthless because you are too short or too fat, or have a long nose or made a mistake,

Accept

yourself.

Be

yourself.

any more than a violin that sounds a sour note is worthless. Don't hate yourself because you are not perfect. You are not alone!

Accept yourself. Be yourself. You cannot possibly realize your potential if you keep turning your back on yourself. Just as it is important for you to recognize and accept your limitations, it's important, if you can, to change those shortcomings. Suggestions for enhancing your self-confidence are found in chapter 3.

Tuning in to Androgyny

Few Questers play gender roles by the book. They possess the best of male and female strengths. In other words, they are androgynous. Androgyny is used to describe people who blend traditional feminine and masculine characteristics. Depending on the situation, Questers are both feminine and masculine, both introverted and expressive, nurturant and assertive, confident and tender. Female Questers are loving and empathetic, but they also have ambition and courage and are open to new experiences. The most satisfied men are assertive, brave, and able to lead others effectively. But they are also comfortable with intimacy and nurturance. Simply speaking, Questers have incorporated the characteristics of their gender opposites. For men, comfort with intimacy and cooperation. For women, ambition and courage.

Androgynous behavior is healthy. It allows you to adapt to a greater variety of situations. It is also more functional. Both men and women should be able to cry, to be assertive, to hug—whatever the situation calls for. Men become manicurists, dental hygienists, or househusbands. Women become crane operators, bank presidents, or breadwinners.

Rigid gender roles can cause conflict that robs you of vital energy. Highly masculine males tend to suffer from high anxiety, neuroticism, and low self-acceptance. The picture is not much prettier for women. Highly feminine women also tend to be very anxious and suffer from low self-confidence. In contrast, androgynous people have much higher levels of self-confidence, are well adjusted, more creative, and have happier marriages.

Because androgynous people have no gender-typed image to maintain, they can remain sensitive to changing situations and engage in whatever behavior seems most appropriate. For them, "masculine" and "feminine" traits simply don't exist.

Almost all people experience some form of crossover as they age. Men and women in their forties and fifties begin to adopt qualities typically thought exclusively male or female. Women may become more independent and strong-minded. Men may become more emotionally responsive and interested in attachment. Older men are often more interested in giving and receiving love than in conquests or power trips. Women may develop exactly the opposite.

Questers tend to start the process of becoming androgynous early. Some in their twenties and thirties are already androgynous. By the time most are in their forties and fifties, they have acquired many of the emotional characteristics of the opposite gender.

Becoming Androgynous

Kathy, whom you met in chapter 1, was androgynous all her life. She was brought up in a mid-sized, Midwestern city. Her father was a lawyer, her mother a homemaker who enjoyed volunteer projects. She had one sister, two years older. Kathy's father encouraged her to be open to new experiences, regardless of whether they were typically "male" or "female." Her mother agreed. As a young child, Kathy had the opportunity to play with dolls and chemistry sets, to play doctor or nurse. She could take dancing lessons or play football, try out for cheerleader or for the basketball team. Because she had no brothers, her chores were both masculine and feminine. Kathy took out the garbage, mowed the lawn, and shoveled the walk. She also washed the dishes, made the beds, baked cookies, and sewed. To Kathy, there was no such thing as masculine or feminine behavior. She did what was appropriate to the situation. As a teenager, Kathy had both male and female friends and she related to both as equals. She considered becoming a lawyer, policewoman, manager, geologist, physical education teacher, interior designer, or dietitian. Because she was a good student with numerous interests and abilities, Kathy had her choice of any occupation. But because she had many options, she had a difficult time deciding. Her parents would have supported her in whatever occupation she chose. As it turned out, Kathy's first occupation was manager with an insurance company. She will soon become a full-fledged lawyer.

Adrian's childhood and adolescence weren't as ideal as Kathy's. Adrian also grew up in a Midwestern city. A middle child, he had an older brother and a younger sister. His parents divorced when he was 10. Adrian's mother worked as a nurse to support the family. Adrian recalls doing a variety of chores around the house. "We all helped at home. I learned that it was okay to do male and female activities."

Parents who are warm and supportive facilitate the development of androgyny, autonomy, and achievement.

Like Kathy, Adrian came from a home where a parent modeled, encouraged, and supported androgynous behavior. Parents who are warm and supportive facilitate the development of androgyny, autonomy, and achievement.

A number of Questers, however, were pushed by circumstance to take on the strengths of the opposite gender when they were in their thirties, forties, or older. They show what goes into the making of a Quester. They remind us that Questers are made.

Women forced by divorce or abandonment to fend for themselves and their children are often marveled at for their pluck, calm, and logic. Wilma started a lucrative typing business in a one-room apartment while her three children learned to become independent by helping out and taking part-time jobs. Elaine completed her social work degree in the evening while she worked during the day to support her two children. Gretchen established her own drugstore while

caring for an invalid husband. Yet, all three, well-indoctrinated in gender stereotypes they never thought to question, had set off into adulthood expecting to find a man who would take care of them. Here's Gretchen's story:

Gretchen was brought up in a small town on the West Coast. She was the only daughter of a merchant and a pampered mother. Gretchen never finished college because she met Matt. Together, they decided she wouldn't need her degree. She would never have to use it. Gretchen worked as a cashier in a bank until they had their first child. Three more came along. Gretchen enjoyed domestic life. When the youngest was in school, she worked as a volunteer two half-days a week at her children's school, watched the soaps, gossiped with the neighborhood coffee klatch, and kept a clean house. Paradise didn't last long. Gretchen was forced to become the breadwinner when Matt was crippled in a car accident. She went back to the bank but didn't like it. By going for broke and cashing in the family's savings, Gretchen returned to school to earn a pharmacy degree. When she completed her education, she got a job as a pharmacist in a hospital. Within five years, she was promoted to director of research, a job she held for six years. The political hassles, coupled with the children's increasing independence and the mid-life transition, led to Gretchen's decision to open her own drugstore. It was hard at first. Gretchen was at work at 7 a.m. and didn't get home until 10 p.m. She was open seven days a week. Today, Gretchen can afford to take it easier. She has two pharmacists and two salesclerks working for her.

Gretchen has learned to be more ambitious, assertive, competent, and confident—the whole parcel of qualities usually associated with men. But she has not lost any of her female strengths, either. She is still loving and lovable, empathetic, warm, and supportive. As a matter of fact, Gretchen, Wilma, Elaine, and other women like them, have assumed male strengths at a remarkable rate. But Gretchen also had other Quester qualities to fortify her. She possessed a willingness to risk, which permitted her to change; she was open to new experiences and she planned for her future. Her need to achieve only surfaced because she had the courage to allow it to, because she had picked up new skills to support it, and because she had the energy to follow through. As director of research, she learned to think for herself. Among other things, Gretchen also has a strong sense of purpose in her life—her children, husband, and a job she enjoyed.

Mike's story is similar. Mike was a macho male. As a young man, he nurtured the classic male fantasy. He ate, slept, played, and worked football. His little remaining time was spent in weight lifting and body building. As he now admits, he was a louse as a husband and father. So, at 35, his wife gone, Mike was left to pick up the pieces of a shattered marriage—a son, 14 and two daughters, 13 and 11. The simple mechanics of being father and homemaker—working, shopping, and cleaning—stymied him at first. But these things were soon learned. It was the idea of intimacy that really threw him. "I didn't understand the language my children were speaking," he said. "I didn't know how to communicate with them. They would come home from school and spill their guts, and I didn't know what to say to them. I knew how to talk to the boys on the team, but this was different. In time, I learned. We learned together. Being a single parent is the most emotionally draining job I've ever had."

In the meantime, football and weight lifting were gradually becoming less important to Mike. The callous views he held as a young athlete had disappeared. He needed another occupation. Sketching and painting caught his interest. Recovering from a broken hip, an athletic injury, he plunged into the paints and a "how to" art book his daughter brought him. He loved it. Next came evening art courses. Now, at 42, Mike is teaching art part-time at a high school and taking more courses. He wants to be a full-time art teacher and free-lance artist. Mike's only involvement in athletics now, other than jogging, is leading a weekly weight-lifting class. He's even marrying a woman he met in art class.

Mike is a good model for younger boys. He has shown that a man is capable of releasing the tender side of his nature without losing his virility. Learning how to care, how to feel, and communicate these feelings to his children and being open to new experiences have made Mike's personality and his life more complete. The new androgynous Mike will probably bring newfound joy and liberation into his marriage. Having the best of male and female strengths allows partners to be equal. Androgyny is an important part of a happy marriage.

Striving to Achieve

Do you have a high achievement quotient? Many Questers do. Most are motivated by an inner drive. They strive to

overcome obstacles, to achieve excellence, to do well at something difficult. This inner drive gives them feelings of accomplishment. Questers tend to seek settings where independence of thought, creativity, and growth are rewarded.

Questers tend to seek settings where independence of thought, creativity, and growth are rewarded.

Success Is Doing Your Best

Because Questers have a high need to achieve, they tend to strive for perfection, to do a good job.

Jason is an achiever. Tall, lean but well-built, with dark hair and blue eyes, Jason is an architect. He began his career in the early 1960s as a junior member of a large architectural firm. In the mid-1970s, Jason decided to go it alone and established his own firm. Now in his early forties, Jason has six younger associates. Because he is a perfectionist, Jason does considerable research before beginning a project. He makes certain that he delivers a quality product. He'll go to great lengths to ensure all details of a home match the personal qualities of the client. Jason particularly enjoys the challenge of doing a big and difficult job well. He feels good about an elementary school he just completed, and so does the school board.

Jason says this about success: "Success is an attitude. It makes you push hard at whatever you're doing. Success means never being satisfied that you've done well, always trying to do better. I work just as hard now as I did in my twenties. If you have passion, it will make you successful. Why else would Michelangelo have lain on his back for three years to paint a ceiling?"

Jason's positive attitude shines through his whole personality. He is driven by the desire to do his best, the need for challenge, and the will to work hard. Jason says, "I love my work. That leads to a strong identification with it and a high degree of motivation. I aim for excellence in whatever I do. Moreover, I have a 'can do' approach. I will try just about anything no matter how difficult it appears—it's a challenge to me!" Jason usually starts work at 7 a.m.. No work appears too demeaning for him. "The more dirty work you do, the more you learn your job." Jason also manages to find time for fitness. He works out at the health club and plays racquetball as often as possible.

Jason admits to being preoccupied when he's working on a project and to neglecting his wife and family. He can also be incredibly messy. But he's trying to improve.

Energy Is Life!

How does he do it? Jason has high levels of energy and can stay with a task until it is completed. Having the energy to accomplish tasks and meet deadlines is vital to the achiever. Jason can go for two days without sleep to complete a project. Like many Questers, Jason's passion for work spills over into his playtime, too.

Feeling "energetic" comes from being alive and involved. You feel wide awake and excited when you are doing things you really enjoy. A number of Questers over 30 have high energy levels because they are optimistic. They set out with high expectations, anticipate the obstacles, put criticism in its place, and find meaning and direction in everything they do. Disappointments and setbacks are taken in stride. Nothing creates energy like living energetically!

Your energy level may partly be determined by genetics. But don't use that as an excuse! You can raise your energy level by having a positive attitude, taking care of yourself (getting enough sleep, eating right, and exercising), becoming in-volved in an exciting job or project, and having an intimate relationship.

Setbacks Are Good Experiences

It's always painful to experience a failure and difficult to examine the reasons for one honestly and objectively. It's even tougher to pick yourself up, dust yourself off, and go back

Failure is

one of life's

greatest

teachers.

into the fray. Yet, failure is one of life's greatest teachers, and many individuals, who have found success, have failed many times. Most manage to make those painful experiences work in their favor by extracting valuable lessons that subsequently help them succeed.

Jason has found success. But he has also failed many times and learned from his mistakes. "Setbacks are important," he says. "Maybe a rejection every few years is essential. It sort of revs up the engine. A number of bids I've made were rejected, so next time, I worked harder. I identified reasons the bids were rejected and tried to address these issues or weaknesses. People usually don't mention their rejections and mistakes, which is too bad, because you think you're the only one not making it. But you know what I found out? That some very successful people have lived through many rejections."

Questers have failed just as frequently and maybe more than most of us. But they don't see themselves as failures or doomed. They've learned not to fall victim to self-fulfilling negative prophecies.

A number of famous individuals failed more than a few times before attaining success. Kevin Costner had many rejections before landing his first acting part. But he persisted in achieving his passion. He is quoted as saying, "Rejection just increased my desire to get ahead . . . . You've got to keep dreaming."

Marjorie Williams, president and chief excutive officer of SHE, Inc., and Laura Caspari, Ltd., two clothing stores that cater to executive women said she failed in her first entrepreneurial venture because she didn't understand her market. Her first business venture was a small exporting agency developed to distribute Indian-made clothing to U.S. retailers. Because she had little sensitivity to the U.S. market, the business failed. This setback motivated Williams to spend the next seven years gaining business tools by working and returning to school. A stint as a buyer at a large department store chain enabled her to get an inside track on the U.S. market. As a result, her former weakness had now become her greatest strength. Williams was the first entrepreneur to spot the special clothing needs of working women. In 1979, Williams launched SHE, Inc., the first U.S. clothing store to cater to executive women. She ensured the success of her business by carefully researching the market and writing a thorough business plan. Her business has grown 1,000 percent since its first year of operation.

Everyone Needs Challenge

Where does the need to achieve come from? Some psychologists believe you are born with "competence motivation," or the need for challenge and stimulation. Babies and toddlers have it. Grade school children have it. Some just have more of it than others.

Joyce is an achieving Quester. She was one of those children who strove to master difficult tasks alone. She recalls, "When I was five, I went to the Ice Capades. I was so excited. I had to have a pair of figure skates so I could do all those fancy tricks myself. The day after Christmas I went to the rink to do 'shoot the duck' on my new skates. It was freezing. I was the only person there. I practiced until I had it mastered. I was cold and wet and my feet and hands were frozen but I felt good. I did it! But I didn't tell anyone. I felt good inside and that's what it's all about for me."

And, today, Joyce is still "shooting the duck." She loved her first job, teaching high school history. Teaching was fun. Joyce liked being around students and enjoyed trying to make her classes interesting and meaningful. Motivating poorly behaved students taxed her, but the rewards were worth it. Besides her classes, Joyce had plenty of other interests. She was involved in a pilot project with her school's English, history, and science departments. She also sat on a state committee that developed a values curriculum. But by the fourth year, Joyce's enthusiasm was waning. Teaching the same old stuff year after year was losing its excitement. A failing marriage added to her lethargy. It was time for a change.

So Joyce took time off to travel and think about her life. She returned to a job offer as principal of a junior high school. Part of the challenge was working with problem students. She plunged in with gusto. Joyce was determined to help teachers deal with difficult students and to help students confront their problems. She introduced humanistic teaching. Then she set up a student-staff liaison committee so both sides could do something about their beefs. Joyce liked having the freedom to solve problems creatively. By now, she's in her fifth year as principal. Joyce has mastered her job pretty well. She wants to move on. To shine, she needs a challenging job she enjoys.

Success and achievement breed even more success and achievement. Joyce and Jason know from previous accomplishments that they can do well. So they set even more challenging goals next time. Every time they succeed, they are flooded with satisfaction. People who do well have the confidence to try and try again.

Revenge Motivates

Revenge can be a strong motivator. You know the feeling: "I'll show them. I can do it!" Some Questers have been prodded to great achievements by people who rejected, mocked, or wronged them. Evelynne, whom you met in chapter 1, had a desire to show the hometown snobs that she could succeed. This drove her to great success. "If someone says, 'You're wonderful, of course you can do that, you can do anything,' and someone else says, 'You can't do that,' you're going to work harder to show that you really can. You just want to prove they were wrong. Sometimes anger can be very constructive."

Boredom May Be Good for You

Boredom can be constructive, too. Oysters produce pearls to stop the irritation caused by trapped sand grains. People produce "pearls" to relieve the boredom eating inside them.

Setting goals beats drinking, drugs, or casual sex. Many Questers quit their jobs because the challenge is gone. Some women take jobs to relieve the boredom of being at home; others leave monotonous jobs and create their own challenges at home.

Wanting to Grow

Most Questers place the opportunity to grow ahead of position, title, or salary.

Everyone needs to grow. Questers, especially. They tend to welcome new experiences, personal or professional. Questers continuously try to improve themselves and the quality of their lives by enhancing these experiences. Psychologists such as Abraham Maslow would say Questers are motivated by self-actualization. They want to become all they can be. Once Questers master tasks, they tend to move on to other new and more challenging ones.

The desire to grow is partly biological. Your nervous system hungers for stimulation. Looking for a job that uses all your talents will allow you to grow. Most Questers place the opportunity to grow ahead of position, title, or salary. A peek at Renee's career history reveals how many Questers seek and develop growth from their jobs.

Renee, now in her late fifties, is like many Questers. She needs work in which she can grow. A speech pathologist, Renee began her career as a management trainee, then manager and head of ladies' fashion in a department store. By 36, she was a professional and financial success. But the meaning and excitement of her work were gone. So, at 38, Renee ventured into speech pathology. With a master's in speech pathology, she went to work as a speech therapist for a school division. She loved it. Eight years later, she took a sabbatical for further training to prepare her for private practice. Renee satisfied another interest in seeing that her community had access to quality education by sitting on the school board.

Happily married to the same man most of her adult life, Renee has balanced a career with a satisfying family life. She took a few years out to stay home when her son was young, but returned to retailing when he started school. Renee's family life hasn't always been idyllic. She admits to some pretty rocky times when she and her husband were in their early thirties. But, true to her nature, she did all she could to save their marriage. Renee sought counseling. "I guess I wanted to know, in my own mind, that I tried everything possible before I gave up on the marriage." Fortunately, because Renee and her husband deeply cared for each other and wanted to make the marriage work, they resolved their differences. Not all Questers are so fortunate. Renee and her husband now have an intimate relationship. They share many things and have a few mutual friends. But Renee also has special friends of her own.

Renee likes serving her community. She wants to see positive changes in the educational system. Like many Questers, Renee feels good when she tries hard. She possesses many Quester qualities. Renee is her own person.

Learning to Be Innovative

Most Questers, like Renee, enjoy finding new ways of doing things. Steve, an 80-year-old Quester who paints, reveals his philosophy: "You remain young only as long as you experiment. When you are content with what you have already done, happy only to repeat yourself, you've reached old age."

Questers express their creativity in many ways. When less creative colleagues of a large department store chain complained that their productivity was being hurt because the central office was ordering and purchasing for local stores,

Aaron, an innovative young manager of a jewelery department, used his creativity to do something about it. He approached his supervisor with a well-developed plan which included monthly profit and loss statements and balance sheets illustrating the kind of jewelery that was most viable for his department. As a result of his department's success, Aaron was promoted to head buyer within three years.

Dustin, a ski instructor turned entrepreneur, delights in dabbling in a variety of ventures. He went from a ski apparel and rental shop to a costume rental business, to a stationery store, to a toy shop. Now 38, Dustin is planning his next undertaking. Molly loves to paint, sketch, and make candles. She just opened a craft shop.

Older Is Better

As Questers grow older, they improve. The accumulation of many experiences has taught them to be realistic, accepting, and caring. Many adults do not develop these traits until well after 35. A number of Questers develop these qualities earlier and more intensely because they dare to experience more.

Research shows that most individuals who possess Quester qualities look younger, feel healthier, and live longer than peers the same age. Questers' happy involvement in activities that give them a sense of meaning and purpose and their optimistic attitudes tend to contribute to their physical, mental, emotional, and spiritual well-being.

Accepting Risk

When Questers are confronted with hard knocks, they tend to view them as temporary setbacks. They perceive setbacks as challenges to be met.

Walter is an aeronautical engineer who lost his job as a result of cuts in defense spending. He went through the typical transition stages of shock, denial and disbelief, fear and anxiety, resistance, anger, acceptance and exploration, and commitment experienced by most dislocated workers (see chapter 4). But he didn't get stuck for too long in the earlier stages. Seeing the glass as half-full, he told himself that he had a lot to offer, that there were positions out there for him, and that he would be employed within two months. He proceeded to work very hard at his job search ensuring that his resume contained a clear objective and reflected his skills and achievements. He attended workshops on how to re-search companies, network, make contacts with employers, market himself appropriately over the phone and during an interview, and follow up an interview. He job searched five days a week and didn't take rejection personally. He believed he would find a job that would enable him to use his skills and make a contribution. Within two months he attained his dream position with another firm!

In contrast, when *Bill* lost his job with the same company, he told himself and others that there were no longer any jobs in the defense industry. Believing the glass to be half-empty, he made a half-hearted attempt to contact employers. A year later, he still had not found a job. Fortunately, he finally enrolled in a career transitions group sponsored by the government for laid-off defense workers and sought some private counseling. With the support of the group and a counselor and a change in attitude, Bill attained a suitable position a year-and-a-half later. Bill learned to become more optimistic by developing a new set of skills on how to talk to himself when he suffered a defeat. He learned to speak to himself about setbacks from a more encouraging point of view.

Being Optimistic

Optimists learn from failure and hope for and expect the best. A crucial component to a happy and successful life, is what we say to ourselves when we experience the failures and disappointments that inevitably come our way. We learn to explain our setbacks in positive or negative styles early in childhood. For some individuals an automatic response is, "It's going to last forever and undermine everything I do." But others are able to say and believe, "It was just circumstances which I can overcome, and besides, there is so much more to life."

A pessimist who is having difficulty with her significant other would say, "Men are tyrants." An optimist would say, "My husband was in a bad mood." A pessimist who is presented with the possibility of having cancer would say, "This lump is probably cancerous. It looks like I may not have long to live." An optimistist would say, "This lump may not be cancerous, but if it is, I will do everything I can to beat it."

Optimists usually achieve happiness and success because they think positively about what they want to happen. Their vivid imaginations about their desired outcomes help to bring these about. Walter saw himself in his desired position, believed he would attain it within two months, and wrote down all the reasons why he would be successful. He reminded himself, three times a day, that he would attain his desired goal, and he developed a plan of action. He kept in contact with positive individuls who supported his endeavors and continued to look after his mental, physical, emotional, and spiritual needs. He worked. He acted confident and successful. Bill, on the other hand, saw nothing but a lack of suitable positions and constantly verbalizd this to himself and others.

You create your own script in life by the thoughts you think.

How you think about a problem can either relieve it or aggravate it. You create your own script in life by the thoughts you think. Fortunately, you have the freedom to change these. You have the choice of making each day terrific or terrible. Habits of thinking need not be lifelong. One of the most significant findings in psychology in the last 25 years is that individuals can choose the way they think. Pessimists, like Bill, can learn to be optimists by changing their attitudes and learning a new set of cognitive skills.

If you want to become more optimistic, practice positive self-talk every day. "I like myself because . . . " "I can . . . " "I will . . . " Write down affirmations, for example, "I can change . . . . " Concentrate on your successes. Create a personal "success" collage by gluing pictures together that illustrate who you want to be and what you want to accomplish. Include the goal you want to attain, how you want to look, and the personal and professional image you want to project. Look at it every day to remind yourself that you are this successful person. Instead of viewing problems as difficulties, look at them as challenges to be overcome. If you lose your job, view it as an opportunity to pursue your dream job or the beginning of something better.

Learn to monitor your self talk by tuning into your own negative dialogue. For example, each time adversity strikes, listen carefully to your explanation of it. When your explanation is pessimistic, actively dispute it, challenge it. Use evidence, alternatives, implications, and usefulness as guideposts to dispute your negative thoughts. Write down all the reasons you can think of to dispute your negative beliefs and thoughts when they arise. Then practice repudiating these by talking to yourself out loud. Replace your negative thought or statement with a more positive or hopeful one. Let this become a habit.

You may also practice focusing your thinking away from your problem and getting the energy moving in your body. Activities which can facilitate movement of blocked energy include drawing, dancing, listening to music, and doing some type of physical activity.

Scientific evidence indicates that optimism is vitally important in overcoming defeat, promoting achievement, and maintaining or improving health. Studies show that optimists do much better in school, at work, and on the playing field. They regularly exceed the predictions of aptitude tests, and when they run for office, they are more likely than pessimists to get elected. Their health is unusually good and evidence suggests they may even live longer.

You, Too, Can Become a Quester

Questers know that surviving in uncertain times means being flexible and willing to risk.

Questers tend to possess many other common characteristics. They have come to terms with the transitions of the different phases of their life cycles. They have dealt with developmental issues, struggled with whether to stay in destructive careers or relationships. Questers have learned how to use life crises, such as accidents, financial reverses, being fired, abandoned, or sudden death, as maturing experiences to take stock of and emerge from them as fuller, better human beings. Most Questers recognize the importance of a healthy lifestyle and strive to strike a balance between work and family, relationships, and leisure activities.

Questers aren't dependent on others for their well-being. They take charge of their own destinies. But they keep their options open, finding satisfaction and success in a variety of occupations and organizations. Questers know that surviving in uncertain times means being flexible and willing to risk. They have the courage to be open to new experiences, to let go of familiar people, places, and lifestyles. Questers have learned to push themselves ahead.

Which of the Questers' personality characteristics of purpose, autonomy, intimacy, self-confidence, androgyny, achievement, growth, and risk are most important? They all are. They all complement one another. Mastering new skills helps Questers gain the confidence to set their sights even higher. They grow and change.

You may not think you are a Quester. But you can become one, if you desire, by small acts of courage. You can move forward, too. Complete The Quester Questionnaire in the next chapter. Dare to take the first step.

Are You a Quester?

re you a Quester? Would you like to become one? We are all born with Quester qualities. You can observe these characteristics in babies and young children. They continuously strive to learn by exploring the world around them. Infants reach out to grasp their parents' ears, eyes, or clothing, and various objects in their cribs or playpens. As they learn to crawl and walk, they have fun exploring every cupboard and object in their homes. Infants and toddlers learn to crawl, walk, and build with blocks by persevering and risking. They are not deterred by setbacks or falls. There is no such thing as failure in their vocabularies. Children feel good about accomplishing challenging tasks, as illustrated by their sparkling eyes, excited waving of arms or legs, and smiles and laughter.

You have Quester qualities within that you can strengthen if you desire.

Unfortunately, as individuals grow older, many lose this excitement for learning; they forget the good feelings that come from accomplishing difficult tasks. Various reprimands, don'ts, shouldn'ts, and shames result in embarrassment or fear of trying and failing. Many adults set up barriers to growth that are manifested in expressions of resistance such as fear, denial, delaying tactics, impatience, false beliefs, and low self-confidence. They lose touch with their inner child and their Quester characteristics.

You have Quester qualities within that you can strengthen if you desire. Contrary to popular belief, the personality that you developed through childhood and adolescent experiences needn't be a wardrobe for life. In fact, you can do a complete makeover any time you want. Naturally, before you do that, you'll need to draft a map of who you are and where you want to go. You should also identify your strengths and limitations so that you can maximize your strengths and overcome your limitations. The Quester Questionnaire can help you find out how you rate on the various Quester characteristics. By responding to the statements and reading the interpretations carefully, you can gain a greater understanding of who you are and who you could become.

The Quester Questionnaire

The 146 statements that follow will help identify how your personality characteristics compare with those of the Questers. Indicate how much you agree or disagree with each statement by circling a number from 5 (very strongly agree) to 1 (very strongly disagree). Scoring procedures and an interpretation of the results are provided at the end of the questionnaire.

Make your responses as honest as possible. Don't choose the answer you feel others would expect of you. This is a test for you, and you alone. Because your attitudes about yourself can also be colored by how you feel at any given time, complete the questionnaire when you are feeling refreshed. For best results, find a quiet spot where you can devote two concentrated hours to completing and scoring it.

One final point: In the field of psychological evaluation, there are no absolute rights or wrongs. This questionnaire does not pretend to be infallible, but you will find it intriguing and revealing. In fact, you may never see yourself the same again.

The Quester Questionnaire	Degree of Agreement				
	Very High				Very Low
1. Facing my daily tasks is a source of pleasure and satisfaction.	5	4	3	2	1
2. I can like people without having to approve of them.	5	4	3	2	1
3. When I do a job, I do it well.	5	4	3	2	1
4. I am determined I will succeed in everything I do.	5	4	3	2	1
5. I often wish people would be more definite.	5	4	3	2	1
6. When I want something, I'll sometimes go out on a limb for it.	5	4	3	2	1
7. When I want to buy something, I rarely consider others' opinions.	5	4	3	2	1
8. It's easy for me to start conversations with strangers.	5	4	3	2	1
9. I don't often contribute new ideas.	5	4	3	2	1
10. Most of my misfortunes and successes were the result of things I did.	5	4	3	2	1
11. It's very hard for me to tell anyone about myself.	5	4	3	2	1
12. I have been doing quite a bit of self-assessment lately.	5	4	3	2	1
13. I have clear goals and aims in life.	5	4	3	2	1
14. I have had moments of extreme joy when I felt I was experiencing a kind of ecstasy or bliss.	5	4	3	2	1
15. I feel I have much to be proud of.	5	4	3	2	1

The Quester Questionnaire

	Very High				Very Low
16. I feel good about doing a job well.	5	4	3	2	1
17. A well-ordered way of life with regular hours suits my temperament.	5	4	3	2	1
18. If the possible reward was very high, I would not hesitate about putting my money into a business that could fail.	5	4	3	2	1
19. I'm self-reliant.	5	4	3	2	1
20. When I'm in a group, I hesitate to make suggestions.	5	4	3	2	1
21. I like a job that demands skills and practice rather than inventiveness.	5	4	3	2	1
22. I cannot really believe that chance or luck has played a very important part in my life.	5	4	3	2	1
23. I always try to consider others' feelings before I do something.	5	4	3	2	1
24. I have experienced at least one traumatic event in the past year.	5	4	3	2	1
25. If I should die today, I would feel that my life has been worthless.	5	4	3	2	1
26. I like to withdraw temporarily from the rest of the world.	5	4	3	2	1
27. I have a great deal of confidence.	5	4	3	2	1
28. I don't have much ambition.	5	4	3	2	1
29. I like to plan all of my activities in advance.	5	4	3	2	1
30. I enjoy taking risks.	5	4	3	2	1
31. I'd rather spend time and energy doing an interesting job than being successful at a job I dislike.	5	4	3	2	1
32. No matter whom I'm talking to, I'm always a good listener.	5	4	3	2	1

Degree of Agreement

The Quester Questionnaire	Degree of Agreement				
	Very High			Very Low	
33. I seldom bother to think of original ways of doing the same thing.	5	4	3	2	1
34. My successes are the result of hard work, determination, and some ability.	5	4	3	2	1
35. I like to play with kittens.	5	4	3	2	1
36. I'm very satisfied with my job.	5	4	3	2	1
37. My close friends are people I really enjoy.	5	4	3	2	1
38. I live only for the present.	5	4	3	2	1
39. I believe that I am as or more successful in achieving my goals as most of my graduating class.	5	4	3	2	1
40. I will never profit much.	5	4	3	2	1
41. I like everything to be in its place.	5	4	3	2	1
42. I would enjoy the challenge of a project that could mean either a promotion or loss of a job.	5	4	3	2	1
43. I refuse to behave like everyone else just to please people.	5	4	3	2	1
44. I'm critical about the dress, manner, or ideas of some of my friends.	5	4	3	2	1
45. I hope to develop a new technique in my field of work.	5	4	3	2	1
46. When I make plans, I am almost certain I can make them work.	5	4	3	2	1
47. I like to cook fancy dishes.	5	4	3	2	1
48. I feel that I'm passing through a transition	5	4	3	2	1
49. I have seriously thought of suicide as a way out.	5	4	3	2	1
50. I can express honestly felt anger.	5	4	3	2	1
51. I wish I had more respect for myself.	5	4	3	2	1

The Quester Questionnaire	Degree of Agreement				
	Very High				Very Low
52. All I want out of a career is a secure, not-too-difficult job that pays enough to buy a nice car and home.	5	4	3	2	1
53. I like to work on problems that have ambiguous answers.	5	4	3	2	1
54. I don't fear failure.	5	4	3	2	1
55. Generally, I don't concern myself with what others think of my abilities.	5	4	3	2	1
56. I feel comfortable with all types of people—from the most wealthy and well-educated to the poorest and least-educated.	5	4	3	2	1
57. I usually continue to do a job in exactly the same way that it was taught to me.	5	4	3	2	1
58. There are many times that I feel that I have little influence over the things that happen to me.	5	4	3	2	1
59. I'm not afraid to take a stand even though it may be unpopular.	5	4	3	2	1
60. I believe the probability is good of finding an acceptable job elsewhere.	5	4	3	2	1
61. I regard my ability to find meaning and purpose in my life as practically nonexistent.	5	4	3	2	1
62. I will continue to grow best just by being myself.	5	4	3	2	1
63. I feel that I am a person of worth at least equal to others.	5	4	3	2	1
64. I would be very unhappy if I was not successful at something I seriously started to do.	5	4	3	2	1

The Quester Questionnaire

	Degree of Agreement				
	Very High				Very Low

65. It bothers me when something that is unexpected interrupts my routine.	5	4	3	2	1
66. I trust decisions I make spontaneously.	5	4	3	2	1
67. What the general public thinks does not affect my standards or beliefs.	5	4	3	2	1
68. I can take a joke when it's on me.	5	4	3	2	1
69. I prefer activities that I know I will enjoy to ones I have never tried.	5	4	3	2	1
70. It is often not wise for me to plan too far ahead because many things turn out to be a matter of good or bad fortune.	5	4	3	2	1
71. I have male and female qualities.	5	4	3	2	1
72. There is much to be gained by staying with my current job the rest of my career.	5	4	3	2	1
73. I would not change my life drastically if I knew that I had only six months to live.	5	4	3	2	1
74. I feel that I would like to make a contribution to society.	5	4	3	2	1
75. I am a useful person to have around.	5	4	3	2	1
76. I have a tendency to give up easily when I meet difficult problems.	5	4	3	2	1
77. I like things to be certain and predictable.	5	4	3	2	1
78. In games, I usually go for broke rather than playing it safe.	5	4	3	2	1
79. I enjoy being a vagabond.	5	4	3	2	1
80. I do not have a small circle of very close friends.	5	4	3	2	1

The Quester Questionnaire

	Degree of Agreement				
	Very High				Very Low
81. I like trying different kinds of foreign foods.	5	4	3	2	1
82. I take my horoscope seriously.	5	4	3	2	1
83. I'm sensitive to the needs of others.	5	4	3	2	1
84. My employer inspires me to do well.	5	4	3	2	1
85. In thinking about my life, I see a reason to be here.	5	4	3	2	1
86. I believe that I am growing and developing as a person and professionally.	5	4	3	2	1
87. I certainly feel useless at times.	5	4	3	2	1
88. I must admit that I often do as little work as I can get by with.	5	4	3	2	1
89. Once my mind is made up, that's it.	5	4	3	2	1
90. Skydiving is too dangerous for me.	5	4	3	2	1
91. I find it very hard to work under strict rules and regulations.	5	4	3	2	1
92. I can like people without having to approve of them.	5	4	3	2	1
93. Few topics bore me.	5	4	3	2	1
94. If I get a really good job in the future, it will probably depend a lot on getting the right breaks.	5	4	3	2	1
95. I'm assertive.	5	4	3	2	1
96. I never think of quitting my job.	5	4	3	2	1
97. My position gives my life meaning and direction.	5	4	3	2	1
98. I enjoy helping younger people both in and out of the workplace.	5	4	3	2	1
99. I cannot accept failure.	5	4	3	2	1
100. I set high standards for myself.	5	4	3	2	1

The Quester Questionnaire	Degree of Agreement				
	Very High				Very Low
101. I think I'm stricter about right and wrong than most people.	5	4	3	2	1
102. I would prefer a stable position with a moderate salary to one with a higher salary but less security.	5	4	3	2	1
103. When I was a child, I didn't care to be a member of a crowd or group.	5	4	3	2	1
104. I feel certain and secure in my relationships with others.	5	4	3	2	1
105. I like to participate actively in intense discussions.	5	4	3	2	1
106. There are often times when I cannot keep my temper or hold back tears.	5	4	3	2	1
107. Men and women should follow any vocation they desire, even if it violates tradition.	5	4	3	2	1
108. I am very satisfied with the way things are going in my life.	5	4	3	2	1
109. I can see past, present, and future as a meaningful continuity.	5	4	3	2	1
110. I believe that I know myself.	5	4	3	2	1
111. I welcome criticism as an opportunity for growth.	5	4	3	2	1
112. I always try to do at least a little better than is expected of me.	5	4	3	2	1
113. I'm in favor of a very strict enforcement of all laws regardless of the consequences.	5	4	3	2	1
114. I try to avoid situations that have uncertain outcomes.	5	4	3	2	1
115. Before making a decision, I often worry whether or not others will approve of it.	5	4	3	2	1

The Quester Questionnaire

	Degree of Agreement				
	Very High				Very Low
116. I would not dare to reveal my weaknesses among friends.	5	4	3	2	1
117. I always feel that I must look into all sides of a problem.	5	4	3	2	1
118. Even when there is nothing forcing me, I often find that I do things that I do not really want to do.	5	4	3	2	1
119. I believe there are no genetic differences between the sexes in intellectual ability.	5	4	3	2	1
120. I try to face reality even when it's unpleasant.	5	4	3	2	1
121. I feel that I have the knowledge and experience to be of great help to family members, friends, and acquaintances when they ask me for advice.	5	4	3	2	1
122. I enjoy doing challenging things.	5	4	3	2	1
123. I always see to it that my work is carefully planned and organized.	5	4	3	2	1
124. I probably would not take the chance of borrowing money for a business deal even if it might be profitable.	5	4	3	2	1
125. It's important for me to have a job where I have the freedom to perform the tasks my own way.	5	4	3	2	1
126. I have a very warm and caring relationship with my friends.	5	4	3	2	1
127. I think of myself as a straightforward, uncomplicated person.	5	4	3	2	1
128. What happens to me is my own doing.	5	4	3	2	1
129. It is possible for women to combine home and career, and do both successfully.	5	4	3	2	1
130. I would like a job that provides good opportunities for self-expression.	5	4	3	2	1

The Quester Questionnaire	Degree of Agreement				
	Very High			Very Low	
131. I can accept my mistakes.	5	4	3	2	1
132. I think I could accomplish almost anything I wanted to if I tried hard enough.	5	4	3	2	1
133. I take things very seriously.	5	4	3	2	1
134. I would enjoy a job where I have to adapt quickly to new situations and to emergencies.	5	4	3	2	1
135. I prefer to have a job where I am not closely supervised.	5	4	3	2	1
136. I am free to express both warm and hostile feelings to my friends.	5	4	3	2	1
137. It is important for me to have a job where I can create original things or ideas.	5	4	3	2	1
138. I feel free to not do what others expect of me.	5	4	3	2	1
139. It's ridiculous for a woman to run a locomotive and for a man to darn socks.	5	4	3	2	1
140. I would like a job where I can fully develop all of my potential.	5	4	3	2	1
141. I feel certain and secure in my relationships with others.	5	4	3	2	1
142. I set high standards for myself and expect others to do the same.	5	4	3	2	1
143. I would take a job I enjoy even if strikes and layoffs are expected.	5	4	3	2	1
144. I would like a job where I can express my own creativity.	5	4	3	2	1
145. A good education is equally important for males and females.	5	4	3	2	1
146. I feel comfortable talking about very personal things with my partner or close friends.	5	4	3	2	1

Scoring

PART A. To determine your score for part A, give yourself 3 points for each 5 (very strongly agree), 2 points for each 4 (agree) and 1 point for each 3 (uncertain or undecided) you recorded for the following statements. Place a 3, 2, or 1 in the blank beside each question. Now, add up your total score for each personality characteristic and place these in the blanks labeled Subtotal.

Intimacy	Self-Confidence	Purpose	Autonomy
8 ___	3 ___	1 ___	7 ___
32 ___	15 ___	13 ___	10 ___
56 ___	27 ___	37 ___	19 ___
68 ___	39 ___	73 ___	34 ___
83 ___	63 ___	85 ___	43 ___
92 ___	75 ___	97 ___	46 ___
104 ___	111 ___	109 ___	55 ___
126 ___	121 ___		67 ___
136 ___	131 ___		79 ___
146 ___	132 ___		91 ___
	141 ___		103 ___
			125 ___
			128 ___
			135 ___
			138 ___
Subtotal ___	**Subtotal** ___	**Subtotal** ___	**Subtotal** ___

Achievement	Innovativeness	Androgyny	
4 ___	45 ___	4 ___	43 ___
16 ___	81 ___	6 ___	46 ___
31 ___	93 ___	10 ___	55 ___
64 ___	105 ___	16 ___	56 ___
100 ___	117 ___	19 ___	59 ___
112 ___	137 ___	20 ___	71 ___
122 ___	144 ___	22 ___	95 ___
132 ___		23 ___	107 ___
		27 ___	119 ___
		30 ___	125 ___
		32 ___	129 ___
		34 ___	134 ___
		35 ___	145 ___
		37 ___	
Subtotal ___	**Subtotal** ___	**Subtotal** ___	

Risk	Growth		Ways to Identify Potential Questers
6 ___	2 ___	105 ___	12 ___
18 ___	14 ___	109 ___	24 ___
30 ___	19 ___	110 ___	48 ___
42 ___	26 ___	120 ___	60 ___
53 ___	50 ___	125 ___	
54 ___	54 ___	130 ___	
66 ___	62 ___	131 ___	
78 ___	66 ___	132 ___	
134 ___	74 ___	136 ___	
143 ___	81 ___	140 ___	
	86 ___	144 ___	
	98 ___		
Subtotal ___	**Subtotal** ___		**Subtotal** ___

PART B. To score part B, give yourself 3 points for each 1 (strongly disagree), 2 points for each 2 (disagree), and 1 point for each 3 (uncertain or undecided). Place a 3, 2, or 1 beside each item under a personality characteristic. Again, add up your scores and place the results for each characteristic in the blanks labeled Subtotal.

Intimacy	Self-Confidence	Purpose	Autonomy
20 ___	51 ___	25 ___	22 ___
44 ___	87 ___	49 ___	58 ___
80 ___	99 ___	61 ___	70 ___
116 ___			82 ___
			94 ___
			106 ___
			115 ___
			118 ___
Subtotal___	Subtotal ___	Subtotal ___	Subtotal ___

Achievement	Innovativeness	Androgyny
28 ___	9 ___	11 ___
40 ___	21 ___	76 ___
52 ___	33 ___	139 ___
88 ___	57 ___	
	69 ___	
	127 ___	
Subtotal ___	Subtotal ___	Subtotal ___

Risk		Growth	Ways to Identify Potential Questers
5 ___	102 ___	38 ___	36 ___
17 ___	113 ___	52 ___	72 ___
29 ___	114 ___	101 ___	84 ___
41 ___	123 ___	116 ___	96 ___
65 ___	124 ___		108 ___
77 ___	133 ___		
89 ___	142 ___		
90 ___			
Subtotal ___		Subtotal ___	Subtotal ___

PART C. Now determine your combined, overall score by adding together your subtotals for each personality characteristic under parts A and B. For example, if, under Intimacy, you scored 9 in part A and 21 in part B, your combined overall score will be 30 (9 + 21 = 30). List each of these combined overall scores in the spaces provided below. You may want to compare your scores to the highest possible totals (far right column). Once you have determined your combined overall score for each personality characteristic, add them up and place the total in the space beside Overall Score. Do *not* include your score on Ways to Identify Potential Questers in your overall score. Read on to discover what your scores reveal.

Personality Characteristics	Score	Highest Possible Score
Intimacy	_____	(42)
Self-confidence	_____	(42)
Purpose	_____	(30)
Autonomy	_____	(69)
Achievement	_____	(39)
Innovativeness	_____	(42)
Androgyny	_____	(90)
Risk	_____	(75)
Growth	_____	(75)
Ways to Identify Potential Questers	_____	(27)
Overall Score	_____	(504)

How to Become a Quester

Your responses to the statements in this questionnaire reveal how closely you resemble the Questers. A high score means you have many Quester qualities. An intermediate score means you are a potential Quester. A low score means you are quite different from the Questers. Keep in mind that your scores are not fixed. When events are going well, your scores will probably rise. Under stress, they will be inclined to drop.

Quester qualities are positive. However, if they become excessive, they lose their value. People with extremely high overall scores may be overly anxious, tense, and unrealistic.

People who seek intimacy compulsively may miss the joys of solitude. Those who have too much self-confidence are arrogant, unrealistic, and may become blind to their own limitations. Those whose sense of purpose is all-consuming may become narrow and boring to others. Overly autonomous people may refuse help even when they need it. Those driven by too great a need for achievement have been known to be ruthless in their single-minded pursuit of major accomplishments. Occasionally, rampant innovators miss the value in the tried and true, and wrongly believe there is value only in the new and novel.

Some people, recognizing the trendy value of androgyny, may foolishly suppress some of the fine strengths of their own gender. A willingness to risk, when carried to extremes, may be hard to distinguish from irresponsible gambling. Obsessive preoccupation with growth can be found among boring people who are too absorbed in themselves.

What does The Quester Questionnaire say about you?

Intimacy

28 or higher: If you scored 28 or higher on Intimacy, your feelings closely match the Questers. You tend to place great value on personal relationships and probably have a small circle of very close friends. Your friendships are emotionally rich. If you are married or living with someone, the relationship is close and loving. You have nothing to hide from family and friends, and readily reveal problems, foibles, or concerns. You are candid and care deeply about others, and your excellent interpersonal skills allow you to empathize with and relate effectively to people from all walks of life. Your self-confident, trusting nature draws them toward you.

15 to 27: You are a potential Quester. Your dealings with people may fluctuate. For instance, you may be empathetic and have a caring relationship with your partner, but find it difficult to start conversations with strangers or hesitate to make suggestions in a group. Go back over the statements and see what you could change about yourself to enhance your ability to enjoy greater intimacy.

14 or lower: You are probably shy, have few close friends, feel uncomfortable being intimate with your partner, or feel ill at ease in social situations. Work on improving your intimacy skills. Your attitudes about love, other people, and yourself may be preventing you from enjoying intimacy. Like anything else, attitudes can be changed. By learning to become more outgoing and a more effective communicator, you can not only improve your intimacy skills, but also take better control of your own behavior.

Tips for Establishing Intimacy

❖ *Get out and associate with others.* The act of mingling and making friends usually requires no more than suffering through the 10 or 15 awkward minutes it takes to get to know someone. Start a conversation. As soon as the conversation starts rolling, see if your shyness doesn't disappear. A hello, a smile, a handshake, a nod, a wink— any one of these tiny little communication devices can help overcome shyness. Force yourself to smile at and speak to someone you previously ignored. During an office coffee break, strike up a conversation with someone new. Go out into the world, even when you don't feel like it. Make small talk. Become more visible. Compliment others or, better yet, ask for their advice. Sit down next to a stranger or a new acquaintance on the plane, bus or train. Pick up the phone. Above all, communicate.

❖ *Enhance your social skills.* Try honing your interpersonal skills at a small task-oriented group, such as a PTA com- mittee, or in a social group, such as a book club. A re- stricted, focused situation is much easier to deal with than the ambiguous, unstructured atmosphere of the party where words can, and do, easily fail most of us. Come to the group prepared to participate. Or, volunteer to collect for the cancer fund so you will feel forced to speak to strangers. Before the party begins, find some- thing fresh to discuss by reading a newspaper or maga- zine. Seek out the host or hostess and ask for introduc- tions. Most of all, be aware of your own body language. Don't close out others by looking away or crossing your arms. Look people in the eye. Set realistic goals. Talk to just a few new individuals each week. And don't feel hurt if someone doesn't respond. Move on to the next person. Introduce yourself to several strangers, then set out to discover three identifying characteristics about each. Next time you meet, you'll be able to put names, faces, and facts together for a fun and fascinating conversation. Probably the biggest payoff from practicing these small steps is that they will help you to stop dwelling on yourself and open you up to the rest of the world.

❖ *Listen to what people are saying to and about you.* To avoid misinterpretation, listen not only to people's voices, but to the tone of their voices as well. Are they saying, "Notice me," "Help me," or "Care about me"? A good listener is an involved participant who shows that he or she understands and cares about the messages others are sending. A good listener hears feelings and probes for thoughts, intentions, and actions, as well as statements. To become a good listener, you must learn to observe (to take special notice of nonverbal cues such as facial expression, body movement, and breathing rates); to acknowledge (to let someone know you are really listening by paraphrasing or by reflecting your interest through nods, smiles, concerns, and comments such as "Uh huh"); to encourage (to invite the speaker to tell you more); and to check out your interpretations so that you know that what you are hearing is what is being said. (You will want to recycle the message back and forth until what is being sent and received are identical.) As you practice these attentive listening skills, try to imagine what your speaker's experiences may feel like. Doing so will help you to better appreciate the message being spoken.

❖ *Say what you feel.* Learn to share your deepest feelings and to express anger without blaming or attacking. Learn how to express affection and discuss problems with friends as well as lovers. Express emotions indirectly or symbolically, perhaps through a gift. Emotions can also be expressed nonverbally through kissing, hugging, crying, or even slamming doors. Such nonverbal demonstrations of emotion are certainly okay. Actions often have greater impact than spoken expression. But feelings and actions that are unsupported by words can be extremely ambiguous. Crying, for example, can express joy, sadness, disappointment, anger, or relief. Direct statements of feeling are much more powerful. Next time you feel upset, say so. Next time you feel excited, tell someone. Most people will readily respond. Expressing those feelings honestly and directly can be done in many ways. Expand your emotional vocabulary by adding these powerful feeling words: pleased, calm, comfortable, satisfied, bored, fearful, confused, lonely, excited, uneasy, silly, surprised, eager, angry, weary, glad, gleeful, content, confident, awkward, anxious, hopeful, sad, proud, relieved.

Using these techniques will help you connect with others more quickly and easily than you may ever have dreamed possible. All it takes is one positive response to send your shyness into seclusion. Being on the lookout only for Number One hinders communication. Remember that if you feel awkward and left out in social situations, so do many others. As you make a conscious effort to be pleasant, others will respond likewise. Pleasing others in this way can be reward enough.

Self-Confidence

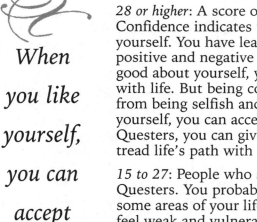

When you like yourself, you can accept life as a gift.

28 or higher: A score of 28 or higher on Self-Confidence indicates that you like and respect yourself. You have learned to accept both your positive and negative qualities. Because you feel good about yourself, you are happy and content with life. But being confident is quite different from being selfish and conceited. When you like yourself, you can accept life as a gift. Like most Questers, you can give yourself permission to tread life's path with enthusiasm.

15 to 27: People who score 15 to 27 are potential Questers. You probably feel quite confident in some areas of your life, while in others you may feel weak and vulnerable. Alternatively, your mood at the time you completed this questionnaire may have a lot to do with your score. Are you being overly hard on yourself? All too often achievement-oriented people set unrealistically high standards, standards that virtually ensure feelings of personal failure or inadequacy. Try to be realistic about what you can and can't do. Perhaps you are a perfectionist and just can't seem to give yourself the credit you deserve. Congratulate yourself on your accomplishments, willingness to risk, and initiative. On the other hand, you may not yet have learned how to translate criticism or mistakes into learning experiences. Go back to the questionnaire and reexamine your low scores. Work on improving these aspects of your personality. Soon your level of self-confidence, and your career development, will begin to escalate.

12 or lower: Your low self-opinion may be taking the fun out of life. With this sort of attitude, you can't possibly hope to feel satisfied or happy, or to establish healthy intimacy or work-related relationships. The gulf between having an inferiority complex and recognizing your own limits is vast but not insurmountable. While a few of your limitations are genetically based, most are due to bad life experiences. Just as it is important to recognize and accept your limits, it is important to try to change those which you can. And to stop agonizing over those you can't change. You are never too old or too young.

Tips for Building Self-Confidence

❖ *Know and accept yourself.* Think of yourself as you really are, rather than as you think you should be. See yourself as others do. Be objective. Don't feel too bad if your clothes are two sizes larger than when you were in high school, or if your viewpoints are occasionally biased, or if you are developing wrinkles and a receding hairline. Compare the picture in your mind to the reality of your presence. You may not like what you see, but to avoid acknowledging these disparities can create immense disharmony, both within yourself and with the people in your life. Know what you can and cannot do and what you want out of life. If you can change your weaknesses, go ahead and do it. But, at the same time, be sure to maximize your strengths. Acknowledge and accept your accomplishments by preparing a list of positive achievements and personality characteristics. Post your list on a bulletin board or a door where you can see it and read it every day. When negative thoughts or experiences creep into your consciousness, look over your list. By competing with yourself, you will be learning how to accept who you really are, not who you think you should be. Don't limit your potential for achievement by only half-knowing yourself. Get acquainted with your strengths and weaknesses, then dedicate life to daily improvements. It's almost guaranteed you will never be bored. Moreover, if you love and accept yourself, others will do the same.

❖ *Be yourself.* Don't be influenced by others who may reject your opinions. You don't have to change to please others. Opinions are extensions of your individuality. Even though others may not like what you say, most will respect your right to say it. Being overly concerned about what others think or trying too hard to please them can result in excessive inhibitions and poor performance. Don't inhibit your creative self or compare yourself to others, but try to maximize your strengths and improve your performance.

❖ *Reward yourself.* Start putting yourself first more often. A little self-indulgence is healthy for your ego. Start your morning by thinking of something positive you can do for yourself. Instead of going to the symphony because you are expected to, stay at home if you feel like it. Start dressing the way you would like to, not the way others say you should. Every time you pull through an experience you feared, give yourself a treat.

❖ *Trust and follow your intuition.* Take time to listen to your inner voice. Your intuition or "inner voice" may present itself to you in a visual, auditory, kinesthetic sensual or mental fashion. To identify and develop your intuitive strength, think about the different life experiences you have had in which your intuition came into play. For example, have you ever met anyone and, without knowing anything about him or her, taken an immediate like or dislike to the person? Did this hunch or gut reaction turn out to be accurate? Have you ever awakened in the morning with a feeling that something was going to happen to you completely out of the blue—that you'd get an unexpected promotion or demotion, for instance, and then what you imagined became reality? What emotions, thoughts, auditory signals, or body sensations were you experiencing at the time of your hunch? Make a list detailing the circumstances. Next, compare the various episodes. When you have a hunch, does a vision flash in your mind or are you apt to hear a voice? If your reactions are for the most part kinesthetic (felt through nerves and muscles), is the sensation always the same? Does it ever vary in intensity or occur in different parts of your body? Does your physical response to a hunch depend on the type of situation? Keep an Intuition Log. Record your intuition "awareness" and note how accurate you are in differentiating your intuition from your hopes and fears. With practice, you will become very good at listening to and understanding these inner cues.

❖ *Enjoy success.* Measure yourself by what you have done, what you are doing now, and what you can do. Keep a daily, weekly, or monthly record of your accomplishments and build on these. For example, develop an exercise routine. Start with five minutes of easy exercises every morning. Then get up three minutes earlier each week to work on it. Add a new routine each week. Mark this down. Be proud of yourself. Remember, change comes gradually. Strive each day to do something just a little better than yesterday. The exhilaration of achievement and growth will help you feel better about yourself.

❖ *Be image-conscious.* Your demeanor—the way you look, act, and express yourself—is your calling card; it's what you leave behind for people to remember you by. Act self-confident and you will be self-confident.

❖ *Use creative visualization.* You can create what you want out of life. Relax and slowly imagine yourself going through an anxiety-arousing situation without the accompanying fear and doubt. Picture yourself as competent and confident. Say to yourself, "I've done this before 100 times and I can do it again with no problem." Record any accomplishments you experience and your responses to them. Imagine yourself trusting all the positive feedback you receive.

❖ *Be heard.* Your speech is often a profound indicator of your level of self-confidence. Take responsibility for what you say. Be heard and be willing to speak clearly, not just loudly or aggressively.

❖ *Believe in yourself.* Affirm yourself. This will allow you to replace negative thoughts with positive ones. Tell yourself, "I am confident, intelligent, caring, and attractive" (or whatever you really want to be).

❖ *Be flexible.* Welcome the new and the unexpected. Listen to your hopes, dreams, and desires. Your creativity is challenged to the fullest by the new and unexpected. Open up, take a risk, explore new possibilities in your life. Be determined enough to achieve your goals, but flexible enough to change directions if required.

❖ *Maintain your perspective.* Time and distance can make once seemingly insurmountable mountains seem like inconsequential molehills. Why let what happened yesterday affect what will happen today or tomorrow? Face each new day and each new challenge with an open mind. They may not be as difficult as you thought.

❖ *Persevere.* Into every life usually comes some turbulence. Weather it out. Power comes from persevering in the face of adversity. Remember, achieving your goals takes hard work.

❖ *Prepare.* Preparation gives you control and the strength to carry on. Keep your hands on the wheel and your road map before you. If you know where you are going, you'll get around the roadblocks.

❖ *Maintain your focus.* Don't look back; look ahead. Keep your energy focused on the challenge and, sooner or later, you'll find a solution.

❖ *Depersonalize failure.* Look upon failure as one step toward growth. You tried. Next time you will succeed.

❖ *Learn to accept compliments.* Accept well-meaning remarks about your appearance or ability with grace and a simple, "Thank you."

❖ *Become an expert.* Learn as much as possible about some subject. Take responsibility for your area of expertise, then enjoy the power and authority that comes from being an expert. An additional payoff will be the renewed confidence that comes from knowing a lot about your particular interest.

❖ *Be responsible.* The more responsibility you assume, the more you will receive. Be responsible not only for performing your work, but also for maintaining your health, developing your personality, and enhancing your lifestyle.

Remember, you are an intelligent person who has succeeded in the past and can succeed again. Acknowledging this allows you to fully enjoy and appreciate your successes without the doubt and anxiety that may have accompanied past efforts. Only you have the power to project a confident image. Exercise it, nurture it, delight in it. You can make anything happen.

Purpose

20 or higher: A score of 20 or more on this section means that, like many Questers, you tend to be involved in activities that give you a sense of purpose, meaning, direction, and satisfaction. You are true to your inner self and have a zest for life. You probably have both short- and long-term goals and you are achieving them. Your various activities such as work, leisure, family, and relationships probably reflect a unity of purpose.

11 to 19: You are a potential Quester. Your goals may not be very clear or they may not reflect your main purpose. Do your job and other life roles help you live out who you really are? Are you having difficulty achieving your goals? You may benefit from the suggestions offered below.

10 or lower: You have little meaning and few goals in your life. You may be suffering from boredom, anxiety, frustration, and a sense of aimlessness. To develop more meaning in your life, you will need to take action to change family, relationships, spiritual, occupational, or other aspects of your life. Reconsider your philosophy of life.

Tips for Developing Purpose

Identifying your mission or purpose will take time, particularly if you are not accustomed to looking inward. A good start, however, is to identify and acknowledge your deepest dreams and hopes. Some individuals have one major purpose or theme running through their lives while others may have two or three which may vary slightly and/or change priorities over the life span. The following activities will enable you to begin to understand yourself better as well as your "raison d'etre."

❖ *Identify what's important to you.* Success may mean something different to you than to your spouse, your parents, or your best friend. When you try to live up to other people's expectations, it's easy to become anxious about failing. The pressure you feel from other people to succeed may be more overwhelming than the pressure you put on yourself. Tell friends and family, in a kind way, when they are placing demands on you to accomplish something you really don't want to do.

❖ *Consider how you would change your life if you knew that you had only six months to live.* Your answer to this question will be very revealing to you in helping you become more candid and straightforward with yourself. If you would make some very drastic changes, then you are not living your current life with absolute integrity. Thinking in terms of six months is useful because it gives you enough time to act on things that are important to you. Remind yourself of your terminal status. If you would change jobs, relationships, locations, friendships, lifestyles, means of communicating with your loved ones, or anything else, then why not get on with it while you still can?

❖ *State what you would do if monetary rewards did not matter.* Ask yourself what you would do if you didn't need money. If you are spending your time struggling at something that has no meaning for you and justifying it by saying that you must do it because it gives you money to pay your bills, then you have made the money more important than your own sense of purpose. You can probably make a good living doing what you really enjoy. Most Questers do. For example, Molly opened a craft shop to display and sell her candles and art, and Ross, a former accountant, makes and sells pottery.

❖ *Identify what kind of personality you would choose if you could begin your life today.* Would you be more assertive, less shy, more humorous, more outgoing, more confident, easier to talk to, more caring? No one forces you to remain shy, anxious, nonassertive. You make these life choices, and you can "remake" them if you really want to.

❖ *Describe yourself without using any labels.* Don't verbalize how old you are, where you live, what you studied in school, your job history, your marital status, your economic status, your hair color and height, or even your name. Instead, describe precisely what kind of human being you are. For example, "I am warm, sensitive, caring, intelligent, creative, intuitive, energetic, enthusiastic, confident, a loving spouse, and I have a sense of humor." If you resort to labels and describe yourself as if you were filling out a job application, then you may view yourself as a statistic sheet rather than as a special human being. And this very image may, in fact, be the reality that you have chosen for yourself. Many people have difficulty finding out what they really want to do because they confuse success, as judged by others, with success according to their own inner feelings of purpose. It is not what you choose to do that will bring you total honesty; it is knowing that the reason you are doing it corresponds with your feelings of self-worth.

❖ *Describe the person(s) with whom you would choose to live if you could live with anyone in the world.* Imagine that you have no legal obligation to stay with your immediate family, assuming you have one, and that you know of no reason why you could not legally live with anyone outside your immediate family. With whom would you choose to live? What's stopping you from living with this person(s)? If you are living in a relationship (family or otherwise) in which you feel obligated (rather than because you genuinely want to be there), then ask yourself why you made this choice and what you can do about the situation to make it more satisfying to all involved.

❖ *Do something worthwhile.* Volunteer your time. Make helping others a goal. Giving away a part of yourself, within reason, makes you a harbor open to all of the good things going on around the world. Adopt a cause. Sign up to work in a senior citizens' home or with the mentally retarded. Make clothes that can be given away to social agencies. Join a citizens' action group fighting for a cause in which you believe. Take a look around your community. You may discover a wealth of ways to get involved.

❖ *Complete the Life Cycle Exercise.* (1.) Think about the various periods of your life (birth to 10 years, 11 to 20 years, 21 to 30 years, and so on) and write down those experiences that gave you a sense of joy and completeness. Also list at least one activity you would really love to do. (2.) Make lists of your strengths and accomplishments, and the qualities or achievements for which you would most like to be remembered. Also, outline the characteristics you admire in others. (3.) Look for the prevailing themes or patterns that run through all these aspects of your life (like to work for justice, to heal others, to learn and to teach, to create, to be an agent of change). Write a statement that represents a mission or goal based on these recurring themes. (4.) Discuss your theme with a supportive partner, relative, or friend. (5.) Brainstorm how your purpose can be expressed in various components of your life. (For example, if your purpose is to help others, you can express it in work by being a social worker, a considerate employee, or a helpful colleague. In family activities, it may be expressed by being a loving spouse, parent, or considerate offspring.) Brainstorming will also help you obtain contacts and practical help. Do not allow age, lack of education or money, or some physical disability to stop you from pursuing your mission. (6.) List the kinds of occupations that would enable you to pursue your purpose. For example, if your purpose is to promote justice, you could express it by being an attorney, a public prosecutor, a policeman or woman, an investigative reporter, a broadcaster, a teacher, a criminologist, or other occupation. (7.) Get your feet wet. Once you've identified your mission, look for ways to get involved in pursuing it right now, without acquiring more skills, credentials, or money. For example, do volunteer work, take a course, participate in a group activity, or commit yourself to a worthy cause. (8.) Write a long-range goal that will make it possible for you to pursue this purpose in an occupational, leisure, or social activity. Visualize this goal. Include as many details as possible. Make some specific plans for the next three months toward achieving this goal (what you plan to do, when, where, with what, and with whom). Be flexible. Realize that your plans, goals, and mission statements may change as you get to know yourself better.

❖ *Make an Inventory of Your Dreams.* Write the things you want to have, do, be, and share. Keep your pen moving nonstop for no less than 10 to 15 minutes. Abbreviate whenever possible. Do not allow security or financial considerations to stop you from dreaming. Create the people, feelings, and places you want to be part of your life. Include a broad sampling of goals and outcomes related to work, family, relationships, leisure, and spiritual activities. Consider everything as possible. Knowing your outcome is the first step to reaching it. Throw away all limiting beliefs. Pick out the two goals you really want to attain this year. Write these down, indicating why you want them and how you will achieve them. Be clear, concise, and positive.

❖   *Do the Guided Fantasy Exercise.* Close your eyes and imagine yourself in a typical workday of your ideal occupation and lifestyle. Describe your whole day in detail, beginning with waking up in the morning and ending going to bed at night. Pay particular attention to the details of your home and work environments, your duties at work, your leisure activities, and your feelings about your various tasks and the people you encounter. Then ask yourself what made you feel excited, happy, challenged, or bored? Your feelings will help you identify the kind of work and lifestyle you really want. Once you know what you desire, you will be more willing to take the risks necessary to achieve your goals.

Autonomy

46 or higher: A score of 46 or more on Autonomy shows you are thinking like many Questers. You tend to be your own person. You believe in yourself and are independent, self-sufficient, and inner-directed. You honestly believe you are in charge of your own destiny and seldom blame others for bad experiences. You try to express your genuine self, your talents, interests, and unique personality. Rather than functioning as an adapted person or following someone else's script, you try to make your own decisions and, when need be, even swim against the tide. Far from being unnecessarily unconventional or prone to illegal or socially unacceptable behavior, you seem to have the courage to transcend your environment when it infringes on your personal and professional growth.

24 to 45: You may be overly concerned with other people's opinions. Status, success, or another's opinions may be

Self-knowledge and self-acceptance are the first steps toward constructive action.

controlling your life. Possibly you believe chance or luck play an important part in your life. Go back over the statements in this section. What kind of changes can you or do you want to make?

23 or lower: You are quite dependent. Your levels of growth, creativity, and self-confidence are probably quite low. You may believe what happens to you is determined by powerful others, fate, or chance. You are influenced greatly by pressure from authority figures and peers, and probably lack clear goals. You may have decided early on to settle for quite a bit less in life than may be necessary. You seem to have chosen to take the path of least resistance by not facing up to the anxiety that accompanies growth. You can enhance your sense of autonomy and control by putting more faith in your own ability to make good things happen.

To become more independent, you must be aware of some basic principles. First, becoming more independent relies on your being aware of and accepting yourself, knowing that you have options in life, and taking action to achieve the goals you truly value. Self-knowledge and self-acceptance are the first steps toward constructive action.

Getting to know yourself better is a process of letting go of old ideas about who you are or should be. Learn to accept yourself, flaws and all, for who you really are. Own your successes. Don't attribute them to chance; they are the result of your efforts and abilities. You'll also need to accept reality. Drive away those rigid or irrational beliefs that are blocking your expression. Accept the fact that your own decisions are just as good, and maybe better, than anyone else's. Besides, the wrong decision may just be a detour on the way to discovering the right one. Stop setting up self-fulfilling negative prophecies. Practice thinking positively about yourself and your abilities. Developing self-confidence can take time, but the results can be phenomenal. Keep an open mind, learn to tolerate ambiguity and trust your own decisions. By seeking out new experiences, you may make some astonishing discoveries about yourself.

Understanding that you do have options is the second step. People trapped in bad marriages, relationships, or occupations do have options. Testing your options may mean trade-offs, but sometimes they're well worth the inconvenience. Knowing that you have a choice in life can eliminate a lot of the distress and uncertainty that accompany difficult experiences. Studies have shown that the more freedom you believe you have, the more able you will be to meet and master the challenges of living.

Exercising your options is the third step to becoming more autonomous. Independent people have learned to act when they are afraid, when they feel like phonies, when they are certain they will do a poor job, when they think they are stupid, and when they don't want to act at all. Independence requires action. Confront your fears. Speak up to your boss, take that vacation alone, or approach your partner or spouse with your concerns. To increase your ability to be more independent, practice the following:

Tips for Enhancing Autonomy

❖ *Believe that anything worth doing is worth doing—even poorly.* Don't let your fear of not being perfect stop you from trying. If you are socially insecure, try settling for less than the perfect date. Learn to speak up, even if what you have to say isn't brilliant. Invite friends over to your home more often. Do what you want to do, not what others think you should. Rather than trying so hard to please others, learn to please yourself. Stop trying to make people like you or to hide your flaws; you are who you are. Learn to become more vulnerable. Anxiety or fear can be major blocks to social independence. Instead of trying to protect yourself from potentially negative experiences, plunge in and see what the results are. You may even enjoy yourself. Accept the fact that you are afraid. Don't fight it. Instead of hiding your anxiety, which will only make you more anxious, tell others you are nervous. Most people will understand; after all, they've been in that position, too.

❖ *Experiment with confronting your irrational or distorted beliefs.* For example, spell out your negative predictions ("People will stare at me if I dine alone"), then devise ways to test them (venture out alone to a favorite restaurant). Now develop a way to measure the outcome (look around and see how people are reacting). Finally, draw a conclusion. ("I can dine by myself.") Keep a record of irrational thoughts and devise experiments to challenge their validity.

❖ *Practice being more intellectually independent.* Follow your own beliefs rather than echoing others' opinions. Intellectual independence increases efficiency, which builds self-confidence, which leads to even more independence. This is the success cycle. As you learn to think more for yourself, you will see that you can start and follow through with those pet projects. You can do so by becoming more assertive and direct, by saying what you mean and want, by being concise, and by letting your opinions stand on their own two feet. Learn to state your preferences, to speak up and to say what you want and feel. Just because others have opinions doesn't mean yours aren't valid. The same principle applies to your tastes in art, music, food, and other cultural pursuits. Own your opinions and preferences. After all, there are few right or wrong decisions, just different results. Practice making your own decisions, and once you do make a decision, follow it through.

Changing distorted beliefs requires an open mind. Seek out and investigate facts that contradict your beliefs. Facts and experiences are the only way to test the validity of those long-held ideas. Instead of being a stereotypical thinker, be a creative thinker. No two people or situations are exactly the same, and just because you have had a negative experience in the past, doesn't mean it will happen again. Broaden your tolerance, develop creative outlets, take time out to think and reflect, and you will be on your way to a happier, more rewarding life.

Learning to become more independent is similar to learning to ride a bike. Repetition helps. Repeat to yourself, "It's better to do as much as possible for myself" or "I can do it, no matter what." Now practice this skill in different situations, starting with the most comfortable, and then progressing to the least comfortable.

Being in control takes time, effort, and transformation. But, chances are, you'll find taking charge of your own life makes you feel better about the direction of your life. Soon, you will discover that you have more choices, more independence, more strength, and more control than you ever thought possible.

Achievement

26 or higher: Is your score for achievement 26 or higher? Like the Questers, you tend to be motivated to achieve by an internal drive such as the desire to do your best, or to accomplish tasks that require skill and effort, or to do a difficult task well. You may be determined to improve and do a better job. If you are predisposed to measuring your effectiveness in terms of achievement, you usually want to know how to improve your effectiveness. You tend to measure success by internal standards, rather than by status symbols or material wealth. You enjoy the whole process of learning, accomplishing, and mastering. You are fortunate to find your work fulfilling, and are probably getting a chance to do things that you are capable of and really enjoy. Your work may also be your leisure. You would rather spend time and money at an interesting job than be an outstanding success at one that bores you. You want the best for yourself and are uncompromising about your standards of excellence. When you finish a project, you want to move on. While your work is obviously fairly important to you, you need to take more time for leisure. What can you do to put more fun into your free time?

14 to 25: You may be a relatively easygoing person who is quite satisfied with your work and lifestyle. Alternatively, you may avoid difficult tasks for fear of failing. Check your low scores for clues, then decide where you can make some changes in your life.

13 or lower: You may lack ambition. If you fall into this category, you tend to have a rather lackadaisical approach to life. You do as little work as possible and have a tendency to give up when the going gets tough. If you are happy with your lifestyle, then that's okay. If you aren't, try accomplishing something you will feel good about. Bake a torte or build a great recreation room. Learn to fix your car. Develop a respectable game of tennis. Perhaps you should be looking for a new job that will give you a better sense of accomplishment.

Tips for Achieving

❖ *Believe in the possibility and desirability of change in almost everything, including yourself.*

❖ *Think in terms of action and consequences or results.*

❖ *Find a hobby or an area of interest and become outstanding at it.* Doing so will also increase your self-assurance.

❖ *Work hard and go the extra distance.* How can you improve your latest project? Set your own criteria for measuring your effectiveness.

❖ *Learn to manage your time better.* Good time management is good life management.

❖ *Assess situations from your own perspective.* Seek guidance, if you wish, but avoid leaving evaluation about situations that affect you entirely in the hands of others.

❖ *Assume more personal responsibility for improving those situations where you have some control.* Try to take the initiative, to demonstrate your energy and drive, rather than leaving the outcome to chance or to the abilities of others.

❖ *Identify a set of goals and develop strategies for achieving them.* Set high goals for yourself, goals that are difficult but not impossible to achieve. Then strive for excellence. Goal setting works better if you decide in advance how you will measure your effectiveness and include a specific time frame for completing these goals. To determine how you are doing, seek constructive feedback from the people around you. Be persistent and patient. Instead of stumbling over roadblocks, seek alternatives, or figure out how to improve the situation.

❖ *Take the initiative.* Demonstrate your energy, drive, and decisiveness, but don't try to run the whole show yourself. Choose colleagues to whom you can delegate tasks with confidence.

❖ *Upgrade your skills.* Perhaps your employer will pay for additional management or technical training you could use.

❖ *Pinpoint something enjoyable in every task you undertake.*

❖ *Be amiable.* Try to show a sense of humor (particularly about yourself) and attempt to draw people to you. In stressful times, these people can be valuable friends and allies.

❖ *Place more emphasis on mastering a task and on improving and innovating.* Don't just focus on avoiding failure. You can find your reward in doing a better job. Money should be a symbol of your success, not an end in itself. Start thinking today about what you could be doing tomorrow to develop a better product or service for your employer.

❖ *Reward yourself.* Pat yourself on the back for completing a task or sticking with a difficult project. Coax yourself along by setting aside time for enjoyable breaks, such as reading a favorite magazine or sleeping in. As you reach milestones along the way, reward yourself with an evening out or a day off. Major projects could be the impetus for larger rewards, such as a ski weekend or trip to the lake.

❖ *Keep a diary of every achievement you have accomplished or hope to accomplish.* Record your successes and desires. Make lists of your successes and place these where you can see them several times a day, for example, on the refrigerator door or the bathroom mirror.

❖ *Eliminate negative thoughts and feelings.* Negative thoughts and feelings produce negative results and tend to block the flow of energy in your body. To change your mental attitude, use positive statements about who you are and what you are doing. Monitor your self talk. Each time you catch yourself using a negative phrase, say "Cancel" and replace the negative thought or statement with a positive one. Additional suggestions for eliminating negative thoughts and feelings are discussed in chapter 2.

With success also comes a sense of purpose and satisfaction. Completing difficult tasks can be energizing. The exhilaration of achievement and growth will make you feel better about yourself. Soon, you will be accomplishing even more difficult tasks.

Innovativeness

Learn to

bring out

the child

deep inside

of you.

28 or higher: You tend to be an innovator. You like change and use your imagination to find new ways of doing many kinds of activities, work-related or personal. Shaping fresh, new perspectives about yourself, life, and the world around tends to bring you great joy. You are a complex, self-accepting person with many interests. You are generally independent, intuitive, and capable of seeing many sides of a problem. To you, routine is boring. You would much rather tread new ground than follow in your colleagues' footsteps.

15 to 27: You may enjoy innovation in your personal life but dislike change in your work routine. Or the opposite may be true; perhaps you are very innovative at work, but conservative at home. To become a Quester, look back over the questionnaire statements and decide which aspects of your personality could use a little creative remodeling. For some ideas, read over the suggestions below.

14 or lower: You probably dislike change. You tend to enjoy the status quo, and prefer the tried-and-true way. If you are satisfied with your life, don't change. But if you want to add more excitement, learn to free and release the creative potential within so that you can express your real self. Learn to bring out the child deep inside of you.

Creativity is a quality everyone possesses. Unfortunately, few know how to tap into it. You can live more creatively and intelligently by following the suggestions below. They are aimed at helping you to develop your creativity by quieting, within you, the voices of reason, disbelief, certainty, time, routine, and social structures. In their rush to point out the rational and logical, these voices can often drown out your intuitive voice. Experiment. There is no right or wrong. Let ideas suggest others. Devise your own ways of freeing your creativity. But, remember, transformation doesn't happen overnight. Be prepared to give the process time.

Tips for Increasing Innovativeness

❖ *Learn to utilize Hurricane Thinking.* Suppose you had to give a talk or write a paper about Cape Cod or any place you choose. First, write Cape Cod in the center of a piece of paper and circle it. This is the eye of the hurricane. Now, write down the first thoughts that come to mind. Place these somewhere around the eye, or main topic. If this process generates related ideas, jot these down close to the parent thought. Draw lines to connect these related ideas. Should a completely unrelated association come to mind, record it on the opposite corner of the page. See if this new idea will produce offspring as well. Continue this process until the page is filled with major points swirling around the calm eye of Cape Cod. What is important in this exercise is not to evaluate your ideas, but to write down all of them that come to mind. Let your mind roam freely to produce as many ideas as possible. Now you will need to organize your cluster of ideas into a formal presentation. Link them up or circle them with different-colored pencils to see where they logically belong. What sequences seem most appropriate? Extend Hurricane Thinking throughout your personal and career life. Be on the alert to those "crazy ideas" that could be the spark of genius.

❖ *Make friends with the imp inside you.* Jot down a list of those things that parents or authority figures always warned you about. Be especially conscious of what you went ahead and did anyway and succeeded at despite their predictions of failure. Examine the attitudes and beliefs you developed as a result of these early teachings. Consider how, given your age and circumstances, these may no longer be appropriate. Admonitions such as "Never question authority," "Boys don't cry," "Never eat in bed," or "Save for a rainy day" may have been useful at one time in your life, but do they really apply today? Examining long-held attitudes and beliefs, particularly those that stifle creativity and change, can open you to new ways of being. No one is encouraging you to throw socially acceptable behavior to the wind. But perhaps it is time you determined which attitudes and values are crucial to your current lifestyle—and which may be cramping your innovativeness.

❖ *Become more playful.* Don't let dogged determination kill your sense of fun. An element of playfulness will make you more creative, more satisfied, and more productive. What people think of fun varies to each individual and situation. However, many individuals find some of the following activities fun: having lunch with people you enjoy, going for a picnic in the country, spending a day at the beach or circus, having a costume party, telling jokes, playing games, painting, attending a concert, dancing, drawing, singing, shopping, gourmet cooking, and gardening.

❖ *Identify face-to-face tensions.* Select two opposing tensions in your life. They may be two contradictory urges or feelings, incompatible goals, two roles you are required to play, perhaps even two duties or responsibilities that conflict with each other. Examples are: independence vs. dependence; career vs. family life; male vs. female; freedom vs. security; friendship vs. solitude. Next, write down all the characteristics associated with each tension. Eliminate those shared by both. Then evaluate the remaining dissimilarities. These are the truly opposing forces in your personality. Explore your creativity. How can these contradictions be resolved? How can these tensions be allied? Keep in mind that there is often strength in diversity, but give some serious thought to how you can lessen some of the tension involved in the opposing forces in your life.

❖ *Try new things.* Learn how to accept and process criticism from your boss, clients, employers, friends, or family members without becoming defensive and angry. Be open to new information about yourself. Play the devil's advocate by arguing the opposite side. Experiment more. Start with a new restaurant; order a dish you never tried before. Make your relationship more creative by surprising your partner with a small gift or favorite meal. Don't wait for a special occasion. Read an unusual book. Give those science fiction books you've been reading for the past eight years a rest and pick up a historical novel or pop psychology best-seller. As you become more comfortable with adding unusual touches to your life, you will find life will become more fun and rewarding.

❖ *Draw or doodle.* Write out a qustion that clearly states what you want to know. Underneath your question, draw whatever comes to your mind or flows though your hands.

Continue to draw until you feel you have nothing to add to the picture. Now, use your intuitive skills to interpret the meaning behind the drawing and the symbols within it. Note the sequence of steps. Pay particular attention to the thoughts and feelings such as joy or sadness you experience as you look at the drawing.

Androgyny

60 or higher: People who score 60 or higher on androgyny closely resemble Questers. If you are one, you tend to possess the best of male and female strengths. Regardless of your gender, and depending on the situation, you can be both nurturing and assertive, competitive and cooperative, confident and tender. You are tolerant, broad-minded, innovative, autonomous, and free from stereotyped thinking. You have probably selected an occupation and lifestyle that suits you and feels comfortable. You don't consider your work to be either a man's or a woman's job.

35 to 59: You tend to have mixed feelings about what is appropriate for men and women. While you may tolerate some androgynous behavior, you may be more traditional about what constitutes acceptable gender-role standards. Back up. See which of your attitudes and behavior are androgynous and which are traditional. Were the statements that you scored low on related to assertiveness, achievement, confidence, intimacy, or to traditional beliefs and values about what constitutes appropriate male and female behaviors? As you become more aware of your feelings, attitudes, and behavior, you can take the first steps to becoming a Quester.

30 or lower: Do you have very traditional views about what is appropriate behavior for men and women? Chances are you attained 30 or less. A score in this range indicates you were low on one or more of the other Quester characteristics such as intimacy, confidence, achievement, or growth. It may also indicate rigid ideas about gender roles that could hurt your health. The energy you are expending trying to deal with this conflict is incredible. Gender-role attitudes and behaviors are learned responses that can also be unlearned.

Tips for Becoming More Androgynous

❖ *Take one step at a time.* Get to know your real self and learn to express this self in personal and work activities. Read over the suggestions offered for developing other Quester characteristics such as purpose, confidence, growth, and innovativeness and see where you can broaden your mind to free yourself from preconceived notions about yourself and others.

❖ *Learn to accommodate other people's values, rights, feelings, and perceptions.* Being open-minded demands the ability to listen, to respond, to interact with others, to be free of the constraint of imposing value judgments on people. You might try developing this quality by becoming more empathetic toward your spouse or partner. Empathy is the ability to get into the other person's feelings and experiences—to walk in their shoes—and to let them know that you understand how they are feeling.

❖ *Try to put yourself in the other person's place.* A man who works in a traditionally male occupation such as electrician, may wish to switch roles with a female colleague for a few days to identify subtle ways which he and his male colleagues may be discriminating against females such as not considering them for certain tasks, training, or promotional opportunities. A man who believes household chores belong in the woman's domain could ask his partner how she feels about doing these household tasks. He may wish to take responsibility for certain traditionally female tasks, such as cooking, for a period of time. Women may do the same. Not all men like performing traditional male chores such as mowing the lawn or fixing things around the home. Women may wish to discuss reassignment of responsibilities with their partner and then take over some of the traditional male roles, if this meets both your needs. Women may also try being more assertive by learning to say what they mean and feel without being offensive. First, practice being assertive in situations that feel less threatening, such as with family and friends. For example, tell that aunt who plans a three-week visit that a weekend visit would be better for everyone. Test your new assertive behavior at home and at work. With practice and time, you'll feel more comfortable.

Risk

50 or higher: Like most Questers, people who score 50 or higher tend to enjoy taking risks. You are also autonomous, you like challenge, are confident, flexible, and given to seeking out new experiences.

26 to 49: Potential Questers tend to score between 26 and 49. The higher your score, the more you resemble the Questers. You may be open to new experiences in some areas of your life, but overly organized or rigid in others. Or you may be reluctant to risk because of family commitments. Becoming a Quester requires determining what changes can help you become more risk-oriented.

25 or lower: You are definitely not a risk taker. You prefer a secure, well-ordered lifestyle. You don't like ambiguity or trying out new things and may fear failure. Change is scary, but if you want to grow and develop to your potential, you may wish to consider making some alterations.

Tips for Learning to Take Risks

❖ *Make small changes first.* Experiment with a different hairstyle. Men might try growing a mustache or beard. At work, offer suggestions about better ways of tackling a job. Change your daily routine. Take a bath instead of a shower, for example. When you feel you are ready to take a bigger risk, such as with your career, carefully read over chapters 8 and 9 to learn how the Questers do it.

❖ *Look upon something new, different, or unknown as exciting—an opportunity to challenge yourself and to grow.* If you don't try something different, how will you ever find out you can do it?

❖ *Have a goal.* A risk without a clear purpose can backfire. Do your homework. Ask questions, know the pros and cons of all choices. Once you know all the facts and have listened to your intuition, act decisively.

❖ *Balance tentativeness with commitment.* Set goals but don't write them in stone. Be open to new experiences. These may enable you to attain your destination using a different path. On the other hand, while you are on this path, you may come across some pleasant coincidences which may entice you to modify your original goal.

❖ *Believe in yourself.* Affirm yourself. This will enable you to replace negative thoughts and feelings with positive ones. Tell yourself, "I can do anything I want." "I am in charge of my life." (Or whatever you really want to be or do.)

❖ *Turn failure into growth,* obstacles into opportunities. Consider "failure" as a temporary setback or challenge to learn from. Failure can be the impetus to move on to bigger, even better projects, jobs, or relationships. It is the beginning of growth. If you deny failure, you run away from growth. Rather than giving up, learn from and depersonalize your setbacks. Ask yourself what you would do differently and then make the necessary modifications.

❖ *Establish a suport group.* Don't try to make big changes entirely on your own. Seek family or friends who are positive and supportive.

Remember, the first risk is always the most difficult. Taking risks gets easier each time. Before you begin your adventure in risk taking, try the Fantasy Risk Exercise. Write your answers on a sheet of paper.

1. Think of an important risk, (such as, taking a credit course at a college, taking a short trip by yourself, applying for a sabbatical, changing your job, taking early retirement, moving to another part of the country), that you would like to take soon, something that is within your control but that you are afraid to initiate.

2. What appeals to you about taking the risk? What would you gain from it? (Be both objective and subjective about your response. That is, take into account economic, family, and other realities as well as your thoughts and feelings.)

3. What is frightening about this risk? What holds you back from taking it? What do you stand to lose if you don't take it?

4. What's the worst thing that would happen if it turned out badly?

5. If the worst thing happened, then what would you do?

6. If you need information to pursue this risk, where could you go for it?

7. From whom could you get support?

8. What could you do to make this less risky? What kind of measures could you build in to make it less urgent? Less irreversible? Less overwhelming?

9. Suppose you were to break the risk into small steps? What would the first step be? How soon could you take it? What would the second step be? How soon could you take it? Proceed this way through each step.

10. Evaluate the outcome of the risk. Did it turn out as expected? If not, why? What have you learned for next time?

11. Celebrate your success. Give yourself credit for taking the risk whether or not it turned out as expected. Gradually, you will see yourself as a risk taker.

Growth

52 or higher: You know and accept yourself. You tend to seek growth in both your personal and professional life by seeking opportunities to develop yourself to the fullest. Your perception of reality is sound and you have fairly good tolerance for ambiguity. You can accept others as well as yourself. You are natural, spontaneous, and innovative. You can also be altruistic. Self-fulfillment and achievement are important motivators for you. When you are no longer growing on the job, you move on to something else that will better satisfy your needs for challenge, autonomy, use of your talents, and self-expression. You tend to possess most of the other Quester qualities.

26 to 51: You tend to be a potential Quester. You may enjoy challenge and be open to new experiences, but perhaps you can't take criticism. Or you may fear failure and have difficulty accepting your own limits. Look over the questions again and note where you picked up low scores. If you want to become a Quester, you must decide what you are prepared to do differently.

25 or lower: You probably like a very secure life with a not-too-difficult job. You may lack confidence, fear failure, and be overly concerned with others' opinions. You don't need to change, but if you want to start small with easily accomplished tasks, try the following suggestions.

Tips for Facilitating Growth

❖ *Take a course in a subject you want to learn more about.* You can often get new perspectives or skills that may help you change your life. Learn how to learn, how to acquire new information, and how to translate that information into constructive experiences. Whatever course you choose, whether it be a new computer language, assertiveness training, or a master's degree in business administration, choose it because you are interested in it and believe it will help you achieve your goal.

❖ *Express your creativity.* Take up painting, writing, macrame, singing, gourmet cooking, photography, woodworking, or carpentry. Creative expression helps you grow by giving you ready evidence of your creativity which can inspire you on to even greater performance.

❖ *Accept and encourage constructive criticism.* Don't take criticism too personally. Listen to what your critics are saying and then find out what you could do differently. If you think the criticism is unfair, say so, but only after you hear out your critic. Especially helpful is criticism from people who have nothing to gain, and possibly something to lose, by giving you feedback.

❖ *Learn how to accept compliments.* Accept well-meaning remarks about your appearance or ability with grace and a simple "Thank you." Trust that the compliment is sincere.

❖ *Depersonalize "failure."* You don't have to get an A in every subject. Failure is just a stage in becoming more fully you and a part of the world, a step toward, not away from, growth. Failing at something means that you at least tried. Next time, you will succeed.

❖ *Develop a sense of humor.* Put some distance between yourself and your problems by thinking about how they will look 10 years from now. Learn to laugh at yourself.

❖ *Be persistent.* Once you have decided on a goal, put yourself into your positive-thinking gear. Be determined enough to achieve your goal, but flexible enough to change directions if required. Don't stubbornly cling to habits, actions, or beliefs that are damaging to your personal or professional life.

❖ *Take time to be silent.* Be guided by your intuition, rather than externally imposed interpretations of what is or is not good. Listen to your body which expresses itself through signals of comfort and discomfort. Communicate with nature—take a walk in the woods, by the water, or find another setting away from the hustle and bustle of contemporary urban life.

❖ *Relinquish your need for approval.* There is great freedom in that choice.

❖ *Review the suggestions offered under Self-Confidence, Autonomy, Achievement, Innovativeness, and Risk.* No matter what your score in these sections, the suggestions can be helpful.

Are You a Potential Quester?

If you agreed with statements 12, 24, 48, and 60, disagreed with statements 36, 72, 84, 96, and 108, and scored in the middle range or higher for most of the other personality characteristics discussed in the preceding pages, then you are definitely a potential Quester. Potential Questers possess some Quester characteristics. Because they are often engaged in serious self-assessment, their attitudes, values, and goals may be shifting. During this time, potential Questers may be thinking about leaving dissatisfying positions or modifying other life components, such as family or relationships that are no longer compatible with their developing personalities, to become Questers. Read over these statements again. They might provide you with some additional insights into yourself and your feelings about your current life and career.

Putting It All Together

330 or higher: The higher your overall score, the more closely you resemble the Questers. A score of 330 or more indicates you are a Quester. You attained high scores on the personality characteristics of intimacy, self-confidence, purpose, autonomy, achievement, innovativeness, androgyny, risk, and growth. You also should attain high scores on The Job Satisfaction Questionnaire and The Job Involvement Questionnaire (see chapter 7).

135 to 329: You are a potential Quester (particularly if you agreed with statements 12, 24, 48, and 60 and disagreed with statements 36, 72, 84, 96, and 108). You may have scored

high on some Quester characteristics and low on others, or you may have scored in the middle range on all of them. Low scores on The Job Satisfaction Questionnaire and The Job Involvement Questionnaire and a high score on The Burnout Questionnaire indicate that, for your physical and mental health, you should seriously consider a job change (see chapter 7 for these quizzes). Chapters 8 and 9 should give you some ideas about how to accomplish this. The list of Suggested Readings at the end of this book contains a number of good books on job search techniques.

You alone are responsible for your growth.

134 or lower: You are a confirmed Traditionalist, at least for now. High overall scores on The Job Satisfaction Questionnaire indicate that you are probably a happy Traditionalist who is satisfied with your job. If your scores are low, you should think about changing your position or another component of your life. This book and good counseling should help you accomplish this.

You alone are responsible for your growth. You have enormous power to change who you are and what happens to you. Learn to use it slowly. Discard those old habits that are holding you back, such as belittling yourself or taking unnecessary precautions. And if the questionnaire you have just taken has shown that you are either a Quester or a potential Quester, don't ignore that discovery. Dare to take the next step.

Career Change:
Up-Down-Sideways

hat makes the
Questers different?
Unlike most people,
they have learned to ask
themselves such questions
as "What do I want out of life?"
"What should I do next?" "Why
am I here?" They have learned to
do a little investigation into their
needs, values, and purpose. They get
answers and then get going. Sound
impossible in today's job market? Not so.
Many Questers have learned you can't put a price tag
on happiness. They understand that they alone are
responsible for their career satisfaction and marketability.
Most Questers have learned to monitor their careers and
when staleness or dissatisfaction starts to set in, they look

for new opportunities. By remaining open to alternatives, they are enhancing their ability to survive in tough job markets. You can do that, too.

Questers tend to take care of their careers by evaluating their development, tuning into their feelings, and being aware of new opportunities. Questers see their careers as ongoing opportunities for personal and professional growth. Their next career assignment is usually lined up while they still have a job, not while they are faced with the many stresses of being out of work. Life is like a tree that branches out before them. The assumption that an implicit social contract guaranteeing their work, status, and income comes with the job just isn't realistic to Questers. Their careers involve periodic assessments of who they are and where they want to go. Are you one of these people?

Finding excitement and satisfaction in a career requires understanding yourself —your needs, values, skills, and purpose.

Finding excitement and satisfaction in a career requires understanding yourself — your needs, values, skills, and purpose. You may enjoy a variety of career directions in the same occupation or want to explore different occupations or even work for yourself. Questers feel free to move up or down the career ladder. What matters is not what others think of your career direction, or what is socially acceptable, but what feels right for you.

Life crises often influence the direction of your career. Questers may have been through a divorce or experienced a death in the family, the loss of a job, job dissatisfaction, frustration with a boss, or even the desire for financial independence. Major or minor, these "determining events" usually lead them to reassess their lives. Events like these can be the catalysts for change.

Because of the influence of past generations—who usually trained for one occupation for life and stayed in it—many people today are not prepared for the idea of change. Therefore, we fear change. But today career possibilities are almost endless. Not only are many traditional occupations still open but opportunities abound in emerging and growing fields including health care, computers, telecommunications, bioscience, business and finance, hospitality, and service. Running your own business and working part-time in two different jobs or returning to school full- or part-time for retraining or upgrading are other options. Just stop and think about it. The world is full of opportunities.

Same Occupational Field

Almost 60 percent of Questers who change jobs stay in the same occupational field. Staying in a job that has a similar psychological climate, they move on to different work environments which provide them with a change, opportunities to grow, to learn something new, to try something different, to achieve greater challenge, responsibility or authority, to make a greater contribution to humankind. Moving on to a new position in the same field can be accomplished in many different ways. You could go from elementary school teacher to special education teacher to school librarian or art teacher. Or you could progress from rehabilitation counselor to social worker to college placement officer. Or how about from bank manager to hotel manager to hospital manager? Even from bookkeeper to clerical supervisor to collection clerk. Why not from surgical nurse to special duty nurse to pediatric nurse? People who stay in the same field often rise to positions of greater responsibility, authority and autonomy, such as manager of a larger bank or hotel. With each move, they gain broader knowledge and experience. Questers who found new satisfaction and success in the same occupational fields often have fascinating stories to tell.

Helen, a physician, is a Quester who has found satisfaction by changing the focus of her attention in her original profession. At 50, still slim and youthful-looking, Helen is looking for answers to the mysteries of human pain. As head of her city's first palliative care unit, a hospice for the terminally ill, her quiet influence extends far beyond the hospital's walls. Helen has true compassion. She has a tremendous amount of medical training, kindness, energy, and consideration for her patients. She listens and cares.

Caring for and helping people was Helen's goal when, fresh from a nursing program, she entered medical school in England. Her career was interrupted only once. At 30, she quit to have two children. Three years later, in 1968, Helen moved with her husband and children to the United States. For seven years, she practiced family medicine in a Midwestern city. Then, at 40, hoping to learn more so she could better help her patients, she returned to school for specialized training in obstetrics and gynecology. As a woman and a mother, Helen already understood many of the concerns of her female patients. She enjoyed her work, and her patients enjoyed her care.

But Helen's true professional calling didn't become evident until she helplessly watched a dying cancer victim writhe in agony while giving birth. Helpless and indignant, Helen became determined to see that terminal patients died in peace and dignity. Through the years, she gained a reputation for dealing sensitively with dying patients and their families. She also fought doggedly for the establishment of a palliative care unit at her hospital. Helen had the ability and tenacity to see her ideas through. It wasn't always clear sailing. While financial problems and uncertain government funding threatened the establishment of the unit, she continued to be optimistic. Now, in addition to heading the palliative care unit, she is conducting research into pain control. To promote palliative care, Helen schedules speaking engagements at least once a week. She also works actively to fulfill her patients' final wishes.

Helen changed jobs because she wanted to serve her patients better. She has all the qualities of a good physician: highly dedicated, selfless, and self-disciplined. She is also healthy and can stand the pressure of working long days and nights, frequently on call. Helen's work gives her a great deal of satisfaction. In fact, her life is her work, although she also enjoys her family, her regular swims, cooking, and gardening. Helen has combined her career and family responsibilities in an enjoyable, rewarding lifestyle.

Len is another Quester who has changed jobs several times in the same occupational field. As a business administration student, Len chose marketing. Marketing research helps companies make decisions by determining what motivates consumers to buy a company's products, how and when products are used, and how much people are willing to pay.

"It was a dynamic field, not routine. I thought it would be a challenge."

Len is 55 now, and he still finds marketing challenging. By now, he's had several positions in the field. His first was with a large consumer food products corporation. He took it because he wanted to get experience, learn about corporate life, and apply his knowledge. "I learned a lot about these things," Len remembers. "I also developed greater confidence and became better at speaking up about my ideas." Five years later, Len moved on. He had mastered the job. Now, ready to explore other products and markets, he joined a large industrial marketing firm and stayed for 14 years. He was moved around sufficiently within the company so he continued to enjoy both new challenges and the opportunity for career growth. During the first four years, Len researched different products in the Midwestern region. Then, he was sent to a foreign country for four years to open a marketing division. Heading up a training and consulting division in the United States followed that. Len liked his job, but six years later, he was ready to move again. He was no longer growing and the work had lost its challenge. If Len had stayed with the company, he might have been given the responsibility of heading a larger division. But the economy was uncertain and he would have had to wait his turn. Len decided not to wait. He was determined to take charge of his own career.

Doing so meant being responsible. Len knew he had to line up a new job before he could leave. That new job turned out to be general manager and marketing specialist for a medium-sized information systems firm. This time, Len was feeling the itch again after just four years. The fact that he didn't agree with the philosophies of the other managers aided his decision. Len recalls being extremely unhappy; his coworkers were uncooperative and seldom agreed with him.

His next move was to his current position, general manager of special products for a medium-sized medical instruments distribution company. The work is exciting. Most importantly, he is in tune with the philosophies and values of the other senior managers. Len has been with the company for four years now and he still finds the work challenging. If he could start over, would he choose marketing again? "Very definitely!" Len asserts. "It's exciting and challenging."

That attitude explains why Len has been so successful in marketing. Both creative and detail-minded, he is well suited to research. Len can see the big picture of shifting economic and social trends, political realities, and changing lifestyles. He also has the right temperament to cope with competition, uncertainty, pressure, constant change, and long hours. Above all, he is extroverted and amiable. Colleagues get along well with him.

Len's personality is what makes him a good marketing person. He knows from experience that many of the most creative and lucrative positions in marketing are the least secure. Being responsible for important marketing decisions leaves him open to both praise and blame. As he says, "In parts of our business, you aren't considered to be good if you haven't been fired at least once. Because if you haven't been fired, you haven't had the guts to take the risks necessary to be successful." For talented, energetic, and creative Questers like Len, marketing is a good career choice.

Chin Yong began university in an architecture program. By the third year, he had switched to civil engineering. It seemed more practical. He's glad he did. Today, Chin Yong is a structural engineer with a California consulting firm specializing in earthquake engineering. He analyzes plans of construction engineers and inspects building projects. He loves the challenge and creativity.

Many Questers have turned hobbies and interests into rewarding careers.

Chin Yong held two other civil engineering positions before be joined his present employer. His first job was with a state department as a transportation engineer, planning, constructing, and maintaining roads, bridges, and airports. That position lasted seven years until he could no longer grow on the job. Then he accepted a job in hydraulic engineering. He designed and supervised the construction of artificial canals and reservoirs and directed water-control projects. His second job also lasted seven years. When the challenge was gone again, he moved to the West Coast to specialize in soil research and earthquake engineering. What does Chin Yong want to do in the future? "Perhaps become a free-lance consultant or learn more about environmental pollution control," he says. "I'm keeping my options open." Chin Yong does know that he wants to stay in civil and structural engineering. "I find it very creative. I enjoy seeing my work come to life."

Many Questers have turned hobbies and interests into rewarding careers. At 31, *Linda* switched gears to turn her interest in carpentry into a full-time occupation. Linda's job as an interior designer had already given her an entry into carpentry skills. But successful as she was, she found herself much more fascinated by the carpenters' work than by her own. She began to dabble. First, she put up a deck and helped friends and neighbors with odd jobs. Then, four years ago, pregnant with her second daughter, Linda got her first big carpentry job. The new addition to her family required a new addition to her home. As she and her husband worked on building an extra room, carpentry got into her blood. Soon, she was dreaming of building an entire house. Linda confided her wish to a neighbor. "I used to dream of things I wanted to do when I was young, too," he said, "but I didn't do them and now I can't." Suddenly, Linda was seeing carpentry in a whole new way. Why should she, like her neighbor, just dream of the things she wanted to do? Why not do them?

Determined to find a more satisfying occupation, Linda enrolled in a carpentry program. Coping with the demands of the program was easier than coping with the resistance she met from well-meaning but dubious relatives and some bigoted union officials. "First, I had to fight with my husband and my mother-in-law. All I heard was 'You should be home with your daughters.' But the more I fought, the more I knew what I wanted," says Linda. Getting accepted into the union, the Brotherhood of Carpenters and Joiners of America, was another hurdle. Fortunately, a senior administrator of the apprenticeship program helped Linda get a job with a construction company as an apprentice carpenter. Linda is now happily spending her days putting up walls, installing Sheetrock, and framing doors. Two nights a week, she also goes to school to complete her training as a journeyman carpenter. And she still manages to find the time to be with her five- and seven-year-old daughters and husband.

Linda's pay is good but the work is physically demanding. She ached all over for three months after starting her new job. "One day, we had to unload a whole truckload of Sheetrock in the rain," she says. "I asked myself, 'Do I really want to do this?' " Even then, the answer was "Yes!" Linda's mother and

116   *Dare to Change Your Job and Your Life*

mother-in-law still don't approve of her occupation, but her husband now understands. He says she's more active and vibrant.

Linda is happy because she's working in a job she enjoys. Yet, carpentry isn't completely different from interior design. Both are in the technical crafts field and are suited to Linda's interests. Without changing occupational fields, Linda has managed to find a more satisfying and rewarding occupation.

Nick went from artist to art therapist. He began as a sculptor and artist, struggling to discover himself. He followed that with a teaching stint in a local high school. When he was 31, he realized art therapy could actually help people suffering from emotional or social disturbances, physical handicaps, or neurological impairments. He entered a two-year graduate program and then created his own job by telling state prison officials about the benefits of art therapy. He's elated about the new direction his career has taken.

Different Occupational Field

About 35 percent of job changers move to an entirely different occupational field.

About 35 percent of job changers move to an entirely different occupational field. These adults move to jobs that have a different psychological climate and often require distinct temperaments, needs, values, interests, and abilities. They usually change for one of two reasons. Some discover a poor match between their personality characteristics (such as interests, needs, values, and abilities) and the requirements of their initial occupation. Others realize they have outgrown their first occupational choice. Their beliefs or life experiences, which were initially compatible, have changed. Many, but not all, Questers who move to different occupational fields have prepared for their moves by taking upgrading or retraining, on-the-job training, or by research and reading.

The Job No Longer Fits

Some Questers have jobs that no longer fit their developing personalities and goals. Their first jobs were often chosen wisely and carefully. They were usually well suited to their positions and were quite successful. But somewhere, over the years, they realized they had outgrown their initial choices.

Lynne became dissatisfied with her childhood career choice as she neared 30. As a little girl, Lynne's dream was to be a librarian. Soon after college, she landed a job as a high school librarian. "I always questioned whether this field was a lifelong occupation, but I really never assessed my career goals," she recalls. Seven years later, at 29, Lynne realized she had to make a change. "It was like the seven-year itch," she says. Watching a play at a local theater, she was struck by the protagonist's rhetorical question, "What am I afraid of?" She realized she had to answer that question, too.

She took a leave of absence. Sometime during that year, she discovered the intrigue of the stock exchange. After investing her money for several years, she was ready to learn more. "When I read The Wall Street Journal or Business Week, I felt like I was reading a foreign language. But at the same time, the field fascinated me." Lynne signed up for a securities course, but began to wonder if there was an entry point for her in what was, in 1981, a male-dominated field. The idea of being in securities scared her somewhat. She wasn't used to taking risks. After working in a job with so much certainty, making such a radical move seemed difficult. "So I asked myself what could stop me. Fear of failure or of trying something new? What did I really have to fear?"

Her first step was to talk to the brokers who had invested her money. By 1982, she was ready to start work as a rookie stockbroker. "I knew I had to cross the line and give up security for growth," she reflects. While Lynne had enjoyed being a librarian, neither the routine nor working with teenagers really interested her anymore. These days, she fits a new baby and a job into a lifestyle that is "exciting and stimulating." Lynne's new position is well suited to her shift in needs, values, and goals. Like many successful brokers, Lynne is thriving on the excitement, tension, and more-than-moderate dose of uncertainty.

Learning to be a stockbroker isn't the only lesson Lynne mastered. She has learned to reevaluate her career choices regularly. She's thinking about her future now. "Maybe there is a third occupation out there for me, too. When you find out what you're afraid of, you can overcome anything."

Ed also had difficulty making the switch to a different occupational field. As a young boy, Ed thought he had his life carefully mapped out. Because he loved mechanics, deciding on an occupation wasn't hard. After high school, he entered a civil engineering program. His first job was with an engineering firm in the Midwest. Ed loved his work. But by the fifth year, his tasks began to seem too technical, detailed, and narrow. Ed started looking around. Finding a suitable job took almost a year. Hired in the operations department of a manufacturing firm at 31, he spent the next several years working his way up to head of his division. Ed liked the work but not the new general manager. Their values and beliefs on policies and procedures just weren't compatible. Determined to leave before he was demoted or fired, Ed, now 42, again started looking around.

Opportunities at Ed's managerial level weren't plentiful. Ed and his family liked the city they had lived in for so many years. Rather than move, he began to consider a different line of work. Soul searching and research led him to real estate. The market was tight and Ed knew he would have to take a cut in pay, but his children were self-sufficient and his wife was considering a part-time job. Armed with a clear option, Ed resigned, took a short real estate course and joined a medium-sized real estate firm. He's happy he did. "I enjoy making a sale, not so much for the money, but because I get a kick out of pleasing my customers," he says.

Making wise occupational choices requires time and understanding.

Poor First Choice

While some Questers discover they have grown beyond the challenges of their first occupational choices, others were never suited to their first occupations. Many plunged into jobs without assessing their own personalities, the job requirements, or the work environments they had selected. Making wise occupational choices requires time and understanding.

Bert is a good example. He went directly from high school to a university science program. He had always enjoyed science, and particularly research, so why not? Hired as a lab assistant while still in his master's program, Bert discovered a new interest—teaching. So with a year of education behind him, he set off to teach science to high school seniors. To his surprise, Bert discovered he really didn't like teaching. "I didn't like policing and being a babysitter to students who didn't want to learn," he recalls. With a wife and young child to support, he could hardly resign. But he could bide his time while he searched for a more suitable position. He applied to a pharmacy program and was accepted, but after further thought he decided he wasn't suited. Then, he took some night courses in real estate, "but it really didn't appeal to me." Frustrated, Bert decided to try to make a go of teaching. Just when he was about ready to give up, Bert found a new interest. He enrolled in a computer programming course. Bert suddenly realized he had found what he wanted to do with the rest of his life. Excited now, he studied by night and taught by day while he saved furiously for the day when he could study full-time. Two years later, with diploma in hand, Bert snapped up an offer from a small oil company to become a computer analyst. Within a year, he was working for a larger company at a larger salary. His new career offered challenge, learning opportunities, and a chance to keep ahead of the computer programming field. "I put up with the red tape because my job is challenging, never boring, and there's always something new to learn," says Bert.

Surprisingly, Bert has also successfully managed to combine his new occupation with his old one. Teaching computer programming to adults helped him realize that he really did enjoy teaching, at least in situations where students wanted to learn. Now 41, Bert is very satisfied with his job, his lifestyle, and his family. But you can be sure that when his job loses its challenge, Bert will once again be searching for a new position.

Jean discovered that dissatisfaction with a job exacts a high toll. Her break was more abrupt than Bert's. One day, Jean walked into her boss's office and quit her accounting and secretarial job on the spot. Jean knew career counselors usually advise against quitting one job before lining up another, but she also knew she'd never be motivated to change directions if she held on to a steady paycheck. "One day I thought, 'I'm not going to sit here grumbling anymore. I'm going to do something about it.' "

Jean spent the next 16 months discovering what her talents and interests really were and then searched for a job where she could use them. Her first step was to sign up at a temporary employment agency so she could continue to support herself. Then she went to the career counseling center at the local university. A battery of tests and inventories revealed a big surprise. Jean's real aptitude wasn't in accounting; it was in language. She had always enjoyed writing but had no idea her skills were so advanced. This discovery was a real ego boost. But Jean still didn't know what she wanted to do. While she floundered, temporary jobs were leading her from typing pool to typing pool. Discouraged, she complained to the agency and asked for proofreading or editing assignments. The agency was reluctant to send her for a job in which she had no experience. "I can read, so I can proofread," Jean insisted. Her determination paid off. A two week proofreading stint led to an eight month editing assignment. Jean loved it.

At the suggestion of a friend, she participated in a workshop on interviewing and job searching. She also got assistance with her resume. Finally, Jean made her first contact with an aerospace firm. Although her lack of a college degree was a handicap, her persistence got her an interview and an opportunity to take an editing test. She passed with impressive skill. But it was several months, and 40 calls later, before she got the job.

That was three years ago. With a recent promotion to technical editor, Jean doesn't doubt for a minute that her efforts were worthwhile. "I'm getting paid for doing something I enjoy," she says with a smile.

Reentry Women

Homemakers are another group who often change occupational fields when they reenter the workforce. A few, like *Edie*, become Questers. Edie graduated from a university on the West Coast with a bachelor of science degree. Her first journey into the workforce was as a microbiology researcher.

Shortly after her marriage five years later, she retired to raise children, run a house, and do volunteer work. Twenty years later, the marriage was over, her children were growing up, and Edie was faced with the task of finding a satisfying occupation that would also support her and three children. She had to earn money. But she wanted more than just a salary. She wanted an exciting, people-oriented job. "Unfortunately, like many women, I thought I didn't have the right to please myself." At a women's career counseling center, Edie found encouragement to complete a master's degree in social work. At first, she was terrified at the prospect. "How could I support myself and my kids? What if I failed? How could I compete with younger people? Who would organize my family? What kind of a job could I get?"

Many married women who return to school or work have similar feelings and fears. Edie overcame hers. With child support from her ex-husband, a student loan, and a part-time job as a salesclerk, she made it. Today, two years after graduation, Edie is doing excellent work as the executive director of a family social services bureau. She got the job because she had the personality, skills, experience, and motivation to succeed. Some of those skills and experiences were learned as a homemaker and volunteer. A social work degree gave her the rest. Had Edie tried to reenter research, she would have been bored. Instead, she is fulfilled.

Homemakers

Not all women want to return to the workforce, but some feel pressured to do so by their friends, family, or society. Others prefer homemaking to the stresses of corporate life.

Verlynne, a 39-year-old homemaker whom you met in chapter 1, enjoys writing poetry and developing games. Verlynne's friends believed she should return to school to prepare for a job outside the home. It seemed to be the thing to do. But she also wanted to be at home to meet the needs of her two teenage children. Despite this, she enrolled in a journalism program at a local junior college with the view to pursue a journalism career. She hated it. Through professional counseling, Verlynne realized that her real mission was to pursue creative pursuits at home in a leisurely fashion. One of her most recent innovations, a doll which you can tell your problems to, is selling well at local stores. Verlynne said, "I'm so happy, I sing all the time!"

Lashonda was a buyer of electronic equipment for a high tech company. On one of her business trips, she met an old male friend at an airport where she was waiting for a connecting flight. The reunion started a romance that led to marriage. Lashonda chose to quit her job and spend the next few years enjoying domestic pursuits such as decorating the home and preparing gourmet meals. The change also gave her the time and energy to devote to caring for AIDS patients at a local hospice. Maybe, in a few years, she will want to return to her earlier profession. In the meantime, Lashonda is keeping her options open and following her passion.

Both Verlynne and Lashonda are fortunate they can pursue activities they enjoy without having to worry about paying for the necessities of life. Not all women have this option.

You shouldn't overlook the dreams of your childhood when you are contemplating an occupational move.

Full-time homemaking is also an option for some men. *Brad* prefers to stay at home to do household chores and look after the two daughters, while his wife, Jan, works full-time to pay the family's bills. Being a househusband gives Brad time to devote to his passion, painting. This arrangement, which works well for Brad and Jan, is an option that an increasing number of Quester couples are selecting.

Questers like Verlynne, Lashonda, and Brad find that homemaking coupled with involvement in activities for which they have a passion gives their lives meaning, purpose, and direction. They prove that homemaking can be a viable alternative for some Questers.

Follow Your Dreams

Finding the right occupation is the key to success and enjoyment of your career. You shouldn't overlook the dreams of your childhood when you are contemplating an occupational move. But it isn't always easy to follow your dreams. Look at *Jane*.

A talented singer in high school, Jane grabbed the spotlight year after year at every musical festival. She loved singing and acting. But when it came time to decide on an occupation, she listened not to her heart, but to her parents' advice. They wanted her to seek a secure occupation such as law. For nine years, Jane practiced law, and didn't really mind it, but singing was still her first love. Every spare moment was spent singing in a nightclub production put on by a local group in her West Coast hometown. Then, it happened. One morning, as Jane rose to go to work, she realized she no longer wanted to practice law. Within two months, Jane was in New York taking singing and acting lessons. The money she had saved from practicing law and from singing in nightclubs helped finance lessons. Two years later, Jane has landed her first small part in a television series. Will she make it big? Only time will tell. But, in the meantime, she is doing what she enjoys. She gave her childhood dream a chance.

Antonio also decided to pursue his dreams. He worked for 22 years in various positions as a chemical engineer with a multinational petrochemical organization. At the age of 42, when he recognized the company was downsizing, he decided to take his career into his own hands. So he took a course to help him identify what he wanted out of the next part of his life and then researched his occupational options. Today, Antonio is working two jobs. He is a crops and sheep farmer and an environmental coordinator for his petrochemical company at a plant near his farm.

Antonio's decision to become a farmer required the investment of a significant amount of time and money. To many, being a farmer means dropping several notches down the career ladder. But Antonio is happy with his new work and lifestyle and so is his family. His status on the career ladder is much less important to him than his health, peace of mind, and job satisfaction. Antonio says," I feel better mentally and physically and I'm doing well financially . . . . My children love the country and my relationship with my wife is better than it's ever been." Antonio has learned to be true to himself.

Antonio is using most of his engineering skills on the farm and the skills and knowledge he's gained from farming also apply to his engineering position. His associates agree that his diverse background makes him a superior problem-solver.

Stress Symptoms

A number of adults not suited to their occupational choice develop stress symptoms because their personal traits are not compatible with their occupational environments. Some of these individuals become Questers.

Terrie, a 48-year-old sales manager, had long been dissatisfied with her job. She stayed because she gradually became convinced she couldn't afford to switch jobs. "To be truthful, I was afraid to," she says. Suddenly, she developed a strange illness. Abnormal lumps formed all over her body. Terrie's doctor could find no physical cause for her malady, but was wise enough to refer her to a psychologist. Testing and career counseling revealed that Terrie was more suited to literary arts than sales. She decided to pursue a library science degree, although history also interested her. Returning to school was intimidating, but a scholarship and her savings saw Terrie through. Now 53, she has been working as a librarian for two years. She loves her work and her health "has never been better." Terrie is also researching and writing a historical novel. She's beginning to sound a lot like a Quester.

Ray developed ulcers when he switched from one civil engineering job to another. Career counseling and introspection finally revealed that he was in the wrong occupation. Ray had an average aptitude for engineering but little real interest. He also had highly developed literary, artistic, and creative abilities, however, which made him well suited to advertising. The stresses he faces now as creative director of an advertising agency are far greater than any he faced as an engineer, but his ulcers are under control because, for Ray, it's positive stress.

Running Your Own Business

What do some Questers do when they find there is no ready-made place in the market for their skills? They go into business for themselves. Approximately one-third of the Questers interviewed for this book established their own businesses. They seemed to be willing to go small in order to be in control of their lives and their careers.

Quester entrepreneurs typify the best spirit of American tradition. Inventive, bold, resolute, eager to meet the challenges that confront them, some become quite wealthy. Others find satisfaction in doing a job well. They prove that it still is possible for someone with a dream to succeed. Entrepreneurial Questers have strong needs for autonomy and independence. Many are nonconformists who picture themselves as individualists and freethinkers. Resenting regimentation, they choose the business world to satisfy their needs. Their talents are very broad, and they have a great desire for variety and flexibility. More than any other type of Questers, they are not afraid to take chances. Their ultimate satisfaction comes from seeing something they have created grow and develop; money is secondary. Entrepreneurial Questers have the perseverance, self-discipline, energy, and stamina necessary to work 12-hour days and forgo weekends and holidays. Many are workaholics. They take it for granted that one of the rewards of their efforts will be financial independence. Entrepreneurial Questers get along well with people. Not only do they have to motivate people who work for them, but they also have to solicit the support of customers and clients. This they do with customary skill.

Business Conducted from the Home

Some Questers operate their business from home. Here is what they have to say about it.

Eleanor started a children's discount clothing boutique because she needed the money. A single parent with two young children to support, she returned to work after her divorce by selling clothing as a manufacturer's representative, a job she had held before her children were born. But housekeepers' salaries, upkeep on her house, and commuting expenses left little from her paycheck. And her 10-hour workday (including three hours of daily travel just to reach the center of her large Midwestern city) was a strain on both Eleanor and her children. When she tried to give needed time to her children, she was fired. Sometime during the six months that she collected unemployment benefits, Eleanor decided to start her own business. The market for children's clothing was good, she had contacts in the fashion industry from previous jobs, and she wanted to be home with her children. The result was a discount children's clothing boutique in her basement.

"For the first time in my life," she says, "I'm independent. I'm available for my children, can go to the school play, take them on holidays, and, because I'm in a child-oriented business, it's okay for them to be here in the background when I'm talking on the phone with suppliers or customers." In the first year, the discount business broke even. Eleanor credits much of her success to her marketing strategy. By dressing her children up in the clothing she sells, Eleanor acquires new customers from among friends and mothers of classmates. Now thinking of expanding her boutique into a full retail store, Eleanor is talking like a Quester when she says, "Everyone dreams of having a successful business. I know I can do it."

Ross, at 34, seemed a success. An accountant moving rapidly up the career ladder in a large firm for the past eight years, he seemed to have a promising future. But Ross was bored with working with numbers. He really wanted to work with his hands. Soon, Ross decided to turn his hobby into his occupation. He started taking pottery courses during the evenings. He loved it. He was also very talented. At first, Ross's wife wasn't too pleased to hear about his plans and hopes. With two children to support and bills to pay, the couple had some heavy responsibilities. But she could see that his dissatisfaction was making Ross irritable and lethargic. So, they decided to compromise. She took a part-time job to help pay the bills, and Ross stayed on part-time with the accounting firm. The rest of this time was devoted to pottery. Ross turned his basement into a workshop, bought a potter's wheel, and built a walk-in kiln in his backyard.

Four years later, Ross is working full-time as a potter. Using his accounting skill to keep the books in order, Ross is selling his wares to specialty shops, galleries, department stores, and private clients. His work is so much in demand that he works long hours just to fill the orders. But he doesn't mind. He's happy with his work and lifestyle. His relationship with his wife and children is better, too. Even though he is busy, Ross has more quality time to spend with them. Everyone has benefited from the changes.

Business Conducted in the Community

Other businesses have taken Questers away from the home. Decorating windows gave *Jennifer* the start she needed to set out on her own. A former occupational therapist, Jennifer went from a window-dressing job for a large department store to designing her own furniture. The frustration of trying to find furniture with clean, simple lines led her to create her own designs. The stark, uncluttered lines were so appealing that people soon began to ask about this young designer. From dreaming up eye-catching window displays, she went on to design inspiring show suites for apartment complexes. Soon she was getting commissions for private homes. Today, she not only does free-lance designing, but also wholesales her ideas to other interior decorators. Her biggest success came while searching for a carpenter. She could hardly believe her luck when she discovered Martin, a top-notch young furniture finisher, and then found he shared a shop with Peter, a first-class cabinetmaker. The three have been collaborating ever since.

Melvin demonstrates you can take a calculated risk and win. When political hassles caused Melvin to quit his senior management job, he had $60 in the bank and a wife and two children to support. Quitting was hardly a spur-of-the-moment decision—Melvin planned his moves—but illness forced him to resign earlier than intended. Determined to market a little-known line of sportswear, Melvin put his convalescence to good use, researching his idea. He even researched bank managers to find out who was the most liberal. Then, putting his idea on paper, Melvin approached the manager he thought would give him the best deal. His next move was to open a store. In four years, Melvin's business has expanded to twenty-one stores spread across the country in eight cities. All smiles, Melvin still can't believe how quickly his idea caught on. He feels as if he's "in Disneyland. It's pure fantasy." Now he's researching a new venture, another specialty line.

Boredom, the desire to do something different, or following a long-time dream aren't the only reasons people start their own businesses. Some are forced to. Being fired, laid off, or discovering that your skills are no longer in demand can be the impetus to starting a new business venture. If you take this path, you begin the process of learning new skills.

Involuntary Change

Job loss due to layoffs or termination is much more traumatic than voluntary change.

Downsizing, layoffs, mergers, company relocations, and bankruptcies have cost hundreds of thousands of people their jobs. Job loss due to layoffs or termination is much more traumatic than voluntary change. Because you have no choice in the matter, it can be frightening and painful. People who had expected to sail into retirement are being cast adrift.

Typically, business and professional women and men blame themselves for failing. They tend to seek explanations by dredging up mistakes of the past. Many tend to be vulnerable to clinical depression, sexual impotence or disinterest, and a variety of physical ailments. Others vent their anger and frustration on spouses or children or abuse alcohol and drugs. For the most part, males in their 40s, 50s, and 60s hold traditional values and attitudes about providing for their spouses and children. Therefore, losing their breadwinner status is a crucial blow to their self-confidence. Most laid off employees come from large companies and go to smaller ones which are in desperate need of their expertise.

A dismissed employee usually goes through five emotional stages which are similar to the ones people experience when told they have a terminal illness. These are: shock, denial, and disbelief; fear and anxiety; resistance, anger, and blame; acceptance and exploration; and commitment. Individuals often move back and forth between the stages, especially the first three. The pace of the healing process usually depends on the amount of introspection and "inner work" the individual has done prior to the loss. For example, those who have come to terms with their developmental issues (see chapter 5) will take less time to heal than individuals who have not.

The first reaction—shock, denial, and disbelief—is characterized by numbness and a general refusal to recognize what is happening. You might think "This is not happening to me!" or "They don't really mean it." These kinds of reactions help protect you from being overwhelmed. Many employees who are told they are targeted for layoffs continue their daily routine as if its business as usual, believing their dismissal is a mistake. Shock is particularly acute for people whose lives center primarily around work. When who we are is our job, we are vulnerable because someone can take it away.

Kent learned that his engineering services were no longer required "out of the blue." He walked around numb for a week. He asked himself, "What's wrong with me?" "Are they challenging my competence?" "What did I do to deserve this?" He said, "It's like getting dumped with a bucket of cold water."

Make no major decisions at this time. Process or absorb the injury, and with time, the hurt will begin to recede. This is the time when you need a sympathetic listener and not necessarily someone to offer advice.

Fear and anxiety follow. You are concerned because you wonder how you are going to manage. You may feel out of control. You may ask yourself, "How am I going to pay for the mortgage? The medical insurance?" "What am I going to do next?" Fear can also escalate to unmanageable levels as in the question "What if I never work again?"

Kent felt terrible because he did not have a plan. He was embarrassed about what he imagined other people were thinking. He felt frustrated and out of control and wondered how his family was going to manage. He felt the need to regroup, to identify a goal, but he could not do it immediately. He walked around aimlessly. His short-term memory was poor for the first few weeks. He felt cold inside, his eyes appeared fixed. Because his goal was interrupted, he felt overwhelmed inside; he had horrible dreams in which he had no destination, no home, no safety.

In this phase, you are mourning the past and resisting the change. You don't want to be disturbed. Letting go of the old way is like confronting a death, a loss. We often resist change because our sense of security is threatened. We feel out of control, powerless, afraid of looking foolish. Kent felt the need for some closure so that he could start healing. He had to create his own closure which he did by retreating and not talking to anyone about his situation for a while.

Do not allow fear to get out of control or refuse to acknowledge it. This can cause panic which can prevent you from acting all together. Acknowledge your fear. Identify exactly what you're afraid of. Are you afraid of the loss of material things? Rejection? The unknown? Learn to manage your fear. Start living in the present. Don't spend time worrying about what might happen, but do what you can to explore the possibilities that lie ahead. This is your opportunity to pursue that job you may have dreamed about for a long time.

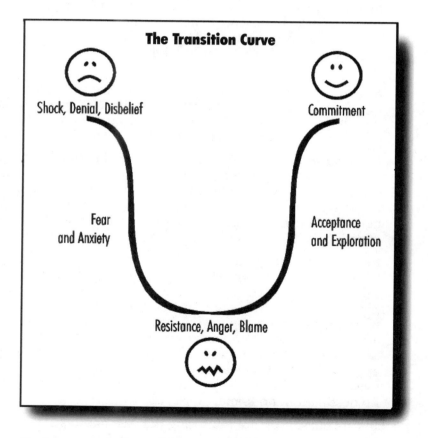

The Transition Curve

Shock, Denial, Disbelief

Commitment

Fear and Anxiety

Acceptance and Exploration

Resistance, Anger, Blame

Resistance, anger, and blame, which are often followed by grief and depression, comprise the next stage. This is the low ebb of the process. Anger, as long as it is a passing stage, is healthy because it means you value yourself. Not everyone is angry, but it is common to complain and blame someone or something. While blame is the first explanation of events, it is rarely the full explanation. Blame is finding someone or something we can hold responsible for our predicament. You may feel physical, emotional, or mental pain. You may doubt your ability to survive the change.

Kent blamed his supervisor and the company. "It was the way it was done . . . I was not involved in any decision making. They could have done it in a nicer way . . . I was not even told why I was being let go."

Anger must be dealt with. Acknowledging your feelings enables you to progress more quickly to the next stage. Talk about your feelings with a trusted friend, relative, or professional. This will help dispel some negative feelings. Another way to vent emotions is to write about them. For example, write about the trauma and explore questions you may wish to address such as "Why me?" "What is the meaning of and the positive potential in this loss?" "How can anger and resentment be transformed into life-affirming energy?" and "What dreams, long put off, can I now pursue?" Translating events into words tends to diminish the stress you may be experiencing and increase self understanding. This will also enable you to present yourself more favorably to others, for example, in prospective job interviews. Writing forces you to address your emotions, cognitively reappraise your situation, and come to terms with your predicament. Exercising regularly, punching a bag, listening to music, participating in community and trade activities, relaxing in a hot tub, and meditating are other activities that may help you get through this tricky transition.

Acceptance and exploration follow. After the period of inner conflict, individuals usually shift into a more positive, future-focused phase. You realize you are going to make it! You begin to look forward to and explore new possibilities. You feel and sleep better. You have more energy to discover and explore new opportunities. You start clarifying goals and are motivated to swing into action. Your creativity is high. You have the ability to move forward.

When Kent started to let go of the loss, to make the best of his predicament, he was able to breathe more easily. He decided he was not going to let the dismissal ruin his life. Kent convinced himself that he was a competent worker. He decided to use the opportunity to pursue his long-time goal of writing. He explored opportunities in the field. Kent felt "on top" of the situation. His goals were now more in tune with his inner desires. His energy level was high and he started to be more friendly with others.

Most individuals who lose their jobs—60 to 85 percent—find new positions within 3 to 10 months.

Don't try to complete the exploration stage too soon or settle for something less than what you really want. Take time to explore and pursue your passion. If necessary, take a survival job while you explore and prepare to pursue your dream.

Commitment involves focusing on a new course of action and adapting to a new situation. You pursue your vision. You make a commitment to finding a new job, starting a business, or going back to school. You have grown and adapted. The future is bright.

After exploring options that would enable him to combine his engineering skills with his long-time interest of writing, Kent decided to pursue a certificate program in technical writing at a local college. He is excited about his future.

Fortunately, most individuals who lose their jobs—60 to 85 percent—find new positions within 3 to 10 months. It may take older individuals a little longer because they face subtle and not-so-subtle age discrimination. Many large companies prefer to hire younger workers who command less pay, are more willing to relocate, and are easier to mold into the company image. Mature workers usually find their expertise is highly valued in middle- or smaller-sized companies. Regardless of age, individuals who have positive attitudes, work hard, and follow their hearts usually come out ahead. The crisis provides them with a stronger sense of themselves, greater control over their careers and lives, and opportunities to pursue their dreams or positions which offer greater personal and professional satisfaction than they had prior to the job losses. Some, although not all, earn higher salaries.

Like Kent, other individuals turned their job losses into challenges, opportunities to work at something they've longed to do for years. They became Questers.

With the help of a therapist, *Gunter*, 50, converted his feelings of anger and frustration into positive energy and action. He began to see his job loss as an opportunity to move in a new direction. A computer technician for the past 15 years, Gunter was bored with his job but afraid to do anything about it because of the depressed economy. A blessing in disguise, his layoff forced him to come to terms with what he really wanted to do with the rest of his life.

Gunter attended a career workshop which helped him clarify his dreams, values, needs, interests, skills, and goals. He also continued pursuing his leisure interest in photography and took skill-building courses to enhance his proficiency. He began subscribing to magazines and newsletters about photography and layout design and initiated a network of contacts. Within four months, Gunter landed an exciting position as a photographer with a growing technical magazine.

Carol headed a learning center at a Midwestern university. But when the center closed down, she was forced to find a new job. As she searched, Carol also turned a hobby into her sole means of support—operating a catering business from home. She explained, "I didn't anticipate what a drastic change it would be to go from Carol, the academic, to Carol, the cook." When the business became too big for her home, she rented space in a large warehouse and hired four assistants. Fortunately for Carol, a bad experience turned into a positive one. She never did return to the academic world. "Starting over was the best thing that ever happened to me," she reflects.

Many Questers, who are jobless or fear they may become jobless, are learning that the best protection may be to lead a more balanced life. They are depending less on the organization and are seeking reinforcement of their self images through a variety of activities and institutions. These include family and social relationships, spiritual practices, leisure and citizenship activities, and fraternal and religious societies. They're also discovering that life doesn't end with a pink slip; it can have happy, new beginnings. Personal dreams, long put off, can now be pursued!

Action Steps to Take to Respond to Change

❖ Schedule periods of rest so you can begin the renewal process and handle the stress.

❖ Learn, practice, and use body-stress relievers that work well for you. These include taking a short nap, breathing deeply, exercising, walking, receiving massages, meditating, and listening to music.

❖ Pay attention to your sleep patterns and diet. Eating healthy will keep your energy level high. Avoid alcohol, which acts as a depressant.

❖ Exercise regularly. This will help recharge your body.

❖ Create a routine and stick to it. A predictable schedule, particularly in your homelife, will help reduce stress.

❖ Get your feelings out. Have family members or a close friend take time to listen to your concerns, fears, and plans. Write about the situation and explore questions you wish to address. If necessary, seek professional help.

❖ Accept the fact that you lost the job. Do not lie about it to yourself, your friends, or your family.

❖ Join a support group for people who are facing the same challenge. If such a group does not exist, consider starting one of your own. Meeting once a week provides ideas, sounding boards, networking opportunities, and positive feedback.

❖ Schedule some quiet time to think and reassess. You need time to consider what you really want to do with the rest of your life.

❖ Develop a positive outlook. Your attitude about yourself will determine how others see you.

> ❖ Put forth effort in your search for a new goal or position. Looking for a new career opportunity is a full-time job.
>
> ❖ Identify your financial status and concerns and develop a budget. If necessary, make some changes in your lifestyle.
>
> ❖ Seek advice and assistance from professionals.

Turning a crisis into an opportunity requires knowing yourself, developing positive attitudes, and believing in yourself and your desired goals. Through hard work and persistence, each challenge you successfully master enables you to take more responsibility for your life.

A dismissed employee reflecting on her experiences with involuntary change shared the following thought. "Change is an irreversible force that sometimes reshapes our lives, bringing new challenges and goals, new commitments to be made. You can use change to your advantage by letting it move you to a new wonderful place you would never have thought to go."

Up or Down?

Up or down? Does it really matter which way you are headed on the organizational career ladder? Not to most Questers. When they change jobs, better social status, prestige, or income are seldom the first issues on their minds. What Questers really seek are satisfying positions that are more compatible with their developing personalities—positions that offer opportunities for personal and professional growth, for service to others, and for greater challenge, autonomy, use of skills, and other desired rewards. Of course, many do end up with more status, prestige, and money. Others don't. They tell us how they perceived their moves.

Don is a quiet, sensitive physician who, at 40, dropped several notches on the career ladder to switch from medicine to education. A caring and successful pediatrician, Don found that after 11 years of being a physician he just wasn't happy anymore. He felt hurt seeing children and adolescents suffer as he stood by, sometimes unable to alleviate their pain. The death of his father a year earlier had made Don realize that life was too short to spend in an occupation he didn't enjoy. Despite reminders from colleagues that he had spent thousands of dollars building up his specialty, Don decided to go back to school to study education. Today, Don is in his third year of teaching biology to teenagers. He is still working with adolescents but these adolescents are not sick and suffering. He has discovered that teaching better suits his temperament.

For many, abandoning a medical practice to become a teacher may seem like a drastic drop in career status. But as a newly emerged Quester, Don is happy with his new occupation and lifestyle, even though he took a substantial pay cut. When Don decides teaching is no longer right for him, he will probably change occupations again. His status on the occupational prestige ladder will be much less important to him than his health, peace of mind, and job satisfaction.

Interestingly enough, occupational prestige studies ranked physicians among the top five percentile. Public school teachers, on the other hand, rank between the twenty-fifth and fortieth percentile, depending on the study. At the bottom are shoe shiners, clothes pressers, waitresses, street sweepers, and garbage collectors. But at least two people who moved from a high-status profession to the very bottom of the occupational prestige scale are happier today because of it.

Until two years ago, *Dwight* was a lawyer with a prominent New York firm. These days, he can be found decked out in badly soiled khaki pants and a grimy army jacket. Since last July, Dwight and 35-year-old *Timothy*, a former administrative assistant to a senior government official, have been driving a garbage removal truck in a town about 80 miles northwest of New York City. Unlike many young people who have been forced to make drastic career changes because of the recession, they are in a usually unpopular job by choice.

Why did Dwight leave law? Because, as he says, "I was getting pretty bored with being surrounded by so many high-powered lawyers working on legal refinements. It just wasn't challenging anymore and I had to wonder how much value I was really contributing to society. I don't want to give the impression that there is more social utility in garbage than in law, but I'm satisfied with what I'm doing now. I wasn't before." Dwight and Timothy are intrigued by the possibility of expanding the garbage removal business into garbage disposal and recycling. After eight hours of guiding a nine-ton truck without power steering along the wooded roads that twist around the town, Dwight's body aches all over. "But I don't feel the strain of the long hours as I used to when I worked at the law firm all day."

When Dwight and Timothy decided to buy the garbage removal company, Dwight and his wife, a graduate of a fashionable women's college, gave up their Manhattan apartment and moved into an average-looking house near the business. Timothy, a bachelor, bought a townhouse. Both have taken substantial pay cuts—Dwight by 40 percent, Timothy by half that. Despite his smaller salary, Dwight says he has much greater peace of mind. "If you're traveling on a superhighway, but going in the wrong direction, you feel insecure. But if you're on a mud road and it's going the right way, that's security."

That's how Questers differ from ordinary folks. Few move up the career ladder just for prestige or money. Instead, they change jobs for the opportunity to grow and develop in satisfying careers.

Ike, a high school dropout who became a civil engineer, advanced from eighty-fifth on the occupational prestige ladder to eighth. But prestige and status were far from his mind when he left his construction job for engineering. Ike just wanted the chance to grow and develop, to use his mind instead of his hands, to make a living.

Over 60 percent of the workforce are in jobs they don't like and approximately half of all employees experience job stress.

The Choice Is Yours

Would it surprise you to learn that over 60 percent of the workforce are in jobs they don't like and approximately half of all employees experience job stress? Stressed workers report that their job stress interferes with their relationships, their health, and their ability to perform work. You probably know many such people and maybe you are even among them. They're the ones who are exuberant Friday afternoon and depressed Sunday evening. As a matter of fact, the number one risk for heart disease is job dissatisfaction; more people die on Monday mornings than any other day or time of the week.

Why then do people stay in jobs they hate and find unrewarding? For many, it's fear of change. They find it easier to stay in comfortable ruts and collect gold watches on retirement. Unfortunately, while the comfortable lifestyle may be materially rich, it doesn't always reflect what people believe is important in emotional life. Even surrounded with every symbol of the good life, you may be suffering from malaise and deep-rooted dissatisfaction. That malaise sets in because many of us have never been encouraged to stop and ask, "Am I doing what I want?"

You are suited to just as many occupations as you are wrong for. You can change to a more suitable job if you have outgrown your position. Even while still employed, you can be planning your escape. Remember, this isn't just a job change. This is your life!

Finding the right organizational fit is important, too. Companies' personalities are just as different as people's. Your company's structure may be rigid or relaxed; it may treasure hard work and reliability, or new ideas and flexibility; it may insist on strict adherence to the hierarchy or form committees that include several levels of employees. In any case, checking out a company is just as important as checking out a job.

Deciding how radical a change you want, and what that change requires, is vital before you even begin to make a career shift. You will need to examine your needs, values, interests, and purpose, as well as any transferable skills you already have. For instance, ministers or teachers looking for personnel work may be able to transfer many of the skills they have already developed (such as advising, mentoring, communicating, teaching, motivating, supporting, arbitrating, problem solving, organizing, scheduling, delegating, planning, and so on). But an artist who decides to become a banker will need a lot of additional training and may have incompatible needs and interests. The unstructured, free-flowing creative skills of the artist don't usually translate into the analytical, highly structured skills required of a banker. Before leaving a job or investing time or money in further education, think over your career change carefully. Give yourself time to make a well-reasoned decision. Find out if you are, in fact, a Quester. Find out if you could become one.

Career Cycle Meets the Life Cycle

dulthood is not a plateau. It is a time of change. Much recent research describes adult growth and development as a cycle that follows an underlying, universal path. Many influences along the way shape this course. They may produce alternate routes or detours, they may speed up or slow down the timetable, or they may stop the developmental journey altogether. As long as you live, this journey continues, following a basic sequence of stages, issues, and concerns. This is called life cycle theory, and it assumes you will pass through these stages as long as you are developing. It cannot predict how you will deal with them.

Your personality or identity is formed by many external and internal influences. Your culture, occupation, social class, family, interpersonal relationships, leisure activities, social roles, image, and participation in the world are the external system. Your internal realm is composed of your genetic makeup, your body build, intelligence, temperament, and vulnerability. Throughout life, your external and internal systems interact to influence your identity and personality. As events in the external system are interpreted by the internal one, crucial shifts in needs and values can throw you off balance. These are signals telling you to change and move on to the next stage. These shifts occur throughout life. Sadly, many people refuse to recognize them.

For each external system, you also have a corresponding inner subidentity. Your identity is made up of several "subidentities" representing your various life roles. You have an occupational identity, a family identity, a social identity, an interpersonal identity, a leisure identity, and a spiritual identity. They may differ quite drastically. Some have large occupational and family identities, with smaller leisure, social, and citizenship identities. With others, the balance is exactly reversed. Still others may have subidentities that are almost equal in size. Moreover, the size of your identities changes as you mature. Those with small children to raise will have larger family identities in their late twenties and early thirties than before their children were born or after they leave the nest.

As the life cycle progresses, you move through developmental and transitional stages. Each presents tasks to be mastered and problems to be solved.

Between each developmental stage are transition periods that allow you to question who you are and where you are going. These give you time to reexamine your needs and values, to take another look at your external life systems, to explore and evaluate potential options, and to make decisions to either deepen or alter earlier commitments. Each transition takes from three to five years. And each developmental period can take from five to eight years.

The transition periods are times of disequilibrium and anxiety. But dangers arise both in moving and staying put. If you stay with a life component after you have outgrown it, you may betray yourself and limit your possibilities; if you break out, you impose burdens on yourself and may fail to find what you seek. Either way there are dangers and losses as well as gains. If you are growing, almost half your adult life is spent in remaking that life.

Every initiation is also a termination of what came before. The developmental periods are necessary for stability; the transition periods are necessary for growth. This process represents the overriding polarity you must integrate in your life, the polarity of change versus continuity, the problem of how to maintain a continuous sense of yourself while growing.

Certain traumatic experiences may cause you to reexamine your life and come to terms with developmental issues.

Developmental periods are just as important as the transitions. If your life contained nothing but transitions, you would feel as though you were being whirled in a centrifuge. But if it contained only developmental periods, you would experience yourself as an inert lump. At one pole, you risk anxiety; at the other, depression. Your life must seek to veer between the two as you try to combine solidity with forward movement, security with risk.

Certain traumatic experiences may cause you to reexamine your life and come to terms with developmental issues. They can be positive, negative, or even somewhere in between—marriage, the birth of a child, the death of a parent, serious illness, travel, loss of a job, or divorce. All may cause you to shift your values and goals.

Adults in transition may be every bit as miserable as adolescents. But those of you who face up to the agonizing self-evaluation and independently set future goals will develop a healthier, happier, and more mature identity. Failure to resolve the difficulties of transitions can cause severe problems. High rates of alcoholism, depression, and suicide are often related to this inability.

Many of the problems and issues adults must deal with appear and reappear in new forms throughout the life cycle. They are not the exclusive property of any age group. Issues of intimacy and occupation, for example, haunt us forever. Compromises are found for a while, then renegotiated. And so it goes.

You may face five or more transition periods: adolescence, age 30, mid-life, age 50, age 60, and others. Of course, you may not face them exactly on schedule. Although the phases are normal, not all people pass through all of them. Some get fixated at one particular stage. They may spend the rest of their lives making futile attempts to work it through. Those who have difficulty making such transitions often resort to familiar, earlier behavior patterns. A three-year-old trying to adjust to a new baby in the family may forget toilet training or refuse to speak. A man in his late thirties may resume the dating behavior (now extramarital) of earlier years to avoid the pain of advancing to another developmental level. While some adults fail to adjust to new stages, those who weather transitions often do so by finding new meaning in their work and other components of their lives. This is often accomplished by making some change such as leaving a dissatisfying job, returning to school, getting married, seeing a marriage counselor, or obtaining a divorce.

Having realistic expectations about impending crises and transitions can ease the stress and the pain of their arrival. If you do some thinking about the transitions in life and prepare for them, you may be better able to cope.

The Beginning Career

Adolescent transition completed (approximately ages 17-23)

❖ First full-time job assumed

❖ Needs for expansion, career mastery, and self motivation prevail

❖ Little self-evaluation occurs

❖ Lifelong patterns may be established

The Developing Career

Age-thirty transition precipitates stage (approximately ages 28-33)

❖ Values, priorities, and goals shift—a more balanced life is valued

❖ Short- and long-range goals pursued

❖ Productivity, fulfillment, excitement, and creativity enjoyed

❖ Occupational and/or job changes may occur

The Maturing Career

Mid-life transition experienced (approximately ages 37-45)

❖ Need for job satisfaction heightens

❖ Creative leadership peaks

❖ Interest in guiding the young blossoms

Age-fifty transition occurs (approximately ages 48-53)

❖ Need for job satisfaction and a balanced life deepen

❖ Innovative leadership and mentoring activities continue

The Continuing Career

Age-sixty transition experienced (approximately ages 58-63)

❖ Career options explored and evaluated, including "retirement"

❖ Continuing opportunities for purpose, meaning, direction, and growth are identified and pursued

❖ Another occupational cycle is completed

Age-seventy transition experienced (approximately ages 68-73)

❖ Decisions to continue paid employment, volunteer activities, or pursue a more leisurely lifestyle are contemplated

❖ Choices are made and plans are implemented to pursue activities which offer continuing opportunities for purpose, meaning, and growth

Age-eighty transition experienced (approximately ages 78-83)

❖ Decisions are made with respect to continued work, voluntary activities, or pursuit of a more leisurely lifestyle

❖ Desire to be involved in activities which provide a sense of purpose, meaning, and direction continue

The Career Cycle: Entry, Mastery, and Disengagement

Your occupational identity is part of your overall sense of who you are. If you are growing as a person and developing in your job, you will have several occupational identities throughout your career cycle. A healthy and vital occupational identity has three stages: entry, mastery, and disengagement. During the entry stage, you make a commitment to the job, become involved, and develop skills and personal meaning that make up your occupational identity. In the mastery stage, you work hard to achieve excellence, acquire experience, and achieve a sense of accomplishment, enjoyment, challenge, and purpose. This is the most productive stage for both employees and their bosses. You gain enjoyment and fulfillment; your boss gains a satisfied and productive employee. During the last part of the mastery stage, you may become confident and even rigid. If your employer cannot or will not alter or expand your tasks, or if you cannot or will not move into another job, the quality of your performance will start to deteriorate. You may no longer be using your skills enthusiastically because

The formation of your career identity is a lifelong process.

you are no longer getting the perks you earlier enjoyed. The challenge, meaning, and fulfillment are gone.

The formation of your career identity is a lifelong process. If, like a Quester, you are growing and developing, you will enter, master, and disengage from several positions. They may be sequential, each building on the other in a logical sequence of increasing skills and responsibilities. For example, one can advance from teacher to department head to supervisor to principal, and so on, up the educational ladder. Or they may be entirely unrelated such as construction worker to teacher to accountant to musician to police officer. A healthy occupational identity occurs when you commit yourself fully to a set of work tasks and master these. When it is no longer rewarding, you move on. You move while your identity is still healthy.

Remember *Kathy* from earlier chapters? Her first full-time job was with a large insurance firm. At first, Kathy was enthusiastic about her position, but four years later, her feelings began to change. She no longer felt alert and enthusiastic. She had moved from the entry to the mastery to the disengagement stage of her job in just four years. By hanging on, Kathy wasn't doing herself or her employer any good. If she had been moved to another position where she could have learned new tasks, Kathy would have kept on growing. She would have been in the entry stage of another occupational cycle. If her employer had expanded her tasks, she might have stayed in the mastery stage for several more years. But Kathy left the company after working in the same position for seven years. Her occupational cycle had lasted only that long. Today, as an enthusiastic law student, she is in the entry stage of her second occupational cycle.

The Cyclical Pattern

Staying in an occupation for five to ten years tends to be a normal career pattern for many Questers. Questers often reorganize themselves, their lifestyles, and career goals every five to ten years. If they are no longer deriving desired rewards from their jobs or progressing in a way that complements their developing personalities, they tend to leave. Throughout their lives, they continue to experience the process of entry, mastery, and disengagement. Most Questers set their own rhythm of change.

The length of your occupational cycles depends on your occupation, the strength of your intrinsic job needs such as challenge, and where you are in the life cycle. Many Questers in middle management have occupational cycles of four to eight years. Questers in occupations such as teaching or air traffic control have similar occupational cycles. However, hairdressers who work for others generally change jobs every three years. Many nurses and individuals who want to take advantage of better advancement opportunities or higher salaries also change positions every two or three years. Examination of the career paths of all these workers, however, reveals a cyclical career pattern. This rhythm of change tends to be related to events occurring in other components of the workers' lives—and the transition periods of their life cycles.

This cyclical pattern of movement is not the same as the changes made by entry-level employees and recent college graduates in the Beginning Career. These young adults, who are still exploring the fit between their personal qualities and occupations or organizations, may stay in jobs for only a year or two as they learn more about themselves and the work world. Some change jobs several times before finding the right fit.

Interaction of the Career and Life Cycles

The career cycles of Questers often imitate their life cycles. When most are in the disengagement stages of their occupational cycles, they are usually also facing transition stages of their life cycles.

Let's look at the Questers to see how their career and life cycles are intertwined. Kathy left her management job during her age-thirty transition. The self-assessment she did during this transition was influenced by her growing job dissatisfaction. Feelings of depression over her father's death also affected her. As she looked more closely at her values and goals, she came to terms with the major issue of her age-thirty transition—changing occupations.

Vern's occupational cycles also coincided with his life cycle transitions. Vern started work as an ambulance attendant and loved it. Six years later, his enthusiasm gone, he decided to disengage. He knew neither he nor his patients would benefit if he stayed put. Vern returned to school to study physiotherapy. Soon after, he married.

Vern's decision to marry and change his occupation were the result of the self-evaluation he did during his age-thirty transition. Vern liked working as a physiotherapist in a hospital. Initially, he derived the job perks he wanted—challenge, variety, scope, and autonomy. But during his fourth year, he became increasingly more frustrated and tense because he felt he had little input into decisions affecting his job. Three years later, he decided to take a year off to sort things out. Vern's "time-out" was part of his mid-life transition and was closely tied to his disengagement from his physiotherapy position. A year off helped him put life in perspective. He returned to school to get some upgrading in physical therapy and then established his own consulting business. Vern, now 47, is in the developmental period of his forties and the entry stage of his third occupational cycle, a physiotherapy consultant.

Today, a number of managerial and professional workers are becoming even more involved in cyclical careers. Many top executives will set themselves a "time horizon" of 4 to 10 years to tackle the tasks, see the results, then move on. Both executives and organizations benefit. The executive has the excitement and challenge of accomplishing a difficult set of tasks as well as maintaining his or her flexibility. The organization has an enthusiastic, innovative manager who can bring fresh new ideas into the company.

It's sad to see so many workers stay 30 or 40 years in jobs they are psychologically disengaged from, watching the clock as the days and weeks pass. With prestige or financial rewards their jailer, they abandon reality, living unfulfilled lives because the thought of starting anew seems humiliating or degrading. Those who lose their jobs as a result of mergers or reengineering are forced to start over. Some who come to terms with their developmental issues find that it is never too late to pursue their dreams and revitalize their lives.

The Beginning Career

Your first developmental period begins with a commitment to your first full-time job. It is a critical time. As you take hold of the adult world, you have to make decisions, commit yourself to a whole new set of roles, and perform tasks that will have a strong influence in later life. Often, the lifestyle and occupation you pursue in early adulthood will be the framework for experiences throughout the rest of your life.

The Adolescent Transition

Let's backtrack and look at the transition that marks entry into adulthood: adolescence. Late adolescence, which occurs from ages 17 or 18 to 22 or 23, is an important period. Many decisions made then about career and life goals will affect your potential growth during adulthood. Remember when many changes were taking place in your inner and outer worlds? Physical growth and sexual maturity were accompanied by the maturation of your thinking capability. Your ability to think in abstract terms multiplied as you struggled with problems, devised solutions, evaluated experiences, and reconsidered your values. You looked at reality from many angles and considered the implications of your decisions. As you finished high school, you wondered what to do next—travel, continue your education, or work.

Work can be the source of pleasure, esteem, and goal fulfillment or it can contribute to disappointment and feelings of failure.

Choosing an occupation is a crucial step. Work can be the source of pleasure, esteem, and goal fulfillment or it can contribute to disappointment and feelings of failure.

Making decisions about a career and other life roles, such as family and sex roles, are major psychological tasks of adolescence. Erik Erikson, one of the pioneers of life cycle theory, called this the search for identity.

There are two essential factors in the attainment of a mature identity, according to psychologist James Marcia. First, adolescents must explore several options before choosing "among life's alternatives." Trying on different roles, adolescents struggle to make decisions about occupations, values, and lifestyles. Second, adolescents must finally come to a commitment, an investment of themselves in their choices. They may be in one of four identity states: moratorium, identity achieved, identity foreclosed, or identity confused. Not all adolescents achieve a mature identity nor do they achieve identity states at the same speed.

Four Identity States of Adolescence

❖ *Moratorium.* In this "time-out" period, adolescents have not yet made commitments nor invested much of themselves in others, and they are still vague about their own values. Even while delaying their commitments, they are actively struggling to find the right roles. Experimenting by "playing the field" with the opposite sex, working at odd jobs, or trying different courses in their first few years at college, they search for roles that fit. Ideally, adult demands can now be put on hold so that adolescents are free to experiment. Most young people in this state are vague about what they want to do. *Kathy* was in a moratorium before she committed herself to an insurance job. She "tried on" several jobs and then went for career counseling before she decided on an occupation. *Vince* also had a moratorium—he dropped out of his first year of college to travel in Europe for two years. When he returned home, he committed himself to a five-year geology program. Kathy and Vince were lucky. Both their parents helped with the finances.

❖ *Identity achieved.* Those who have reached the state of identity achievement have explored their options and have made commitments to desired values and goals. They know who they are and what they want to do. They have developed strong, healthy identities by experimenting, carefully evaluating various alternatives, and making their own decisions. Efforts to resolve questions of identity may have taken these adolescents onto paths of overzealous commitment, emotional involvement, alienation, or playful wandering. Flexible and inner-directed, they set realistic goals and are unlikely to subscribe to authoritarian values. They have committed themselves, at least for a while, to occupational goals. They have experienced a moratorium and are often older than those in the other groups.

❖ *Identity foreclosed.* The identity foreclosed group have made commitments but have not explored their options. They seem very sure of what they want to be. James, a fourth-year medical student, studied hard to get good grades to enter medical school. His parents thought medicine was a good profession to be in—it paid well, had prestige, and provided financial and job security. Judy, the daughter of a prominent New York banker, went to finishing school, and then a prestigious women's college because that was the family destiny. In many instances, the family destiny will define a certain value to strive toward intellectual achievement, independence, power and status, or societal contribution. James, Judy, and other adolescents like them made commitments without exploring options. They have passively accepted the identities their parents (or other significant adults in their lives) cut out for them. They have never seriously evaluated their own goals and values. People with foreclosed identities are generally more brittle, authoritarian, and conventional than any other group. Adolescents in this group have not yet "broken loose" from the significant adults in their lives. They are "locked in." Until recently, most young women in our culture were part of this group.

❖ *Identity confused.* The identity confused group have not yet consciously explored their options nor have they made commitments. They have shrunk from the task of defining who they are or what they want to do. They perform well enough in school and social roles, but they also feel like misfits. They tend to "opt out" of situations to avoid commitment. Often, in the early attempts to define themselves, they become immobilized by feelings of inferiority. But unlike those in a moratorium, they do not seem to be compelled to do much about it. Some young women in their early twenties, who seem to live in a state of suspended animation, are in a confused state. They can't bring themselves to make career commitments, nor any extended plans for that matter, until they know whom they are going to marry.

As you passed through the adolescent transition to achieve greater maturity, you probably experienced confusion and depression. The task of bringing together the pieces of your life into a coordinated and clear self-identity is difficult and time-consuming. Those who can consciously explore their options and make commitments to desired values and goals at this turning point often emerge stronger and more in control of their destinies.

Of course, your identity is never static. Each time you pass through a transition phase and reevaluate your values and goals, you are reformulating your identity. An identity foreclosed young adult may become an identity achieved adult—a Quester—as he or she comes to terms with the career decisions made during the age-thirty, the mid-life, or later-life transitions. How you deal with the transitions in your life will determine whether you become a Quester.

The Beginning Career Develops

Your need to expand and your career drive are likely to take precedence during the Beginning Career. Young people are busily engaged in the increasing responsibilities of career, marriage or relationships, and acquiring knowledge. They do not have much time for self-evaluation. The road ahead is exhilarating, conflicting, and sometimes overwhelming. But most young people are certain they will have what it takes to overcome any difficulties. They want to shape a dream, to create a lifestyle, and "make something out of their lives." They are getting started in occupations, learning the capacity for intimacy with spouses or partners, becoming involved in leisure activities, and establishing circles of friends of varying degrees of intimacy. Career will play an important part in the realization of their vision, but young people must also strike a balance among work, love, and leisure.

Two impulses, as always, are at work now. One is the need to build a firm, safe lifestyle for the future by making strong commitments. The other is to explore and experiment, to create structures that are easily reversible, to satisfy the cravings of the riskier self. Both can be easily taken to extremes. Like the identity confused group, young people who are too tentative tend to be transient and unstable. They spend their twenties bopping from one job to the next, one personal encounter to the next. On the other hand, young people who, like the identity foreclosed group, commit themselves too strongly tend to be fearful, rigid adults who cling too tightly to their choices. Striking a balance between tentativeness and commitment, exploring alternatives, keeping options open, avoiding strong commitments, and not clinging too tightly to the choices made are all important to maintain occupational flexibility and adaptability.

The Beginning Career is more stable than the transitions that lead to and from it. It begins with a commitment to a full-time job to prepare for a life of work. For many, the process starts in the early twenties and ends with the age-thirty transition. However, given permission to experiment, prolonged schooling, and ample time out, it is not unusual for some Questers to be nearly 30 before they start on their Beginning Careers.

The Beginning Career is a mastery stage when young people gain positive feedback, achieve competence, and become self-motivated. The positive feelings that flow toward them fill them with self-confidence. Devlin, a 25-year-old middle manager, says of his career goals, "Success and greater responsibility provide me with greater motivation to reach my career goals with my employer . . . . I'm interested in obtaining more efficiency in all aspects of my personal and business dealings."

The Beginning Career is a mastery stage when young people gain positive feedback, achieve competence, and become self-motivated.

The future path of your career starts with the Beginning Career. Patterns that will affect your future lifestyle often begin here. Many older Questers in the Maturing or the Continuing Career started here. But these patterns can be changed. Some current Questers were Traditionalists or Self-seekers in Beginning Career but moved to the Quester track as they acquired knowledge, experience, and the will to risk.

Most Questers in Beginning Career have confronted the challenges of the adolescent transition. They have committed themselves to occupational goals and are working on implementing these. They have struck a balance between tentativeness and commitment. They have committed themselves to a career, but they know that technology and their own development will one day change the pace of their lives. Both Kathy and Vern were young Questers who recognized the need to be tentative.

A number of Beginning Career Questers may seem quite like their Traditionalist and Self-seeker peers, but they have been through many broadening experiences. They may endorse several values, but personal and career development matter most. From their jobs, they want to get such valuable rewards as autonomy, challenge, and opportunities for self-expression. They also desire quality from other life components. They are not afraid to work hard for what they want. Many put in long hours on weekends to achieve their goals. They also may make many material sacrifices to reach these goals.

Take *Aaron*. His goal was to own a jewelry store. To get enough money and experience to set out on his own, Aaron took a job as a management trainee with a large retail chain, and, at the same time, worked evenings sorting mail. During weekends, Aaron threw all his energy into designing jewelry. His wife didn't mind. Designing and making jewelry was one of her hobbies, too.

Rob is another Beginning Quester who sees work as a major source of satisfaction. After trying out a variety of courses and programs at college, Rob wound up in physical engineering. He likes his first full-time job as an engineer for a large consulting firm. He enjoys the challenge, is involved in his work, and relishes the positive feedback. Working gives him a sense of competence and confidence. Unlike many of his Traditionalist colleagues, Rob's sense of competence is inner-directed. Money and promotions come second to the feelings of accomplishment he gets from completing a challenging task. Moreover, he is less concerned with socializing just to get ahead. For him, the status, affiliations, and external guideposts many rely on don't really count. He places more value on a self-defined lifestyle and career goals. To Rob, his job is an "opportunity for challenge, freedom, a sense of identity, autonomy, involvement, or creativity." His career goals are open-ended. He wants "to learn, to experience, to grow."

Petite, attractive and 27, *Susan* is another young Quester with similar values and goals. A journalist for three years, she is happily involved in her work and has also managed to combine work and marriage successfully. Susan and her husband of two years have worked out a system of sharing domestic responsibilities. And like some young women approaching their late twenties who have postponed having children or decided against parenthood, Susan is more satisfied with her life than many of her Traditionalist contemporaries. Late motherhood is a bona-fide pattern among some female Questers under 30.

Questers in Beginning Careers, who have been in the same job for four or five years, may begin to feel stale or bored. Company policies incompatible with their values may also trouble them. A few years earlier, they simply didn't care. But now, the excitement, romance, and challenge that made their jobs something special are beginning to disappear. Questers who feel this way are in the late mastery or early disengagement stages of their first occupational cycle. A series of jolts in other areas of their lives are beginning to wean them from their earlier illusions. Their experiences with a career, marriage, or the death of a parent are preparing them for the age-thirty transition. At the same time, their feelings, needs, and values are beginning to change. So the Beginning Career ends.

The Developing Career

Often, the need to change begins slowly, a vague but persistent sense of wanting to do and be something more.

The Age-Thirty Transition

The Developing Career is ushered in by the age-thirty transition. Many people begin to question their past decisions. They may realize they have ignored important needs, interests, and desires. Now, new choices must be made and commitments altered or deepened in all major areas of life. For some, this period may be marked by turmoil and confusion. For others, it may involve an intellectual inquiry into the past.

As you progress through this transition, you may feel confused, sluggish, and dissatisfied. The desire to try new things is beginning to take precedence over safety needs. Apparent restrictions are the outgrowth of decisions made in the late teens or early twenties, choices that were perfectly appropriate at the time. Now the fit feels wrong. It may make itself felt suddenly, emphatically, sometimes precipitated by an external event. Often, the need to change begins slowly, a vague but persistent sense of wanting to do and be something more.

Remember *Al,* the farmer in chapter 1? As he approached the age-thirty transition, he began to feel that his life and his job no longer had purpose and meaning. Al's age-thirty transition was tied to his occupational cycle. At 28, after working in computers for five years, he was in the early disengagement stage of his job. The meaning and excitement had disappeared. Negative feelings arose about his job. This, coupled with the birth of his child, began the reassessment of his life and career goals.

How you look at time can also change. You will become aware that your life is finite. Death is still an abstract fear. You still have time to do it all. New experiences are waiting. You are impatient to get on with your life but the desire is not yet urgent.

The severity of the transition phase is reflected in the moratorium of one or more years many Questers took. *Adrian,* a happy entrepreneur, "walked away from the world" during his transition. He needed time to rethink the direction of his life. Adrian was particularly restless as he approached 30. While he performed his management tasks dutifully, he was in the disengagement stage of his occupational cycle. The job seemed frustrating and restricting. Adrian emerged from his moratorium with greater self-understanding and renewed confidence to move forward in his new, self-determined career. He and his wife became partners in a variety of entrepreneurial projects. Today, Adrian describes his job passionately: "It represents a future; it gives me an economic base to pursue my own lifestyle." Now 34, Adrian is working on the goals set during the transition. When he is no longer challenged, he will probably seek greater challenges.

Janet also experienced a moratorium. A creative and assertive young woman, she quit her job as a news photographer to travel in Europe for a year. She had no definite future plans. Even though she liked her colleagues, she no longer felt challenged. The marital problems she was experiencing aggravated her feelings of depression and lethargy. Counseling sessions with a psychologist gave Janet the necessary support and courage to "get away from everything for a while."

"While in Europe, I smiled for the first time in years. I returned home a different person. I felt happier, more at peace with myself, than I had felt in a long time." Janet changed both her job and her marital status. But it was a difficult process. "When I was in Europe, I prayed for help in making the right decision about my marriage in every church I visited as a tourist . . . and there were plenty of them!"

Questers who experienced time-out periods show it can be helpful. They emerged from their breaks with greater self-understanding, renewed confidence, and courage to move forward in their self-determined careers and lifestyles.

Roman may become a Quester. Currently, he's recovering from surgery. He has a four-year business degree and has worked as a manager for the past seven years. Roman has some hard decisions to make about his career and life goals. Until now, he has been doing what everyone around him told him to do. That's probably why he's ill. Not feeling good about your job does have physical costs. You only deceive yourself if you think it doesn't.

Many Traditionalists in their late twenties or early thirties are experiencing similar thoughts and feelings as Questers. But they modify their lives to place higher value on family needs and leisure, building directly on the past and making few real changes.

Men may feel anxious making it through the age-thirty transition, but women face an even more turbulent time. Women have more options and, therefore, decisions to consider. The biological clock increases the pressure to make decisions about when and if they want a family and how long they are prepared to delay a decision to enjoy a career. For some, occupational change means dropping out of the work world to have children and stay home with them. Many say they would like to return to work in a few years. A few feel they have had enough.

Beverly, another Quester, is a good example. Beverly spent the married years of her early twenties as a graduate student engaged in occasional research projects. Her age-thirty transition was accompanied by a strong desire to trade career for family. For the next seven years, Beverly was deeply engaged in the domestic life. Then, when she was 37, she began to think again about returning to work full-time. She felt she was "getting narrow." That's part of the complexity of women's development.

Clearly, the passage into the thirties stimulates a psychological changing of gears on all fronts. For Questers, this transition brings the desire to broaden their lives and make some changes. Many tear up the part of the lives they spent most of their twenties so carefully building. Those who have been in a corporate slot feel narrow and restricted. Some Questers decide to open their own businesses. Others return to school to prepare for new occupations. Yet others decide to enjoy life by traveling for a while. If they have been in training, such as graduate study, for a long time, now they eagerly look forward to starting a new job. If they have been single, they long for marriage and emotional attachments. Women who have been pursuing a career may decide to have a family and become more domestic. Moreover, self-assessment is often linked to other life crises such as divorce or job dissatisfaction. As experiences snowball, self-evaluation, a necessary prerequisite to passing successfully through the transition, takes place.

During the Developing Career, most Questers deepen their commitments and invest more of themselves in their work, family, and other valued interests.

Transition problems occur whether people are entering or leaving jobs. But the solution most Questers found was constant. They were willing to listen to their inner voices and willing to risk. Even if no overt action is taken during the age-thirty transition, there is often an unseen shift, a change in the way a person feels about his or her life that will most likely lead to later changes. The equilibrium regained by reaching the other side of 30 makes it easier for people to reexamine their origins and gradually acknowledge parts of themselves that were left out by earlier choices.

The Developing Career Begins

For the Questers who remained in the work world, the decision to make a commitment to another position marks their entry into the developmental cycle of the Developing Career—the entry stage of another occupational cycle. This is a productive, fulfilling, exciting, and creative period in their lives. Both their personal and occupational lives seem fuller and richer. During the Developing Career, most Questers deepen their commitments and invest more of themselves in their work, family, and other valued interests. They pursue their short- and long-range plans and goals.

The reappraisal of the age-thirty transition leads a number of adults to shift their values, priorities, and goals. Many adults become more self-aware and more interested in sharing their understanding of themselves and others. They place more value on the quality of life. Leading a more balanced life, becoming more family-oriented, and developing relationships may take priority. Job satisfaction suddenly becomes more important than climbing the corporate ladder or earning higher wages.

Questers also become more aware of their strong needs to become self-fulfilled, to derive challenge and independence from their jobs, and to make use of their skills. They have outgrown their earlier choices. All want to avoid stagnation. Questers' reappraisals help them arrive at the decisions to leave their jobs when they feel stagnant. The age-thirty transition is usually interrelated with a job transition. Many Questers have completed one occupational cycle and are eager to get started in another. But their decisions do not come easily.

Tall and well built, *Mark* has blond curly hair and brown eyes. He is good-looking and well liked by his peers. Mark completed his college degree at 22 and entered a management training program with an international banking organization in a large western city. His decision was largely influenced by the fact that his father was the president and major shareholder of a large manufacturing firm and his older brother was a successful executive in the family operation. Mark's goal was to become a senior executive. He enjoyed his work, especially the contact with his colleagues and subordinates. But over the next seven years, he gradually came to realize he just wasn't "cut out" to be a manager.

"Two factors influenced my self-appraisal and consequent decision to leave management—the breakdown of my marriage and the fact that my father, who was in his mid-fifties, was struck with two heart attacks. These events helped me realize that I wasn't going to live forever and that if I only had one life to live, I shouldn't be wasting it. I should be involved in doing something I enjoy." Then 31, Mark decided to enter broadcasting, a longtime love and hobby. The only experience he had was at his college radio station, years before. Combined with some initiative and his willingness to take a salary cut and change his lifestyle, it was enough. He got his foot in the door in a small town 100 miles from his hometown. Now a disc jockey and part-time announcer, he loves his work.

Some Traditionalists, who shift their work and life orientation dramatically as a result of the age-thirty transition, may become Questers. Talking about the changes in her values and lifestyle over the past few years, *Alice*, a new Quester, says, "Position, status, and power were extremely important to me in my twenties. Now I'm different. I'm more self-aware and I'm more interested in the quality of life, work, and leisure. I also know that I need a job that gives me autonomy, scope, and challenge . . . . I have taken steps to do something about changing my status. I've made plans to enter a profession."

Brian is also in the mastery stage of his second occupational cycle. He dropped out of high school at the end of his sophomore year for a job doing office work for a railway company. He did well. Promoted to supervisor and then to management, Brian completed his high school diploma at night school. His first job lasted 13 years. Then, he began to feel restless. He remembers feeling trapped as he rounded the corner to his twenty-eighth birthday. "I wanted to do something different . . . something I felt better about. Helping people meant more to me than financial rewards." But Brian had a wife and two children to support. Could he do it? The deciding factor was the death of his mother two years later. "Life is too short not to do what I wanted to do," he thought. So, at age 31, he quit his job and went back to school to get a degree in occupational health and safety. "My wife was great about it," he says. A former dietitian, she went back to work to support the family. By taking extra courses at night, on weekends, and during the summers, Brian completed his degree in three years.

Two years into his new occupation, he admits to loving his job. "I feel very good about life in general. I understand myself better, I'm a better person, and I think I've become more broad-minded and liberal . . . . We have more conversa-

Questers often

feel a sense

of exhilaration

from a

challenging job

well done.

tions as a family, and I know where the children are coming from now."

Most women Questers marry later than their Traditionalist contemporaries and have fewer children—on the average, only one. Those who waited are usually happy. These Questers enjoy all three—marriage, career, and motherhood. They have relished pleasure in love, family, and work. Many are willing to spend extra time on their work. But they are not willing to allow their love or family relationships to disintegrate just so they can attain professional or business success.

Far from vagabonds, most Questers who set out to find more satisfying careers need roots. Questers who tore up the structure of their twenties are particularly keen to build a solid base. As he decorates his new apartment, Mark, the disc jockey who had to move to a new town, says, "I want to feel I'm a very stable citizen."

Many Questers aren't bothered by work pressures. They don't feel helpless in the face of continuing distress. Questers often feel a sense of exhilaration from a challenging job well done. They feel in control of their work and lives.

Bill, a Quester who is currently disengaging from his second occupational cycle, is an example. A sensitive, reflective, diplomatic man who describes himself as "a loner and a lover of people," Bill worked in a government department after he completed his master's degree in forestry. He was promoted up the ladder at regular intervals but at a slower rate than he would have liked. Gradually, Bill became bored, disinterested, and disenchanted with his job and lifestyle. When an offer arrived to teach forestry at a two-year college, he willingly accepted. "Teaching was something I always wanted to do. I thought it would provide me with more meaning, interest, and freedom than the government job and it does." Four years later, Bill was still teaching but was thinking that in the future he might like to devote his time to writing. He had been married for 12 years, but was not particularly happy. Bill and his wife had been through two separations and it looked as though their relationship might not survive the next few years.

Bill is in the process of disengaging himself from both his marriage and his second occupational cycle. The unhappy marriage and his desire to try something new are precipitating and aiding the self-assessment that accompanies a transition. For Bill, it will be the mid-life transition.

Many Questers who have been involved in their new occupations for three to four years are also making transitions. They are beginning to think about what they want to do next. They have mastered their second set of tasks and are enthusiastically looking forward to conquering new ones. Bill, for example, is still interested in writing. Others, like Melvin, are pondering expanding their businesses. Still others are considering returning to school to make more dramatic occupational shifts.

The Maturing Career

The Mid-Life Transition

The mid-life transition acts as a link between the Developing Career and the Maturing Career. The transition can occur anytime between ages 35 to 45, and, in some cases, even later, depending on when the earlier transitions began and ended, how many life crises occurred, how they were dealt with, and where a person is in his or her existing occupational cycle.

This transition is the beginning of what many authorities have called "the crossroads of life" or "the halfway mark." We become aware of advancing age and death. Time seems scarce. We begin to think about time left to live, rather than time already lived. We become aware of our lost youth and our faltering physical powers. We question the stereotyped roles we adopted and we realize that we do not have all the answers. We may wonder, "Is this all there is to life?"

Our source of identity moves from outside to inside. It causes men and women to switch from one set of goals in their twenties to a different set by their forties. We begin to notice previously hidden masculine and feminine aspects of our nature. Men are caught by surprise as a more tender, feeling side emerges. Women are amazed to discover a more aggressive, rational side surfacing. We become aware of developing a more ethical self. An old part of us is dying—and we are troubled.

During this transition, we question every part of our lives. To pass through this "authenticity crisis," we must listen to our inner voices and critically evaluate ourselves and our goals. We must identify and accept our suppressed and unwanted parts and integrate them into our real selves. Now we must shelve the phony self we created just to please others. This is also a time when we must master other tasks. Commit ourselves to goals that have meaning and value to us. Come to grips with the decline of our bodies and eventual mortality. Feel free to express what we previously considered foreign.

Psychologists and psychiatrists, who have helped investigate adult development, believe failure to resolve the difficulties of the mid-life transition helps explain the high rates of alcoholism, depression, and suicide that occur during this period. It explains why many creative and industrious people burn out in their mid-thirties and why others blossom only after that age.

Quite often, people who considered themselves successful during young adulthood become disenchanted with their work, spouses, or lifestyles. Many will question how important and fulfilling their work really is. Earlier career stages may have required compliance with demands at work that may have interfered with the development of an achieved identity. If you have been in a job for 10 or more years without promotions or lateral moves, you are probably already in the disengagement stage. You may be feeling stale, tired, anxious, unattractive, restless, old, burdened, or even unappreciated. You may be thinking of getting back to your original career "dream" after being nudged away from it through the adaptational demands of earlier career experiences. Ulcers, anxiety, or other emotional problems may be taking a toll. Being in charge of your life and your career is important. You want to be able to produce something lasting and worthwhile. Many who did nothing about their careers in their early thirties may be feeling panicky. "This is my last chance!" they cry. Some are forced out of their jobs by obsolescence or technological change. Other adults also flee from well-established bases such as marriage. Or they may decide their life is just fine as is. Any of these alternatives are okay if they feel right for you.

Psychologist Daniel Levinson and his colleagues pointed out that this is a time of paradox. They describe the dilemma a man faces when, on the one hand, if he doesn't make a switch, he will never become his own person; if he does, he risks hurting the people he loves by failing. "Having made his bed (marital, occupational, or other), he cannot continue to lie in it. Yet to change is to tear the very fabric of his life, to destroy much that he has built over the last 10 or 15 years."

Now you can see that you must evaluate your life not by external symbols of success (prestigious job or big house), but by internal symbols (feelings of accomplishment or peace of mind).

Bertrand is one Quester who is thinking of changing jobs again. For the past six years, he's been teaching law school at a Midwestern university. Before that, until boredom came calling, he practiced law in the same city for seven years. Now 43, Bertrand likes his job. He has independence and variety. But, once again, he is feeling stale and restless. In a few years, he would like to do something else. Maybe start a business, something he can be enthusiastic about. A very creative man, Bertrand's needs for challenge and growth are stronger than many others. Because he understands himself, Bertrand knows he will need some changes soon to keep his occupational identity healthy.

Ill health or misfortune forces some people in this transition to make changes that cause them to become Questers. *Kit*, a brilliant man of 42, was the controller of a large corporation. He worked his way up with a master's degree in accounting. Kit's position, salary, and lifestyle were the stuff dreams are made of. He had a beautiful wife, well-behaved children, a large home with a swimming pool and sauna, and took luxurious vacations. But he was frustrated and uneasy. Psychiatric counseling was necessary. His doctor referred him to a career counselor. It was apparent that at least some of Kit's frustrations were related to his career. He was in a figures-and-paper job. He belonged in a selling-and-people-persuading position. Kit was lucky. He could ask for a move to a sales department where he could use his accounting skills. By night, he studied marketing techniques and strategies. Two years later, he was sales manager.

Martha has a similar story to tell. A married woman of 38 with three children, she was feeling "out of sorts" and didn't know why. The feelings came on gradually. Night after night, she lay awake. Her relationship with her husband and children faltered. She thought she had everything she needed—a loving husband, well-behaved children, a nice home, and enough money to buy the things she needed. Martha let a friend talk her into counseling. It was a wise move. During the counseling sessions, she learned she was letting her own needs play second fiddle to what she thought her husband and children wanted. Martha's whole world revolved around her family. She deprived them of nothing—she gave them her time and even sacrificed many pleasures. A year later, Martha had the courage to talk about her feelings. To her surprise, her family understood her needs and supported and encouraged her to pursue a longtime goal to become a dietitian. Soon after, Martha began to follow her dream. As a young woman, she was not motivated to complete the home economics program she began because she was too busy having a social life. Today, Martha is in the final year of her program. She is talking like a Quester. She feels great.

For many adults, the mid-life crisis is so great that they fail to make a smooth transition. A long process of frustration and failure follows. A woman whose children no longer seem to need her may become depressed or decide to have another baby. To bring back the excitement of years long past, many men will try to reassert their masculine prowess through vigorous physical activity or invest in risky stock ventures. Alcohol can become an escape route leading nowhere. Many of these problems are a result of job dissatisfaction and disengagement. Staying on the job physically, while far removed from it intellectually and emotionally, causes many dissatisfied workers to wither. Those adults who weather the crisis often do it by finding new meaning and purpose in more satisfying positions or leisure activities.

The Maturing Career Begins

For many Questers, the Maturing Career begins about age 40. Relatively stable and contented, they understand themselves a

The creativity of leadership peaks during the Maturing Career.

little better. They are in tune with their needs. They are more real, happy, warm, mellow. They feel alive! Their families are still important to them, and so are their friends. But having some time to themselves is becoming more important.

A number of Questers are in the mastery stage of their next occupational cycle. Their job satisfaction is high. So is their productivity. They are creative but their creativity is more "sculptured" than in earlier years. They form and fashion a product, work and rework the material, act and react to what they are making. Rather than the intense, spontaneous, and often unconscious creativity of the twenties and early thirties, the creative process is more deliberate, conscious, and analytical. It may continue for years. The creativity of leadership peaks during the Maturing Career. Leadership abilities in education, law, and industry are at their highest in the forties, fifties, and sixties.

Along with leadership ability, the need to make a lasting and significant contribution to a profession or organization is strongest in middle age. Because development of a future generation of leaders is a significant and highly satisfying contribution, interest in guiding the young blossoms now.

Betty, a Quester politician, radiates a star quality that belies her age of 50. She refused entreaties to run for a seat in the Senate because, as she stated, "I want to be a mentor rather than a power broker." Betty and other Questers like her become role models to the young women who will succeed them.

Men and women in the Maturing Career may also become interested in people-related work. Adults in people-oriented occupations, such as teaching, social work, sales, and politics, find immense satisfaction in helping others.

Erik Erikson called adults who have dealt with the mid-life crisis "generative." They are nurturing, protective, productive, and creative in a new sense. They feel voluntarily committed to guiding new generations as parents, as mentors of an occupation, as members of society. In contrast, those who haven't dealt through the crisis successfully are egocentric, nonproductive, self-indulgent, depressed, and lack the ability to truly care for others.

Peter left his senior management position to teach accounting in a two-year college. He traded his plush office—its deep pile rug, brown leather sofa, windows overlooking a lake, and private secretary—for a cubbyhole with no windows, no rug, and a secretary shared with seven others. Peter seemed to make the decision to leave his career of seven years quite suddenly. It happened when he spotted an ad for a business administration instructor. He phoned. Several hours later, he was interviewed. There was no hesitation when the offer came. "I was ready for a move," Peter said. "It was a matter of time . . . I was beginning to feel stale in my position. Even though I liked and respected my colleagues, I couldn't see myself spending the next 20 years of my life there." Peter, now 45, did considerable self-evaluation during his mid-life transition and discovered he really did want to change positions. He was in the disengagement stage of his managerial cycle and was ready to change when the teaching opportunity presented itself. Now in the mastery stage of his teaching job of four years, Peter muses that he would like to do something else in a few years, perhaps work in staff development with his previous organization or write. Like a typical Quester, Peter is keeping his options open.

Evelynne (who you met earlier) is another 45-year-old Quester who is keeping her options open. Evelynne made the decision to start over during the self-appraisal she did at 40. Today in the mastery stage of her entrepreneurial cycle, Evelynne is thinking about getting involved in something new a few years from now.

By the time Evelynne, Peter, and many other Questers in their mid-forties reach their fiftieth birthdays, they will probably modify or change their plans again if they feel they are no longer growing. These shifts in careers will be associated with their age-fifty transitions. Many adults will be trying to come to grips with recurring issues, such as jobs, and issues they haven't dealt with, such as faltering relationships.

Murray came to terms with his growing dissatisfaction when he was 51. Principal of a junior high school for eight years, Murray was tired of political hassles. Art and interior design had been longtime hobbies, and, for many years, he had

Many women in the Maturing Career stage can't get their children out of the nest fast enough so they can return to work.

dreamed of spending more time on his leisure activities. So he decided to open a furniture store in the suburbs of a medium-sized, Midwestern city. At last, Murray could put his interests and knowledge of art and interior design to use. The management and people-related skills he developed and used as a principal were invaluable in his new venture. Murray had begun his working life as manager of a retail organization. His age-thirty transition found him returning to school for teacher training. In seven years, he was principal. A Quester throughout his working life, Murray has found his disengagements from occupational cycles always coincided with life cycle transitions.

Brady, like Murray, has undergone the same transitions. He left his dentistry practice when he was 47, traveled the world for a year, then returned to America to take a lower-paying job as a researcher. Brady felt he was getting stale. He needed to expand, personally and professionally. "I feel more alive now, and believe I am a better husband and person. I'm also more productive as a professional." His family and colleagues agree. Brady is a good example of the growing number of professionals in their late forties and fifties who leave secure positions to pursue new interests.

For Traditionalists, the era from age 40 to retirement is often called the maintenance period. Established in their careers, they enter a plateau. Usually holding their own at work, they try to maintain what has already been achieved. However, in an economy characterized by downsizing, layoffs, mergers, company relocation, and bankruptcies, they may not be able to remain in their comfortable ruts.

Many women in the Maturing Career stage can't get their children out of the nest fast enough so they can return to work. Some studies of American women between 35 and 65 indicate that they are feeling extraordinarily good about themselves, their lives, and their futures. These feelings are shared by women in all kinds of roles, from housewives to executives. Some are just now becoming Questers.

Many are the beneficiaries of a new social climate created largely by the women's movement. Not so long ago, the common perception was that women aged 50 or older were over the hill and unemployable. Today, the numbers alone challenge the old stereotype. Women who have reached or passed 50 are frequently regarded as glamorous and desirable. Women such as Lauren Hutton, Lena Horne, Jane Fonda, Sophia Loren, and Joan Collins have popularized the appeal of "older" women.

Many women who are 50 or older are going back to school and literally starting new lives. *Kate,* who has six children, went to school to study economics at 50 and now works in the trade department of the federal government. *Anne* is becoming a student again. Being 50 can be a special time for a working woman, too. Shirley MacLaine won her first Oscar for Terms of Endearment when she was 50. Gloria Steinem and many other women in their fifties and sixties are setting goals they hope to realize over the next 20 years. These women are aware of how much age has to do with state of mind. Studies show women who are homemakers tend to be physiologically 10 years older than women in the workforce. It's not the work. It's a result of the lack of control, dignity, respect, stimulation, and company. Today, diet and exercise are changing the way women look and feel about themselves. Nowadays, your only limits are energy level, drive, motivation, and goals. At 50, you've just begun to come into knowledge and experience you've spent a lifetime piecing together. Many women over 50 feel a new sense of independence and strength. They feel good because they're doing the kind of work they want to do. They are keeping young. That such changes are commonplace even into the sixties surprises many young women. Yet, this bloom in the middle of the female life cycle is a signal that it's never too late to find wholeness.

The career patterns of reentry women often resemble those of young adults in the Beginning Career. Women who have been out of work for a while tend to have strong needs for career expansion and mastery. They appear to be making up for lost time. At the same time many of their husbands want to slow down and lead a more balanced life.

Looking for jobs to replace the outlived purpose of mothering is particularly difficult for the middle-aged women of today. Their generation was never adequately prepared, emotionally or educationally, for the reality that paid work is central to the self-confidence of middle-aged women. And, yet, they rally. All at once, a "sense of accomplishment" becomes vitally important. Middle-aged women who point the way to younger women's futures are the only ones in recent studies who rate accomplishment as their most important long-range goals. Mobilizing their strengths and pouring their energies into doing paid or unpaid work outside the home is one way of handling stress. This sudden, strong emphasis on achieving something worthwhile brings exhilaration and a renewed sense of purpose.

Moreover, most Traditionalist women don't do much about achieving their identity until after their mid-forties. Now, at 46 and older, they begin to establish a firm sense of their own identities for the first time. Many women, who have weathered the crisis of the mid-life and age-fifty transitions, see their fifties as the happiest times of their lives.

The developmental period of the fifties comes to an end when we start wondering what to do about retirement. Should we work full-time or part-time if we have the choice? Or should we disengage ourselves completely from the marketplace?

The Continuing Career

The Age-Sixty Transition

The age-sixty transition marks the boundary between the Maturing Career and the Continuing Career. As we progress through this transition into late adulthood, we again question and explore our inner selves in relation to our external world, examine our careers and other options, and settle on a course that will give us opportunities for continuing growth. If you can come to terms with issues that lie before you now, you will acquire a clearer and fuller sense of who you are. You will develop greater inner strength and become more capable of pursuing your goals.

Individuals who remain active and involved in their work or leisure activities during their middle and later years will be healthier, happier, and live longer.

One issue almost all of us must deal with is whether or not we will accept the compulsory retirement included in the employer-employee contract of a number of organizations.

New attitudes toward aging, improved diet and exercise programs, and medical advances have prolonged life expectancy. In 1900, only one American in 25 was over 65. By 2000, one in five will be 65 or older; and by the middle of the twenty-first century, one in four will be 65 or older. During the twentieth century, we have gained 25 years of life expectancy.

Unfortunately, many individuals and organizations still cling to outdated ideas about retirement and aging. For example, they believe that retirement at age 65 or younger is an effective and efficient use of human resources. Sixty-five was the retirement age set by German chancellor Otto von Bismarck in 1881, when few Germans lived much beyond that age!

Now, although mandatory retirement is usually 70, many healthy and productive individuals in their fifties or younger are being "retired" early due to mergers, new technologies, or other factors. It is doubtful whether this practice will be able to continue as the baby boomers reach their fifties and sixties. How will the decreasing number of younger people be able to support the increasing number of active and healthy seniors?

Today, retirement means different things to different people. For some, loss of work means a loss of part of themselves—they feel as if a piece of their inner self has disappeared. Retirement raises the specter of unwelcome inactivity. To others, retirement means escape from a dreary and frustrating job—freedom to do things they had no time to do before. Yet others consider retirement an escape from suffocating pressures. Decisions about your post retirement life may be related to how long you want to live. Research shows that individuals who remain active and involved in their work or leisure activities during their middle and later years will be healthier, happier, and live longer.

For many Questers, "retirement" means continuing growth and revitalization. During the age-sixty transition, many are in the late mastery or early disengagement stage of their fifth, sixth, or seventh occupational cycles. Some cycles have been sequential, a logical succession of increasing skills and responsibilities. Others have been as unrelated as athlete, artist, and mechanics teacher. Questers are continuing to find work in which they can grow.

Fortunately, at the same time, some Traditionalists are also becoming Questers. *Wally* worked for the same bank for 40 years until recently, when he began to think like a Quester. His retirement plans are still tentative, but he can hardly wait to get started. Wally believes retirement will give him a chance to do something different, to be more flexible and autonomous. For Wally, compulsory retirement doesn't mean disengagement or diminished activity. It means greater challenge, scope, and freedom.

Some people who seem to be Traditionalists are "retiring" early. *Cliff* spent his life in a blue-collar world as a building custodian. Cliff decided to retire early and enter an entirely different field of work. He took courses to help him prepare for his new occupation—selling real estate. "One of my strengths is that I'm a creative person, and that type of individual always searches for new experiences," he says.

But for most Traditionalists, retirement can be difficult because it often requires dramatic changes. Finding out you have nothing to do, or are just in the way, can be devastating when you have been a good provider or wage earner for 35 years. Death rates increase dramatically for retired men and women. So do illnesses that have no physiological causes.

The Continuing Career Develops

When many Traditionalists are retiring, most Questers are in the entry or early mastery stage of their next occupational cycles.

Phyl is a good-looking man with gray hair and sparkling blue eyes. He walks with a spring. Now 70, he has had an amazingly diverse career—news photographer, newspaper reporter, school principal, magazine and newspaper editor, politician, writer, and television producer. Phyl dropped out of school after repeating the tenth grade and managed to get a job as a photographer's assistant with a local newspaper. From there, he moved to newspaper reporting. During the age-thirty transition, he went back to school. Phyl earned his education degree and got married in the same year. He taught school for six years, then became principal of a school in the same city. At 45, he was off to work as editor of a newspaper and then a magazine. By age 60, when most men are planning for retirement, Phyl ran successfully in state elections. He left politics for writing and working as a television producer.

When Phyl is asked which job he enjoyed the most, he replies, "I enjoyed them all. I have enjoyed whatever I was doing when I was doing it. My various positions have a common thread running through them . . . I need to work with people and to communicate to others."

Phyl has some regrets. Most involve interpersonal relations: "I have been so immersed in what I'm doing that I have neglected friendships and family at times. Much of my success is due to the energies that I have put into the work at hand . . . . I have sometimes wondered why I work with such single-mindedness. It is not for the financial rewards nor is it for the renown. If there has been a dominant drive, it has been a deep need for challenge . . . for variety, scope . . . for personal satisfaction. However, I would still lead a similar life if I had my life to live over again."

Phyl has this to say about his career goals. "I am by no means certain what I will do next. I will certainly continue to write." Like many Questers, Phyl's career goals are still open-ended.

Growing old is not a death warrant for mental activity. Many outstanding people did not reach their prime until long after 50. Pablo Picasso was still painting at 91, Grandma Moses at 101. Arturo Toscanini gave his last performance at 87 and Giuseppe Verdi composed Falstaff at 80. Konrad Adenauer was chancellor of West Germany at 87. Artur Rubinstein excited audiences with his piano artistry well into his nineties. So did the late centenarian Eubie Blake.

Sociologists say that with more people living active, youthful lives well past 60, public perceptions of later adulthood are changing. College students fresh from high school share classrooms with 65-year-olds. Gray-haired athletes enter marathons. Retired workers become entrepreneurs. Artists become world travelers. "A few years ago," says a fashion expert, laughing, "the sight of a woman over 40 dressing in jeans and riding a motorcycle was thought bizarre, or at least inappropriate. Now women are expected to be fit into their seventies and jeans have become so haute couture that only women over 40 can afford them." Nowadays, whom can we tell to "act your age?" The rhythm of life has changed in other ways, too. A man and woman can become father and mother again at the same time they become grandparents. Puberty arrives earlier and menopause later. Grandparents are getting younger and living longer. You truly are "as old as you feel."

Attitudes are going through immense changes and people have many new and interesting alternatives. *Kay* was a principal until she retired at 65. Everyone was amazed at her energy level and wondered how she managed to find time for skiing, singing, and other projects, in addition to her heavy work schedule. When she retired, Kay and her husband spent a year traveling around the world. Six months later, she was bored and restless. To keep challenge and meaning in her life, she approached the school board and asked for a job. Her first project was to coordinate a group so that it could attack the problems of inner-city schools. This was followed by the evaluation of private schools. Kay, now 72, is still working on educational projects. She also has time for social activities. She is feeling great and hopes to continue with her present lifestyle.

Frank worked for the railway for 42 years, first as a mechanical apprentice, next as a tradesman, then as a supervisor. He climbed the organizational ladder until he was in his mid-fifties. Then his career reached a plateau. To keep involved and enthusiastic about life, Frank volunteered to do first aid with the Red Cross during his spare time. At 61, he retired early to become a full-time first-aid worker. When most of his railway friends were retiring, Frank opened up a practice in reflexology (a form of therapy based on manipulation, anesthetization, or cauterization). Now 70, Frank is still a vital man. "Age," he says, "is a matter of attitude more than years." Frank plays tennis and skis during his spare time. He's also remarrying.

Contemporary career development is a continuing quest to improve the fit between your occupation and your developing personality. Only you can establish your rhythm of change. It's never too late!

Job Satisfiers

he rewards Questers get from their positions depend on their personalities. But most are seeking higher-level needs: freedom, growth, independence, challenge, achievement, variety, involvement, altruism, plus a sense of purpose and identity. They tend to enjoy their jobs as indicated by their use of such adjectives as "fun," "excitement," and "pleasure." *Phyl*, the energetic 70-year-old, now in his seventh occupational cycle, says it best: "There is nothing more thrilling than creating something out of yourself. To follow a strong drive toward a goal and find yourself, to work at what you want to do and do it successfully, to risk everything when the chances for success seem so small, to give everything to your work and get everything back from it, this is the ultimate satisfaction."

How different Questers are from many Traditionalists. *Lorne,* a 50-year-old writer in the civil service, is thoughtful when he considers why he works. Then he says, "For bread and butter. It's a necessity, a way of making a systematic life for me in that it gives me a place to go, even though it's no longer fulfilling because it is no longer challenging. I'm not learning anything. I'm not reaching." Lorne acknowledges that he misses the challenge and stimulation his career earlier provided. Now in the disengagement stage of his occupational cycle, he has, quite simply, outgrown his job.

The sense of resignation in Lorne's voice is echoed when we hear Jessica describe her job. A 40-year-old bookkeeper and former homemaker, Jessica sees her work as "an escape from housework and doing routine tasks." Her job may be more rewarding than housework, but she's far from satisfied.

Unfortunately, while a number of Traditionalists do derive a sense of identity and sometimes challenge from their work, their careers tend to satisfy little more than lower-level needs: money, security, prestige, and something to do. Many Traditionalists are missing the intense feelings of satisfaction that drive Questers on to further challenges. Ultimately, they will pay for it.

How Satisfied Are You?

Because your job needs are dynamic, they usually reflect your reactions to your current work environment. For example, as you gain competence, a job that first seemed challenging may become boring.

Why, then, do some people seem satisfied to do the same work over and over again, day in and day out, without complaint? Because their need hierarchies may be very different from most Questers'. Less important needs can be satisfied much more easily than higher-level needs. So, for instance, if you have a high need for social contacts and your job gives you many opportunities to satisfy that need (assuming other important high-level needs are also met), you will have a high level of job satisfaction. But if you took a job that offered few chances to make social contacts, you would be very dissatisfied.

As you grow and develop, your needs constantly jockey for position. As a result, in middle age, you may seriously consider changing the direction of your career. A young person with a job that demands extensive travel may be very satisfied. But once married and with children, being away from home may become so displeasing that a new job with limited travel demands will be sought. Whether or not you're satisfied with your job depends on the degree to which your needs are being met.

A look at the job satisfiers many Questers seek will give you a better idea of where your career fits into your need hierarchy. Following is a summary of what many Questers consider in the often difficult task of finding true career satisfaction.

Who hasn't been asked, "What do you want to do when you grow up?" A more appropriate question is "What kind of a person do you want to become?"

Emerging Identity

Part of the search for career satisfaction is finding an occupation that will fit your personality and self-image. Your career is a statement about you. Knowing who you are and who you want to become and receiving recognition from your work are essential to satisfaction. The desire for self-awareness and recognition will last throughout your life.

Your career plays a major part in how you represent yourself to society. The recognition you get from your job is an important part of your life. A career charts your path in the human community. Asked who they are, many people will respond by telling you what they do. Children also face this. Who hasn't been asked, "What do you want to do when you grow up?" The proper answer, of course, is "a doctor" or "a police officer" or "an astronaut." A more appropriate question is "What kind of a person do you want to become?" The expectations of others tend to encourage most people to emphasize the work they do rather than who they are.

The importance of a job to one's sense of identity is evident when speaking to the unemployed. Many feel worthless without a job. Grace, an assistant vocational rehabilitation counselor, was depressed to find herself out of work even though she puts her husband, her 12-year-old son, and her home before any job. "When I was working, my husband was proud of me, my son was proud, and then all of a sudden I had nothing," she recalls. "Though I never really blamed myself, I felt emotionally worthless. There's more to life than staying home and it's bad when getting your unemployment check is your big day out."

You are judged not only by what you do, but by the industry in which you do it, your responsibilities, and your company's reputation. A person who craves responsibility might be quite happy working in a small company. But someone who identifies with prestige and status may accept a much lower position just to join a large, renowned company in a prestigious industry. Much job dissatisfaction can be traced to the mismatch between a worker's identity needs and his or her employer.

Of course, as you grow and develop, your identity will change, too. In fact, most Questers are constantly reshaping their identities. They commit themselves to occupations only as long as the jobs fit their personalities.

Finding Purpose in Work

Everyone needs something to believe in. People who feel they have a reason to exist are healthier, happier, and live longer. Your career can give you a sense of purpose. Your purpose may be the same throughout your life, or it may be modified as you progress through life. Having a sense of purpose means being open to and accepting change. It also means being honest with yourself. Questers periodically ask themselves, "Who am I?" "Whom do I want to become?" "What do I really want to do with my life?" They also want to know how they can better guide, teach, or help others, as well as how to make useful products.

Most people want to improve themselves or some aspects of their lives, but many are afraid of letting go. They are too dependent on security, money, prestige and power. This dependency often results in a sense of meaninglessness, frustration, and anxiety. Questers, in contrast, seek higher level rewards (such as meaning, purpose, love, altruism, joy, harmony, growth, beauty, and truth). They strive and struggle to reach the goals that will help them attain these rewards.

Brock exudes happiness, a sense of inner peace, and good health. A politician now, the 55-year-old Quester has been an actor, salesman, market research analyst, and stockbroker. He thought he'd take early retirement, but he just couldn't do it. After a year of being idle, Brock decided he preferred to work even though he didn't need the money. "After a year, I felt parasitic and indolent. I have to be involved in something I can believe in, can enjoy, can commit to, and from which I can be of use to humankind. To energize myself, I needed something that would make me push myself to the limits." He moved into politics and now Brock feels he is making his country a better place to live. "It's a wonderful feeling to be involved in something you love," he says earnestly after election to the provincial legislature. "It gives you a sense of purpose and meaning—and feeling needed."

Kim, 30, a human resources consultant, says, "My mission is to learn and to teach." Kim states that she knew this as a young child but lost her passion to pursue these goals when she was raped at age 10. A workshop she attended recently helped Kim "reconnect with my inner child, to reclaim my purpose, and commit myself to this dream."

As a child, you often know what you want to do. But various experiences such as traumas and learned belief systems disconnect you from your inner self. By breaking down the barriers and asking yourself specific questions you can recon-nect with your life goal. This will give you the courage to believe in yourself and commit yourself to pursuing activities that give your life meaning. Kim describes purpose "as a rough diamond. As you become more and more in tune with it, you can make it shine more brightly. This will give you the strength to follow your dream."

The Need for Challenge

Questers usually need more challenge than most. As soon as many master one challenge, they are off to tame yet another. Why? Differences in genetic makeup and early socialization experiences give some people a greater thirst for challenge. But the workplace can also play a big part.

Employees who enjoy sufficiently challenging jobs are enthusiastic and involved.

The Work Environment Influences Your Happiness

Learning new tasks, having control over your work, and being responsible for decisions all involve mental challenge. But what happens when your work doesn't provide enough challenge or opportunities for mastery and achievement? The result is usually boredom. Employees who enjoy sufficiently challenging jobs are enthusiastic and involved. Those who feel responsible for the actions and outcomes of their work will strive harder because their total personalities are involved. Coping with challenge also requires effort and commitment to your goals in life.

Challenge, of course, is dynamic. Once you have mastered a difficult task, you need new challenges. The quest for challenge corresponds to a growing person's occupational cycle.

Achieving Psychological Success

You can get a better understanding of the cyclical relationships between challenge, achievement, involvement, self-confidence, goal attainment, and job factors from the diagram illustrating psychological success. Achieving your goals leads to feelings of psychological success. Below are the prerequisites for feeling good about your job:

❖   Challenging work

❖   Autonomy

❖   Support from others

❖   Feedback

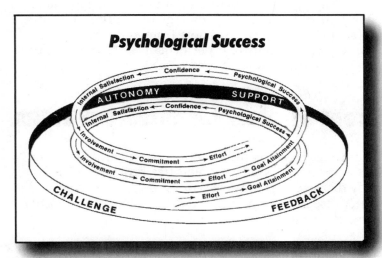

As mastering each task pushes you to newer levels of competence, your satisfaction increases. So does self-confidence. As a result, your involvement in your job will probably increase, too. These increased feelings of success, confidence, involvement, and commitment will usually lead you to set more difficult goals. When this cycle is occurring, you feel "turned on" by your work.

To set work goals, you will need a healthy degree of autonomy. Close supervision may make you feel that your performance reflects more on your supervisor than on your own efforts.

However, getting support when you try a difficult task (regardless of whether you succeed or fail) spurs you on; it also facilitates the development of your creativity. Feedback is necessary to help you evaluate your performance. This tends to give you feelings of accomplishment.

Glen is a good example of what happens when an employee receives support and encouragement. As an accountant for a meat-packing plant, Glen persuaded his boss to allow him to plan and install a new management information system. Extensive research went into his plan. Its success was overwhelming. His confidence bolstered by this success and the discovery of a whole new set of skills, Glen asked for a transfer so he could develop his management potential. Now general manager of a division, Glen is again happily involved in the entry stage of a new occupational cycle.

The good feelings of success and satisfaction that Glen and other Questers derive from their jobs come because they tend to have challenging positions that are interesting and meaningful. They are able to set their own goals, work independently to achieve them, gain support from supervisors, and get useful feedback about their performances. Because of this, Questers are satisfied they are doing good work.

Different Strokes for Different Folks

Challenge comes in many different forms. At one end of the stimulation spectrum is the commodities broker who makes potentially disastrous trades every minute. At the other end is the product researcher who may develop a new product only once or twice a year. Both are challenged—with different timing.

Just as too little challenge may cause you to be dissatisfied, so can too much. If the level of challenge is so great you can't cope with it, you are in the wrong job. Moderate challenges, which make success difficult but possible, will give you the most pleasure and satisfaction.

Questers—who understand how to match their needs for stimulation to the right job—could find challenge in many different occupations. What do you need to find challenge? And how much is right for you?

Variety Adds Spice to Life

Questers tend to enjoy work that allows them to accomplish many different tasks. They appreciate jobs that require some thought, have some unexpected challenges, and allow them to use their own ingenuity.

Sandy gets plenty of variety in the Peace Corps. A broad range of experiences, skills, and interests have prepared her to succeed at this often frustrating job. Before she married, Sandy, now 51, was an agricultural agent. While she gave up her career for motherhood and marriage, Sandy kept busy with volunteer work. She headed a political campaign, lobbied successfully for a home for battered women, developed a youth employment center, and chaired many committees seeking better facilities for the mentally retarded. "I love challenge and variety. I want to help others."

Her husband died when she was 49 and Sandy needed a job to support herself. She was well qualified for the Peace Corps. Although her position as a director is often difficult, she treasures the variety. "Every minute, every hour, is different. I get to work for world peace, travel, meet people from all walks of life, and help with all kinds of projects in agriculture, education, social work, and medical care. I even answer phones for the African relief hotline."

The Need to Achieve

Psychological growth occurs when there is opportunity for achievement.

Understanding why many Questers are so involved in their work requires knowledge about the need for achievement. People who derive feelings of accomplishment from completing a difficult task feel satisfied and proud. How successfully they cope with a task determines how competent and proud they feel. Psychological growth occurs when there is opportunity for achievement.

To see how important achievement really is, you must meet *Omar*. He raised $275,000 to start his own Italian ice cream store, the first of its kind in a large Eastern city. The store drew 160,000 customers in just six months. Strange as it may sound, Omar didn't really care how much money he made or how famous he became or whether he could beat the competition. What he cared about was his product. "I had a product that I loved and believed in and I wanted a perfect gelato store that looked attractive and authentic and gave people something wonderful." To achieve that, he was willing to pay his employees well.

Persistence Is the Mother of Invention

Inner toughness, the ability to stick with a dream or an ambition even when it's not going well, tends to set Questers apart from a number of Traditionalists and Self-seekers. Instead of panicking and packing it in when their dreams seem about to fall apart, they size up the problems and figure out alternative solutions. As they have discovered, the paths to success are many.

Shawna learned that when she decided to go to college. Divorced and with two children to support, she worked day and night just to make it through her program. By the time she had obtained her B.S., she had to face facts. She was just too poor to afford her longtime dream of becoming a doctor. So she took a job as a junior biologist, then as a technical writer, moving from a computer company to a small medical electronics firm. While she seemed to be drifting, Shawna was actually questing, constantly "fine-tuning" her abilities.

By 1975, Shawna had saved enough money to start her own company making electrosurgical equipment, the same product her last employer had specialized in, only better. Her company's best-seller, a high-tech scalpel, made her rich. Shawna's interest in medicine had finally paid off, but in a much different way than she had envisioned.

Hard Work Is Energizing

The accomplishments of many Questers usually take a tremendous amount of hard work. Omar held a full-time job at an investment firm while working nights to research gelato recipes. His new position still keeps him going day and night. Shawna went to night school and studied weekends. Getting ahead as they did without succumbing to exhaustion or self-doubt takes enormous determination and single-mindedness.

But hard work can be very energizing. Hard work has its own rewards, such as positive feedback and the feelings of satisfaction that accompany a sense of accomplishment. Like many Questers, as you gain competence and become more fulfilled and involved, you will also gain energy. You may even learn to approach your job with verve, as if you are playing an exhilarating, although serious, game.

Successful activity, no matter how intense, leaves you with comparatively few scars; it causes stress, but little distress. Work wears you out mainly through the frustration of failure or boredom. Many of the hardest workers in almost any field live a long life.

Information Is Power

If many Questers don't know something, they tend to find out, pronto! Omar tells his employees that "there's no such word as 'can't.'" While some salesclerks sit around waiting for customers, many Quester salesclerks hound their bosses to teach them how the businesses operate. Questers know that every bit of know-how they pick up can only help to make them more resourceful.

When they're not studying, a number of Questers are evaluating what they've learned. This thirst for information heightens their chances for succeeding when taking risks. Omar found market research invaluable when he approached possible financiers. While the banks had a million facts and figures to show why another ice cream store just wouldn't make it, Omar had the research to prove it would. "I might have stopped right there, but I had done my own research and I just had a feeling that gelato would go."

Confronting Fear of Failure

Questers seldom risk their resources on impossible dreams. While they take chances, their actions are based on sound knowledge of the facts plus planning and intuitive feelings. Omar's friends were appalled when he left his well-paying position. But he had done his homework so well that opening the store felt like the next step in a well-conceived plan.

Risk takers have to confront the fear of failure. Losing job security and possibly pride is risky. Questers tend to deal with this by waiting until the signs look good—and then plunging ahead. They work out their anxieties by acting, not agonizing.

When you are generous with your own talents and time, your efforts are usually rewarded many times over.

Because setbacks are inevitable, Questers train themselves to look at reversals as learning opportunities, not signs of personal inadequacy. "Failure is good for you," Bernadette says confidently. "It's a kind of bruise that makes you tougher. If I've done my absolute best and still goof, I say, 'Okay, I'm human.' I forgive myself. Then I sit down and take a look at what went wrong."

Enhancing Your Potential

How can you develop your achievement potential? Set personal and professional goals and then start realizing them one step at a time. For example, start and stick with a training or savings program. At work, figure out how long a single project will take you to complete, then try to do it 10 minutes faster, then 20 minutes faster. Not only will increased efficiency raise your feelings of competence, but it could prompt your boss to give you even more responsibility and challenge.

While you are raising your own sense of competence, try to avoid competing with the experts around you. Instead, enlist their help and support. Many Questers are backed up by efficient and loyal support teams. When you are generous with your own talents and time, your efforts are usually rewarded many times over.

Self-Confidence Empowers

Confident people stand out. They seem so comfortable and so in control of their lives. But self-confidence is often the result of accomplishing something. It also stems from learning to accept one's negative qualities.

Many Questers don't feel rejected for long if they have been passed up for a promotion or some other form of recognition. Because they are self-confident, they tend to have the courage to move on to occupations that do satisfy their needs. Their confidence also gives them the courage to take other risks leading toward goals that are important to them.

Studies in the workplace have found that most managers and professionals select "feeling that my work is worth doing" as the most important factor contributing to their sense of self-confidence and self-respect. Listed below are other contributing factors:

❖ An equitable salary

❖ A sense of accomplishment

❖ Growth opportunities, such as freedom, independence, authority, and creativity

❖ Sufficient feedback and recognition

❖ Ability to advance within the company

❖ Two-way communication

❖ Enjoyable work

❖ Company security

Highly self-confident employees get more pleasure from succeeding at their work than from any other factor. They are more likely to:

❖ Value challenging tasks

❖ Find the pleasure of achievement to be intense and enduring

❖ Want promotions for reasons of justice

❖ Desire responsibility over status

And they are less likely to:

❖ Value prestige, approval, and verbal recognition as sources of self-assurance

❖ Be emotionally affected by criticism

❖ Experience conflicts and feelings of anxiety on the job

❖ Be defensive and employ defense mechanisms (Less confident employees will often project their failures onto other people or circumstances.)

How did they become self-confident? They developed it through work, practice, determination, and achievement. You can develop self-confidence in the same way. Start by realizing that at your core is an inner strength that you alone have the power to bring to the surface. The ability to tap that resource is what long-distance runners call "digging down." Once you've grabbed hold of your own power and felt the magical quality that you possess, you'll see that self-confidence can truly turn your world around.

Bette learned that lesson while she was still young. A shy, quiet little girl, she stayed pretty much to herself. "If you had known me then, you would have said that I was one of the most unassuming and unambitious children you ever met." But Bette had a secret. While other kids were outside playing, she was pouring over her mother's magazines and trying to copy the high fashion togs on her sewing machine. "I wasn't too successful at the time," she remembers, "but I knew somewhere deep down inside me that as long as I could play 'dress up' in my life, I would be happy. As I look back on it, I realize that even then my career was growing inside of me."

Bette's interest in sewing was translated into the desire to become a good dress designer. "Not to say it was a piece of cake. It wasn't!" She studied and worked very hard. Though still just a frightened little girl at heart, she traveled to Paris and New York to learn her trade. She took risks. "But the important thing is that once I made my decision to work toward this goal, I gave myself every opportunity to achieve it." These days, when she recalls her past insecurities, Bette thinks that she, like the legendary glass of water, was half full, not half empty. "Now, I design dresses that other little girls dream about!"

Bette didn't acquire self-confidence overnight. Nor will you. Self-confidence develops as you work on and achieve small goals. Like learning a language, developing self-confidence may sometimes leave you feeling awkward and uncomfortable. You will make silly mistakes and you will feel as though it's someone else, not you, doing those things. But the more you practice, the easier it becomes and the more natural you feel.

Ultimately, you alone are responsible for the decisions you make. The final results—self-confidence, knowledge, and success—are the results of those choices. To become more like the Questers, you will have to act like the Questers.

Autonomy Is Being in Control

Questers tend to have a strong desire to control their own work. They perform best in jobs where they have the freedom to use their own ideas and knowledge, pioneer new procedures, take responsibility, and prove their competence. Questers need the freedom to persist, to take risks, and to fail without fear of being reproached or fired.

Few large organizations today provide employees with the opportunity to be autonomous. That's why so many Questers go into business for themselves or work for small companies. A National Science Foundation study showed that small firms produce about four times as many innovations for each research development dollar as medium-sized firms and about 24 times as many as large companies.

Mauro, now 55, owns one of these small companies, a factory that manufactures statues, fountains, and tombstones. During his career, he's been a copywriter, salesman, and middle manager for a large manufacturing firm. He left the last position because he was frustrated by the bureaucracy. Unable to use his own ideas, he felt stifled. "I had little input to decisions affecting my job and little creative input. The position was becoming really watered-down." Feeling emotionally drained and physically ill from his lack of power, he soon developed ulcers. "I felt like I was wearing a straightjacket." When Mauro decided he just couldn't take the feelings of powerlessness anymore, he left. Friends who knew him when he worked for his old employer are startled by the way he changed. His wife, Sandra, is happy with the new Mauro. "Mauro is more relaxed now. He was an old man 10 years ago. Now, he's young again." In control of his life and his health, Mauro feels good about himself again.

Frustration caused by lack of work autonomy can lead to serious consequences.

Nothing breeds success more than success, nothing blocks it more than frustration. Frustration caused by lack of work autonomy can lead to serious consequences. Unrelieved tension or distress, usually accompanied by feelings of helplessness, is a threat to your personality and self-confidence. Ongoing frustration can weaken the body's immune system and result in physical and psychosocial illnesses such as peptic ulcers, migraine, high blood pressure, or back pain. Low self-confidence, job dissatisfaction, lack of creativity, and low aspirations usually accompany the feelings of general ill health and malaise associated with lack of autonomy. For employers, the cost is measured in high turnover, dissatisfied employees with low levels of motivation and morale, reduced productivity and creativity, and ineffective management. Some organizations are now involving their employees in decision making and providing human relations training. Employees are taught to alleviate frustration and stress through relaxation exercises. They are also encouraged to talk to a trusted friend, counselor, or relative when they feel tense.

Fitting In

Corporations often fail to tolerate creative employees who are the force behind many innovations. In an organization's eyes, these highly creative people may seem impatient, egotistical, obnoxious, and perhaps even a bit irrational. As a result, some Questers may have a difficult time convincing prospective employers to hire them. If hired, they may not be promoted or rewarded. The frustrations of seeing creative efforts go ignored is what causes a number of Questers to move on.

Fortunately, some Questers can continue to be themselves and find autonomy in large companies. A few organizations give employees plenty of autonomy. These companies encourage employees to take practical risks and, even if they fail, support good efforts. They know that many employees have to be allowed to experiment and even fail. The companies have learned that "turned on" employees can accomplish miracles. By creating small, independent divisions that give managers control over hiring, firing, finances, and purchasing, these organizations breed loyal, dedicated managers who make better decisions than centralized departments ever could. The absence of paperwork and overplanning is as conspicuous as the internal competition. Unlike many organizations, managers who take on additional responsibilities outside their own divisions are even rewarded.

Jack is a bright, young Quester who works for a progressive company. Encouraged to take risks, he has the freedom to persist and the freedom to fail. At 32, this enthusiastic chemical engineer developed a new medical adhesive product. Supporting and protecting Jack in the development of his product, his manager sympathized with Jack's occasional failures and celebrated his frequent successes. Jack appreciates the support he received. "Without the freedom to persist and fail, I never would have discovered the product." Once developed, the product has been so successful that Jack's employers have given him even more autonomy and incentives to promote further development and marketing.

Coping with Forced Autonomy

Not all Questers find a company they can fit into. But unemployment has motivated many a Quester to become more independent and autonomous. *Carol*, the educator-turned-caterer, is just one Quester who had to learn to cope with forced autonomy. Today, these Questers are adamant that they will never again let anyone else control their careers. *Simone*, manager of an insurance agency, is another who learned coping mechanisms.

Five years ago, Simone found herself suddenly unemployed when her insurance company folded after she had advanced from policy typist to branch supervisor. It didn't take long for Simone to turn a crisis into an opportunity. "I realized there were only two ways to do things: work for somebody else or work for myself." She decided to open her own agency. She had already prepared for the change by taking night courses. Most Questers are thinking ahead long before fate or fortune causes them to move on.

Among many Questers, the yearning for independence is a familiar feeling. Hasn't everyone, at least once, dreamed of owning a business? These dreams come true more frequently now as the economy and various job frustrations prompt more and more employees to strike out on their own. But can you really do it? Of course you can, if you're willing to put in the time and work and to take the risks involved. Most Questers have—and very successfully, too. Why can't you?

Involvement Is Excitement

Questers are generally very involved in their jobs. Psychologically, they identify closely with their work. They take their positions seriously, and their moods and feelings are significantly affected by their work experiences. Their jobs must satisfy the needs and values that are important to them. People who are highly involved in their jobs are more likely to feel either extremely satisfied, or dissatisfied, depending on what's happening at work. On the other hand, uninvolved employees tend to have less extreme emotional reactions to the same job experiences. If carried to extremes, such job involvement can become a neurotic compulsion. Although wise Questers want to immerse and enjoy themselves in their work, they have learned to balance their jobs with the many other dimensions of their lives.

Job involvement is related to job satisfaction. Some authorities say the orientation to work is learned early in childhood and is hard to change; others think it may be related to biological makeup. Most agree that while work orientation can be developed, it is also related to certain personality characteristics and work environments.

Enthusiasm Is Good for You

Involved employees have an infectious enthusiasm about their work that employers can't help but admire. One company president remarked that he'd forgive just about any mistake, at least once, that was made out of enthusiasm. The president came away from his first meeting with the new company lawyer (a woman selected after much hesitation) glowing with admiration. He was involved in a legal battle that his company was almost certain to lose. Did she tell him he could win? "No," he said. "I know better than that and if she had, I'd have fired her. What she did do is to outline all the steps she could take to limit our loss and all the ways she could press the other side to settle. She was so enthusiastic about it that I came out of our meeting feeling pretty good about the whole thing. Any lawyer who can make me feel good about losing a million dollar case is unusual. Given a case she can win, this lady is going to be a real tiger!"

The excitement of being involved in your job affects other people. *Joyce*, the schoolteacher from chapter 2 who left her job to become a principal, moved on because she was no longer enthusiastic about what she was doing. "Enthusiasm is catching," she says, "and if I can't be enthusiastic about what I'm teaching, neither can my students." The intensity of high-energy performers and actors is the result of their deep involvement in their work. They can't be boring. They're too interested in what they're doing.

Enthusiasm is no less valuable in your private life. More love affairs and marriages die from lack of enthusiasm than any other reason. Nothing is more wounding than indifference or boredom. Even in sex, how much energy or interest you put into it pretty much determines how much pleasure you get out of it. Sex is a need like other needs and often is treated only as such. But the real need could be fulfilled by masturbation or routine intercourse. An interesting sex life is one in which people share their feelings, energy, and passion. It's surprising what a satisfying sex life can do for your image. And why not? The better you feel about yourself and your life, the better your image will be. Same with your job. The real secret of having an exciting image is enjoying what you do.

Passion Provides Perspective

For some Questers, work is a passion. *Gerald*, the eye specialist from chapter 2, calls himself a work addict, but a happy one. "I love my work," Gerald remarks. "Helping people see is

rewarding. On occasion, I've met my wife at a party at six in the evening when I've been working since six in the morning. I haven't had time to wash or change to black tie, even if that's what all the other men are wearing. I might be completely exhausted, but when I think of what I did with my day, I feel good inside."

Financially successful people are involved in occupations they like and value.

Passionate involvement in their work helps many Questers deal with problems that do arise. Gerald says even if he starts the day feeling sick or out of sorts, he forgets about it. "When you are working at your best, you forget your negative feelings. At that moment, nothing else exists."

Money Is a By-product

Financial reward is often the result of a growth process that begins with a real interest in your work and a love of accomplishment for its own sake. After all, earning power is just the by-product of doing a good job. Even in today's turbulent society, a number of people without family money or social connections are growing rich on their own initiative. They are not hotshot investors, intellectual geniuses, money grubbers, or ruthless competitors. In fact, studies of the personalities of financially successful people claim that these traits actually impede moneymaking potential. Financially successful people are involved in occupations they like and value.

Andrea, vice-president of a western investment firm, was divorced and unemployed with two children to support when she discovered her life's work. From secretary to administrative assistant for a financial services company, she has blossomed into a six-figure employee. Andrea used her position as a springboard to learning what was previously foreign to her—finance. Studying largely on her own, she borrowed money for some night courses that helped her earn a broker's license. "I learned a lesson that I wanted to get across to other women whose husbands left them," Andrea says with determination in her voice. "When you're on your own, you can't afford to be a financial sleeping beauty." Andrea's financial planning series for women is an ongoing success.

The Joy of Helping

Financial rewards or prestige are not the primary motivators of Questers. What they do value, however, is an occupation that will give them opportunities to contribute to the welfare of others. Feelings of altruism or concern for others' well-being usually develop around the mid-life transition. The middle-aged become more committed to being mentors—guiding and helping others. A number of Questers seem to develop the need to be altruistic early in life and many look to their work to satisfy this need.

Take *Christopher.* Until two years ago, Christopher, now 31, was doing extremely well as a lawyer for a large insurance company in a Midwestern city. Then, suddenly, he quit and took off to do some wandering and put his life in perspective. He turned up two years later in a storefront legal office funded by the Office of Economic Opportunity. Christopher explains that his insurance position, defending the company against plaintiffs who had been struck by cars, was the first rung on the career ladder. His next move would have been to become a personal injury lawyer. Had he stayed with the company for the usual—"heaven forbid!"—25 years, Christopher would have retired with almost $400,000 in profit-sharing receipts. He laughs. "Once the novelty wore off, spending 10 hours a day defending an insurance company was a waste of time. With the education I've got, I might as well do something useful."

Today, Christopher is satisfied that he is doing something more useful. He's still a lawyer, but now his clients include single parents, senior citizens, new Americans, and people struggling to overcome landlord-tenant disputes. He represents juveniles in trouble, blacks abused by police, inmates caught in the state penitentiary system, and people dumped into the streets as a result of overcrowding in state hospitals. Happily involved in a challenging new position, he charges one-tenth of the going legal fee. "Every day is different," he says with real pleasure. "I can work four days straight, 16 hours a day, and never feel tired. Until my eyes start falling out . . . then I know I have to go to bed. "

Unlike his new position, the insurance company was all competition. "Everyone was trying to push the other guy down and crawl all over him to move up. If you didn't, you knew he was going to do it to you. God, the days dragged! I'd have a stack of 100 files on my desk, and all I could do was make checkmarks or go into court and make the same motions, day after day. And why? To save the company money."

Legal problems aren't the only ones that concern Christopher. If a client has an emotional problem, Christopher calls a psychologist. If the problem is lack of job skills, he encourages the client to go back to school. "They're so pushed down, so depressed. You get to know them intimately. I call them by their first names. We've been to each other's homes. After five o'clock, I never even saw the people I worked with at the insurance company. I would never have shared my thoughts with those people. But I would with my clients."

These days, money or fame are the furthest things from Christopher's mind. Helping his clients is reward enough. But he also realizes the immensity of his task. At times, he feels overcommitted, overextended, and powerless, but Christopher has few regrets.

Many Questers feel the same way as Christopher and commit themselves to helping others. Some are even able to work happily within the bureaucratic constraints that Christopher finds so frustrating.

Soft-spoken *Meagan* has been called the Indiana Jones of her state's child welfare system. Each day, she slashes through a jungle of red tape to safeguard the rights of government wards. Why did Meagan, a former political scientist, abandon a prestigious consulting career to become a community social worker? "I think, more than anything else, for the challenge of developing something new that might have a chance of helping deprived children," she says thoughtfully.

Tigers Rarely Reach the Top

Popular myths aside, wealth and success don't have to be achieved at the expense of others. Wealthy and successful Questers didn't claw their way to the top, heedless of whom they hurt along the way. Many Questers made their contributions through inspiring others, promoting teamwork, and developing other people's abilities. Of course, Questers must be competitive to succeed. Those who own businesses know the importance of being acutely aware of how their products and services stack up to their competitors'. But most Questers are less intent on getting ahead at the expense of others than they are on achieving. This is what *Ryan*, a factory owner, says about competition: "I know what my competitors are doing and I keep 10 steps ahead of them. I can meet them any way they want. But not to cut their hearts out. We all have to make a living." Other more ruthless competitors have come and gone. Ryan is still in business.

Growing on the Job

Whether or not a job rewards you depends on what you want from it. For most Questers, this equation is easy—they seek occupations in which they can thrive, develop, and mature. They want to develop their own personalities, to exploit their talents, to innovate, to get the job done without having to follow rigid regulations. Questers' drive for growth is closely related to such other job satisfiers as challenge and autonomy.

Nicole has left several jobs that didn't offer the rewards she wanted. Petite, vivacious, with expressive brown eyes, Nicole at 38 is a magazine editor. Before that, she was a staff writer for an institution that published health care literature. And long before Nicole began her writing career, she was an elementary school teacher. Loved by her fourth-grade students, Nicole was flattered by the power she wielded as a teacher. "But I felt I wasn't really using enough of me," Nicole says. So she took a writing job. Much as she loved reading and writing, that occupation just wasn't right for her either. "When I first got my job, I came in early and stayed late," she recalls. "I would work a project to death and get it really done right and then ask for more. But I found I was out of place. No one else was devoting as much passion to their jobs as I was and they didn't want to be reminded of it." So, she settled down and conformed, divorced her mind and spirit from her work. Like her colleagues, who were just as capable as she, Nicole ceased to care. "I played cards for three hours at lunch or went sunbathing or shopping," she says. "It was a very comfortable job and it was despicable." Because Nicole's company expected less than she offered, she felt she was forced to play the game by its rules. "But I couldn't. At the end of the day, I felt that I had not accomplished anything. I was furious, I felt humiliated and used." Predictably, it wasn't long before she quit.

The difference between her last position and her new one shows in Nicole's face. Blossoming as an editor, she is delighted that her new job offers her the freedom to develop her writing, editing, and other skills. The magazine's readership has doubled since she became editor, but Nicole is constantly concerned about improving its quality.

Nicole, always highly independent and innovative, will change jobs again, if necessary, to avoid stagnating. Like many Questers, she is more concerned with acquiring a position and a lifestyle that matches her purpose, interests, needs, abilities, and goals than with seeking material rewards.

Brad satisfied his love of challenge by opening his own business. His success story started with a belt and a buckle. While in his second year of college, Brad received a beautiful belt buckle as a gift. Intrigued by the possibility of designing his own belt, Brad splurged $50 on leatherworking tools and materials. Soon, he was selling his unusual, handmade belts to friends. "The business really snowballed from there," he remembers fondly. As his belts began selling at art shows, Brad expanded his work to include caps, wallets, key cases, and other small leather products. Suddenly, Brad realized that he could be a business success. "The more involved I became in running the business, the more I realized how much I enjoyed the challenge." Today, he has 25 stores and is a multimillionaire.

Persistence Pays

Genius or a natural talent such as Brad's aren't the only prerequisites for success. The word "persistence" crops up again and again when Questers talk about their accomplishments.

Ryan is a 64-year-old entrepreneurial Quester who, like Brad, loves to innovate. He, too, has kept expanding his business for the sheer joy of seeing it grow. From a newly built factory on the outskirts of a large industrial city, Ryan manufactures coin and vending machines, vending machine parts, and video games. He's thinking of expanding into computers.

With $500 borrowed from a bank, Ryan started his first business, a pinball game parts factory. As he kept adding new products, his business developed into a successful enterprise. Ryan admits he's not an engineer, but he does love to create mechanical parts and products. "I love to see a piece of iron do some work," he says with a sparkle in his eyes. "I have an idea and then I see if I can make it work. I love what I do," he explains. "I persist, and I keep on top of things."

Innovativeness Is Action

Many Questers understand that the difference between being creative and being an innovator lies in the ability to bring ideas to life. Innovators do things; creative people think of new things. While there is no shortage of potentially creative people, there is a shortage of people who have the courage to innovate. Innovative Questers have the know-how, energy, daring, and staying power to venture beyond convention. They may—and usually do—fail somewhere along the road to success. But their determination drives them on to bigger and better projects and eventually they will succeed. They are not geniuses. They are merely persistent and willing to fail. That willingness is what separates creative people from innovators.

Keeping Options Open

Having the ability to succeed is one thing; deliberately setting out to do so is another.

Having the ability to succeed is one thing; deliberately setting out to do so is another. Questers tend to achieve because they set career goals related to their needs, values, interests, and abilities. They also listen to their inner feelings. Careful to keep their options open, they have the freedom to develop and to find challenge. Their career goals may range from open-ended goals to five- or seven-year plans. But all represent an active and independent commitment to career management. Questers are in control of their lives. Most Questers will move on to new goals that better satisfy their developing personalities. Having made at least one occupational move, they are not afraid to make others when they are no longer growing.

And a good many, aware that they might be approaching a dead end, have searched for and found a new road. They are usually adept at anticipation—imagining future bends in the road and preparing to shift gears in advance.

The willingness to manage their own careers and to anticipate their future needs is what tends to separate most Questers from many Traditionalists. Questers have learned to maintain a balance between tentativeness and commitment. Committing yourself to and becoming actively involved in a job that satisfies your goals is admirable. But Questers are usually the masters, not the slaves, of commitment. With a clear understanding of their own needs and goals, they can balance the two with skill as they travel tentatively along the sometimes rocky road to career satisfaction.

In today's economic climate, being flexible, resilient, and open to change are the best protections against obsolescence. Most Questers have learned to ignore the dangers and focus on the opportunities. Open-ended career goals permit them to react quickly to the changing marketplace and high unemployment levels.

Having a satisfying career and life isn't always easy. But to most Questers, the easy life is usually not worth living. Consider your own career and lifestyle. What kind of life are you leading?

Rate Your Job Satisfaction

re you satisfied with your job or does it make you feel moody, depressed, and discouraged? It's normal to experience career ups and downs, but if your lows become much more frequent or last a lot longer than your highs, you probably need to give serious thought to whether or not you are in the right position. You can find out by asking yourself specific questions about your job and work habits. The three questionnaires in this chapter—The Job Satisfaction Questionnaire, The Job Involvement Questionnaire, and The Burnout Questionnaire—are designed to help you do just that. The questionnaires will also help you determine whether your work attitudes and habits may be leading to burnout and what you can do about it. Directions, scoring procedures, interpretations, and suggestions are provided.

As you read the items in each questionnaire, think them over carefully. The more honest you are, the more you will benefit. Let your feelings be your guide.

The Job Satisfaction Questionnaire

Each of the 44 items in this questionnaire evaluates one job facet. Understanding how well your job satisfies these facets will give you a good picture of your overall degree of job satisfaction.

For each facet:

1. Circle +2 if you are very satisfied.

2. Circle +1 if you are satisfied.

3. Circle -1 if you are dissatisfied.

4. Circle -2 if you are very dissatisfied.

5. Circle 0 if you are not sure or if the facet is not present in or appropriate to your job.

Grade each facet with your present job in mind. Scoring directions and an analysis of your responses follow the questionnaire.

	Ratings				
	VS	S	? or N/A	D	VD
1. Personal growth and development.	+2	+1	0	-1	-2
2. Working alone.	+2	+1	0	-1	-2
3. Security.	+2	+1	0	-1	-2

	Ratings			
	VS	S	? or N/A	D	VD
4. Appropriate salary level.	+2	+1	0	-1	-2
5. Self-esteem or self-respect.	+2	+1	0	-1	-2
6. Participating in decision making.	+2	+1	0	-1	-2
7. Accomplishing something worthwhile.	+2	+1	0	-1	-2
8. Having authority and/or leadership.	+2	+1	0	-1	-2
9. Assisting others.	+2	+1	0	-1	-2
10. Social status and prestige.	+2	+1	0	-1	-2
11. Time to pursue leisure activities.	+2	+1	0	-1	-2
12. Money to pursue leisure activities.	+2	+1	0	-1	-2
13. Desirable locale.	+2	+1	0	-1	-2
14. Opportunity to develop friendships.	+2	+1	0	-1	-2
15. Varied responsibilities.	+2	+1	0	-1	-2
16. Professional development.	+2	+1	0	-1	-2
17. Seeing work results.	+2	+1	0	-1	-2
18. Feedback on performance.	+2	+1	0	-1	-2
19. Fringe benefits.	+2	+1	0	-1	-2
20. Merit promotion.	+2	+1	0	-1	-2
21. Paid study leaves and/or time off for courses.	+2	+1	0	-1	-2
22. Opportunity to change jobs within organization.	+2	+1	0	-1	-2
23. Use of special skills/abilities.	+2	+1	0	-1	-2
24. Respect and support from subordinates.	+2	+1	0	-1	-2
25. Compatibility of personal goals and values to organization's.	+2	+1	0	-1	-2
26. Resources to do adequate job.	+2	+1	0	-1	-2
27. Respect, fair treatment, and support from superiors.	+2	+1	0	-1	-2
28. Physical surroundings.	+2	+1	0	-1	-2

	VS	S	? or N/A	D	VD
29. Interesting work.	+2	+1	0	-1	-2
30. Amount of pressure.	+2	+1	0	-1	-2
31. Relocation possibilities.	+2	+1	0	-1	-2
32. Aesthetic contribution(s).	+2	+1	0	-1	-2
33. Using own ideas.	+2	+1	0	-1	-2
34. Time to spend with family.	+2	+1	0	-1	-2
35. Amount of job involvement.	+2	+1	0	-1	-2
36. Amount of unrelated/clerical work.	+2	+1	0	-1	-2
37. Ability to organize work.	+2	+1	0	-1	-2
38. Clients' and/or customers' appreciation.	+2	+1	0	-1	-2
39. Challenging work.	+2	+1	0	-1	-2
40. Work hours.	+2	+1	0	-1	-2
41. Using creativity.	+2	+1	0	-1	-2
42. Having a sense of purpose.	+2	+1	0	-1	-2
43. Having autonomy.	+2	+1	0	-1	-2
44. Having a sense of identity.	+2	+1	0	-1	-2
Subtotals					
Total **Satisfaction** Score					
Total **Dissatisfaction** Score					
OVERALL JOB SATISFACTION SCORE					
(Satisfaction + Dissatisfaction)					

Scoring

To determine your job satisfaction score:

1. Add your subtotals for your VS, S, D, and VD scores and write them in the space provided under Subtotals.

2. Determine your Total Satisfaction Score (add the VS and S ratings) and your Total Dissatisfaction Score (add the VD and the D ratings) and write these in the spaces provided.

3. Determine your Overall Satisfaction Score by adding your Total Satisfaction Score and your Total Dissatisfaction Score.

The highest possible score is 88. The lowest possible score -88. The higher your score, the more satisfied you are with your job. The lower your score, the more discontented you are.

Interpreting Your Score

50 or higher: If your needs and values are being met thoroughly in each job facet, your Overall Job Satisfaction Score will be 88. This rarely happens. But if your score is over 50, you are still quite satisfied. However, there probably are some aspects of your job that could stand improvement. Find out what these areas are by reviewing your low scores. Think about how you could better satisfy those needs.

20 to 49: If your Overall Job Satisfaction Score is between 20 and 49, you are moderately satisfied with your position. Your job situation is in need of some changes, though. Can the facets in which you got negative scores be improved? If you answered no, you need to assess your current job in relation to your career goals. Exploring other career options in your current or another organization should be considered. View your work as a continuing opportunity for growth and development. Some jobs are good; they are regenerative and the longer you keep them, the more they increase your value. Other jobs diminish your value; they are repetitious. The longer you do them, the older you get, the more you lose your flexibility and opportunity to grow, and the more easily you can be replaced with someone who is younger and cheaper.

20 to -10: A score between 20 and -10 indicates that you are a candidate for a job change. You are tolerating a number of on-the-job conditions that make you unhappy. Perhaps you should consider moving on. Don't remain in a deadening work situation. Circumstances often force people to take jobs that are incompatible with their needs and abilities. Selecting a job out of economic necessity is understandable, but choosing to remain year after year in a blind alley is detrimental to your health and well-being. Don't put off for long your resolve to do something about this situation. If you do, you might end up in the next category within a few months.

The key to an ever-evolving career is to monitor your own career development and stay attuned to new opportunities.

-11 or lower: If your Overall Job Satisfaction Score is -11 or lower, you scored yourself D for most job facets, indicating that you find many of your job conditions dissatisfying. You have a serious case of job blues. Obviously, you need a change, perhaps even a dramatic shift to a totally new field. Considering that you have so few satisfiers in your position, it's amazing you can even motivate yourself to go to work. Your position may be affecting your health. If you suspect that you would have answered this quiz in a similar way six months or even a year ago, you may also be a procrastinator who is waiting for someone to force you to make a move. Wait no longer. Put your career back into your own hands.

Appraising your job satisfaction should be an ongoing process. Do it whenever you need to clarify where you are in your career and what your next step should be. Do it to get to know yourself better. Do it to get ahead. The key to an ever-evolving career is to monitor your own career development and stay attuned to new opportunities.

Further Considerations

The Job Satisfaction Questionnaire should have helped you pin down your major sources of job frustration. Now you have to decide what to do with this information.

Many men and women hope their discontent will go away on its own. It rarely does. Others throw themselves into their work in an attempt to compensate for their feelings of self-doubt. Some distance themselves from their work, which often leads to poor performance or problems with the boss.

All these reactions to job dissatisfaction are part of a "survival mentality." Too many individuals often put up with unhappiness in their work that they wouldn't tolerate in other areas. Rather than trying something new, they adjust to the old.

They don't select, they settle. These people may regret that they never even tried to find out what really might have been right for them.

This is the big question. You may tolerate your work because it pays the bills. You may even like it because it's familiar and easy. But is it what you want to be doing years from now? As you reach the end of your life, will you have regrets about how you managed your career?

What can you do if you feel stuck in a position you dislike? If you could create the ideal job for you, what factors would you want to include? The Job Involvement Questionnaire and The Burnout Questionnaire should give you additional insights into the feelings you have about your work.

The Job Involvement Questionnaire

Do you identify closely with your job? Are you absorbed in it? Does it give you a sense of purpose? Are your moods and feelings significantly affected by your work? One way to find out is to complete the The Job Involvement Questionnaire. Evaluating your job involvement can also give you additional clues about whether or not you are satisfied with your position, whether you are happily involved in your work or a compulsive neurotic, whether you are a candidate for burnout, and if you should stay put or move on.

Answer the statements below by circling either Yes or No. If you are uncertain about a question, circle the response that most closely describes your feelings. Once you have completed the questionnaire, add your scores. Scoring procedures and an interpretation follow the questionnaire.

1. The most important things that happen to me involve my job.   Yes   No

2. I am really a perfectionist in my work.   Yes   No

3. Most things in life are more important than my work.　Yes　No

4. My work is one of the most rewarding and fulfilling parts of my life.　Yes　No

5. I would probably work just as hard as I do now even if I did not have to support myself and my family.　Yes　No

6. Most of my friends would probably agree that I usually have a great deal of energy and I get much of my energy from my work.　Yes　No

7. I never work on weekends and holidays.　Yes　No

8. I am so involved in my work that it is hard for me to take vacations.　Yes　No

9. I would never think of breaking a date or canceling an appointment so that I could get more work done.　Yes　No

10. Most of my interests are centered around my job.　Yes　No

11. My involvement in my work never causes problems for my family and friends.　Yes　No

12. Most of my goals are not job-related.　Yes　No

13. I often do some extra work for my job that isn't really required.　Yes　No

14. Even though I'm efficient, I work harder than most other people doing the same type of work.　Yes　No

15. I live, eat, and breathe my job.　Yes　No

16. I feel depressed when I fail at something connected with my job.　Yes　No

17. I'll stay overtime to finish a task, even though I'm not paid for it.　Yes　No

18. For me, mornings at work really
    fly by.   Yes   No

19. How well I work does not affect
    the way I feel about myself.   Yes   No

20. Sometimes, I'd like to kick
    myself for the mistakes I've
    made in my work.   Yes   No

Interpreting Your Score

Points

Give yourself one point for each Yes answer to
questions 1, 2, 4, 5, 6, 8, 10, 13, 14, 15, 16, 17,
18, and 20.

Give yourself one point for each No answer to
questions 3, 7, 9, 11, 12, and 19.

Add your points.

Total Points [   ]

The maximum possible score is 20. The higher your
score, the more involved you are in your work. A low
score suggests lack of involvement. Read on for additional interpretation of your results.

Are You Happily Involved in Your Work or Are You Neurotic?

A score of 13 or higher suggests you are very involved
in your work. Your work is probably central to your
identity. You take your position seriously and your
moods and feelings are significantly affected by your
work experiences. Answer the questions below to
determine whether or not you are happily involved in
your job.

1. Does your family support your work
    habits?   Yes   No

2. Do you have autonomy at work?	Yes	No	
3. Does your work provide you with sufficient challenge and variety?	Yes	No	
4. Do you get enough recognition, support, and feedback from your supervisors and coworkers?	Yes	No	
5. Does your job make you feel good about yourself?	Yes	No	
6. Is there a good match between your needs, values, interests, skills, and job?	Yes	No	
7. Are you in good health?	Yes	No	
8. Do you avoid drug and alcohol abuse?	Yes	No	
9. Do you take time out for fun?	Yes	No	
10. Can you organize and manage your time?	Yes	No	
11. Do you set realistic work goals?	Yes	No	
12. Do you see friends outside your work situation?	Yes	No	
13. Do you have a regular exercise program?	Yes	No	
14. Do you feel you have control over your life?	Yes	No	
15. Do you thirst for novelty and challenge?	Yes	No	
16. Does your work give you a sense of purpose?	Yes	No	
Total Points			

If you answered Yes to 10 or more of these questions, you are probably happily involved in your work. You generally feel good about yourself. You are independent, growth-oriented, and enjoy intrinsic rewards. Your position satisfies the needs and values that are important to you and gives you a sense of purpose. You may have an infectious enthusiasm about your work that communicates to other people.

You will spend at least a third of your adult life on the job or commuting to and from it.

Some people may call you a "workaholic." The word "workaholic" may have negative connotations but fortunate indeed are those who find work they passionately want and do it successfully. After all, you will spend at least a third of your adult life on the job or commuting to and from it. The label "workaholic," for those who are happily involved in their positions, is a positive, not negative, term.

If you are a happy workaholic, you are fortunate. But do learn to relax. Spend more quality time with friends, family, leisure pursuits, and yourself. People who are contentedly involved in their work are usually flexible and can cut loose to enjoy the many other dimensions of their lives.

There is a distinction, of course, between happy job involvement and neurotic compulsion. If you responded No to 10 or more of the above questions, you may be driven by a neurotic compulsion. Neurotic workaholics don't enjoy leisure pursuits that differ from their work routines and may feel uncomfortable in social settings. You may feel distressed, anxious, and dissatisfied when you are not working. Your family life and relationships may be crumbling. If your work is always with you, and you are constantly tired, irritable, and withdrawn and feel that you have no control over your life, you may be headed for burnout. Complete The Burnout Questionnaire and follow the suggestions offered.

Are You Moderately Involved in Your Work?

A score between 7 and 12 suggests that you are probably moderately involved in your work. If you are happy with your work and feel that you lead a balanced life in which your career, family, leisure, and other activities all contribute to your sense of well-being, that's fine. However, if your job satisfaction is low, you should probably do something to improve it.

Take charge of your work and your life. Don't just react to your boss or other people around you. Instead, take the initiative and create your own ways to reach your department's goals. With your boss's help, see if you can shape your position so that you are doing more of what you like to do and are good at, while shifting or delegating other duties and responsibilities to coworkers with complementary talents. Don't hold back or be afraid of being thought of as too enthusiastic. Try to develop your own challenges. Visualize what would happen if another highly motivated person was promoted to your position. How would he or she tackle it? What challenges would another person find in your job? If it's not possible to develop challenges or change your current position—and sometimes it isn't—then maybe you should consider another job or a transfer. Explore other occupational options.

Are You Really Suited to Your Job?

A score of 6 or lower indicates you are not even slightly involved in your job. Perhaps other aspects of your life are more interesting to you. Good! But low job involvement indicates a lack of interest and enthusiasm in your work. It may even suggest poor health.

If your scores on both The Job Satisfaction Questionnaire and The Job Involvement Questionnaire indicate that you are dissatisfied with your position, you should probably do something about changing jobs or even occupational fields. To find an area in which you'll excel naturally, do some self-analysis. Just why do you dislike your position so much? What would you rather be doing? What's stopping you from going after it? Reading chapter 9 and completing the inventories located there should help you answer these questions.

The Burnout Questionnaire

Psychologists and physicians consider career burnout a chronic stress syndrome.

Do you experience chronic fatigue? Are your thought processes dulled? Are you irritable? Are you progressively withdrawing? Do you feel physically unwell? Is your work always with you? Do you wonder why? If you answered yes to more than two of these questions, you may be headed for burnout. Psychologists and physicians consider career burnout a chronic stress syndrome.

Work conditions that promote burnout include lack of support, challenge, autonomy, variety, flexibility, and security. Heavy work loads, ambiguous job descriptions, rude customers or clients, lack of knowledge or information, and impersonal work environments are other job stressors. Certain personal characteristics, attitudes, and habits also facilitate the development of burnout. These include poor planning, inability to manage change, inability to relax, and failure to care for one's physical, intellectual, emotional, spiritual, and social needs.

Burnout affects the whole person. This syndrome is not just limited to physical symptoms or poor job performance. It influences the intellect, feelings, relationships, and the spirit as well. Burnout is a progressive and slow process, eating and wearing away at the individual a little at a time. Its victims report reduced personal energy, diminished vitality, and dampened enthusiasm for life. Burnout is similar to the disengagement stage of the career cycle; both syndromes are stress symptoms which are influenced by lack of job satisfiers, particularly autonomy, challenge, and a sense of accomplishment and confidence that come with challenge.

Burnouts are often successful in their fields—that's what burns them out. Some bright women and men work terribly hard, make tremendous sacrifices, soar to the top of their occupations or professions, and then seem to run out of fuel.

To find out if you are on the path to burnout, complete the questionnaire below, then read over the explanation that follows. Circle "Yes" for the symptoms of burnout that apply to you and "No" for those that don't.

The Burnout Questionnaire

1. Are you increasingly irritable and impatient? Are you more disappointed in the people around you? Are you having more arguments with your spouse, friends, or even strangers lately?	Yes	No
2. Do you feel irreplaceable? Do you go to work even when you feel ill? Do you accept extra duties out of obligation?	Yes	No
3. Are you always tired? Feel fatigued rather than energetic? Does sex seem like more trouble than it's worth?	Yes	No
4. Do you have very little to say to people? Are you seeing close friends and family, even if you live in the same city, less frequently?	Yes	No
5. Do you fail to establish an enriching and satisfying life separate and distinct from your work?	Yes	No
6. Do you take work home only to find you don't complete it? Do you find that even though you don't do it, the work dominates your environment, provoking guilt?	Yes	No
7. Have you overtaxed yourself at work or home? Do you feel persistent pressures—too much to do and too little time? Are you too busy to do even routine things like make phone calls, read reports, or answer correspondence?	Yes	No

8. Are you increasing your use of drugs, such as aspirin, sleeping pills, tranquilizers, alcohol, or tobacco, to cope with job pressures or to unwind from work?   Yes   No

9. Are you preoccupied with thoughts of self-blame, guilt, self-recrimination, anxiety? Do you feel powerless about certain aspects of your job? Do you lack feelings of success or challenge?   Yes   No

10. Do you feel as if nothing is going well? Do you find yourself talking mostly about work and are your conversations mostly negative?   Yes   No

11. Are you developing uncharacteristically rigid ways of thinking and/or losing the ability to adapt to change? Are you adopting rigid "by the book" approaches to problems rather than developing individual solutions?   Yes   No

12. Are you turning excessively to colleagues for help in coping with emotional or physical problems or with business and professional responsibilities?   Yes   No

13. Do you use more board/workbook activities, audiovisual materials, or support staff lately to remove you from direct contact with subordinates? Have you taken a large number of sick days lately?   Yes   No

14. Are you forgetting appointments, deadlines, or personal possessions?   Yes   No

15. Are you suffering physical complaints— aches, pains, headaches, or lingering colds? Have you had more severe physical/emotional illnesses—ulcers, high blood pressure, hypertension, colitis, or nervous disorders lately?   Yes   No

16. Is joy elusive? Are you often invaded by a sadness you can't explain? Are you unable to laugh or joke about yourself?   Yes   No

17. Do you hate going to work? Do you turn off as you enter your workplace? Do you feel as if you are operating like a robot that doesn't care enough to care? Do you get a knot in your stomach when you realize the next day is a workday?   Yes   No

18. Do you constantly say, "Is this all there is?" about your job?   Yes   No

19. Do you fail to achieve desired professional goals (for example, financial gains, attainment of status, perception as an "expert," respect from others, or validation from patients)?   Yes   No

20. Are you pessimistic about life? Do you always emphasize the bad, down, or failure side of things?   Yes   No

Total Points

Interpreting Your Score

Give yourself one point for each Yes. The maximum score is 20. If you answered Yes to 11 or more questions, you may be a candidate for burnout. The higher your score, the greater your chances. A score of 12 or higher indicates you need to take quick action to change your work habits or job. While no one sign of burnout is serious on its own, when many are present, you may already be well on your way to burnout. Burnout is not only preventable, but can be temporary and treatable.

If you are prone to burnout, you probably have several of the following symptoms:

❖ Feelings of recrimination about work problems

❖ Cynicism

❖ Long workdays to compensate for diminished productivity

❖ A one-track life with little social or love life, or a chaotic family life

❖ A one-track mind which may lead to interpersonal problems

❖ Loss of energy and inability to relax; fitful sleep and possibly frequent headaches, stomach aches, back pains, or even ulcers

❖ Drug use as an escape from stress

❖ Little or no time for play

❖ Anger and hostility to others—friends, colleagues, children, even pets

❖ A loner lifestyle

❖ A sedentary lifestyle

❖ A continuing restlessness that drives you to constant activity

On the other hand, if you thrive on long work hours, you may have the following characteristics:

❖ The ability to postpone thinking about problems

❖ Prompt reactions to signs of fatigue

❖ Avoidance of drug abuse

❖ Enjoyment of scheduled vacations

❖ Stable domestic situations

❖ The ability to organize and manage time

❖ The ability to make a distinction between your personal and professional life

❖ The ability to set realistic work goals

❖ The ability to maintain friendships

❖ A regular exercise program

❖ A belief that you have control over your life rather than feeling controlled

❖ A thirst for novelty and challenge rather than familiarity and security

❖ The ability to derive inspiration and energy from work

Preventing Burnout

Burnout can be a catalyst for growth. The pain of burnout may advance you to higher levels of maturity as you choose new and more productive attitudes and behavior patterns. A life change, an altered direction, a new attitude, or a humorous twist may all help you acquire more energy.

Most Questers stay healthy because they are committed, challenged, have control over their destinies, and feel supported by family and friends. Surprisingly, these people tend to be challenged most by adversity. Many have learned to use stress as a constant source of energy that helps them get things done and feel good about what they have accomplished. Perceived this way, stress can be valuable. But it must be managed wisely. If you can adopt attitudes like theirs, you may cut your chances of becoming ill in half. To survive, you need to recognize the possibility of burnout and act to stop the syndrome before it strikes or becomes worse.

Stress Busters

❖ *Find something to stimulate you each day.* Make your life full and rich by seeking challenge. Let each day bring new, manageable, and exciting opportunities for growth. Make your career a cherished, inspiring, living, and developing part of you.

❖ *Respect yourself.* Reward and reinforce yourself. Engage in self-talk. Tell yourself, "I am doing all I should right now." "I'm okay just as I am." "I'm human and I will make mistakes." Brag about yourself. Realize that you don't need to perform to prove anything or to beat anyone because you already know and like who you are.

❖ *Have a positive outlook.* Look on the rosy side. See the glass half full instead of half empty. Reinforce the positive in yourself and others. Most of all, keep your sense of humor; learn to laugh at yourself once in a while.

❖ *Readjust your attitude.* The Serenity Prayer by Reinhold Niebuhr provides a good start: "God grant me the serenity to accept the things I cannot change, the courage to change the things I can, and the wisdom to know the difference."

❖ *Keep problems in perspective.* Mistakes and setbacks, even outright failures, can be learning experiences. Accept responsibility for your actions.

❖ *Get away from it all.* Have other interests besides work. Learn to play. Make family, leisure, and relaxation times fun. These activities are necessary to maintain physical and mental health.

❖ *Learn to relax.* Relaxation techniques such as Transcendental Meditation and creative visualization can help emotionally rejuvenate your weary mind and soul.

❖ *Rest and sleep.* Leave your worries outside of the bedroom and try to get at least seven hours of sleep each day.

❖ *Eat well.* Eat lots of fresh fruit, vegetables, and grains, but don't stuff yourself. Go easy on sugar, coffee, pop, and alcohol.

❖ *Smell the roses.* Enjoy life's small pleasures such as walking in the park, gazing at the stars, smelling the flowers, or watching infants and toddlers explore their surroundings.

❖ *Exercise regularly.* Don't just be a passive observer of sports activities. Do get actively involved in some athletic or physical activities to play and relax.

❖ *Develop support systems.* Cultivate rich and meaningful relationships. Your interpersonal support systems can be built from a variety of people including friends, work associates, family members, spiritual acquaintances, neighbors, clients, store clerks, service people, or club members. Blow off steam to trusted individuals. Don't keep all your disappointments or frustrations to yourself.

❖ *Manage your time wisely.* Make lists and prioritize your tasks. Plan each day to include the things that are important to you. Don't let your work overwhelm you. Don't try to control everything. After all, you are in control from within. Stay on top of your work, but don't let it overwhelm you. This goes for housework as well. Consider paying for housecleaning help and using your extra time for relaxation or enjoyable activities.

❖ *Listen to your inner self.* Pay attention to your hopes, dreams, sorrows, and beliefs. Listen to what your body, mind, spirit, and emotions are really saying and then do what you feel is right. If you long for more time to watch your children grow, don't play golf with your colleagues. If workaholism is encouraged or demanded by your boss, decide whether salary or status is more important than a healthy lifestyle. You may have to change jobs. Set aside time each day to listen to yourself, even if it's only five minutes. Staying in touch with your spiritual core will enable you to enhance your sense of commitment, enthusiasm for living, and sense of purpose.

❖ *Add spice to your life.* Try doing something different once in a while. Although unusual activities vary between individuals, you might try having a costume party, playing a game you enjoyed as a child, making a snow angel, going to an avant-garde movie or gallery, going "skinny dipping," or ocean kayaking.

❖ *Restructure your work time.* Make lists of all the factors that drain you and all that energize you at work. As much as possible, spend your time with the positive aspect of your position and intersperse the negative activities with short breaks and rewards. Avoid all unnecessary meetings and learn to delegate.

❖ *Seek professional help.* Many good books and articles on both burnout and relaxation techniques are available in your local bookstore or library. If you can't cope on your own, most hospitals or mental health professionals can give you good advice on how to deal with burnout.

The Will to Risk: Psychological Aspects of Decision Making

he will to risk is a difficult quality to cultivate. It requires great strength—strength that is built on wounds, failures, and losses. People who become Questers tend to draw their strength from every dimension of their lives so that they can become resilient and enduring.

Making a change requires letting go of the familiar.

Making a change requires letting go of the familiar. You will feel exposed and vulnerable. But that very stress gives Questers the determination to go through with change. It provides the heightened awareness that offers hope that change will be worthwhile.

Questers' sense of inner control determines their success in new ventures. The link between a sense of inner control and the willingness to risk is a strong one. Having a sense of purpose and some plans for the future strengthens Questers' assurance that they can have a positive impact on future events in their lives. Moreover, because most Questers believe in what they are doing and expect that they are going to succeed, they generally do. Most Questers believe their expectations are realistic even though they are reaching for their dreams. Many Questers have learned to risk.

Part A: Decision-Making Styles

How do Questers go about making risky decisions? What is their decision-making style? Most Questers take planned risks. The majority do not move on impulse, but give careful deliberation to their decisions. Making decisions rarely comes easily to them. They often harbor numerous doubts about themselves and their work options. Many will struggle with doubts and uncertainties about their futures, their jobs, and the consequences of their actions. They will evaluate their purposes and their personal characteristics, as well as their occupational alternatives. But once they make a firm commitment to change, the rest of the process becomes easier.

Questers tend to be flexible risk takers. The risks they take are a response to feedback from the environment, colleagues, friends, and their own emotions. Questers do not discount security. Many take measures that carry them through a crisis.

Most Questers try to establish a balance between the intellectual and emotional, between the rational and the intuitive aspects of decision making. Although they will consider a broad range of alternatives, Questers will eventually select one. They are realistic enough to know that there really is no one right decision, only one that feels good for them at a particular time. They anticipate both good and bad outcomes. The process usually takes from six months to two years. Even after they arrive at a probable decision, Questers will remain open to new information and ideas. But once they have made a big decision, Questers usually stick to it. Most evaluate the results after they act. Questers tend to learn from mistakes.

Melissa's Story

Small, dark-haired, attractive, energetic, intense, warm, *Melissa* belies her 44 years. Dressed in a dark gray suit and a becoming gold blouse, she projects a businesslike, yet feminine, image. Melissa is impulsive and intuitive but she plans her risk taking. Currently, Melissa is director of training and development for a large retail outlet. After her first full-time job as an airline stewardess, Melissa returned to school to study education. She had grown tired of her nomadic existence. Her desire to challenge her mind led to three years of college, then to a job as a high school English teacher. But six years was enough of that. Her desire for new challenges led her into a management training program for a large retail outlet. Melissa was an extremely good manager. A promotion to manager of women's fashions in a large department store gave her a chance to exercise her flair for fashion and well-developed people skills. But by the time six years were up, the old familiar, uneasy feelings were back. Increasingly restless and tired, she looked around for other opportunities inside her company. Nothing seemed particularly attractive. Melissa knew she needed a change, but to what?

Now 43, she was anxious about her future. An amalgamation with another retail chain had resulted in regressive policies and procedures. Incensed with her lack of control over purchasing and personnel, and frustrated by both lack of autonomy and yet total responsibility, she quit. Resigning may not have been very wise, but Melissa chose to trust her instincts. "I felt like I was in a straitjacket." Unemployed and scared, Melissa turned to friends and family for support. But there was none. "They thought I was crazy to give up this position, even after I told them why I had to leave." With no support from friends and family, sticking to her guns took real guts.

Actually, the decision to change jobs had germinated some time before. Long before she quit, she had begun salting away large chunks of her salary. A full year before she left, Melissa attended a seminar on career change that helped her identify abilities and transferable skills. It was no accident that Richard Bolles's book, *What Color Is Your Parachute?*, rested on her bedside table. Still, there is a difference between leaving one job for another and quitting with no prospects. Quitting was an impulsive (and perhaps even irrational) act, something Melissa had never done before. Only the knowledge that she was at the breaking point propelled her forward.

What to do? First, Melissa assessed her net worth. By giving herself permission to live off rainy-day resources, Melissa could manage for 10 months. The next move was a visit to a talented career counselor who could help sort out her feelings, identify her strengths and other personal characteristics, explore occupational options, and set some career goals.

Melissa's self-appraisal revealed that she had knowledge, skills, and experience in retailing, teaching, managing, coordinating, communicating, and public relations. Testing told Melissa what she already knew: She had high abilities in English comprehension and expression, analytical reasoning, and supervision. An interest inventory gave her top scores in leadership, business, supervision, human relations, and teaching. Other inventories revealed that she had high needs for autonomy, variety, achievement, challenge, altruism, and creative expression. With these characteristics, Melissa could do almost anything! Further exploration helped Melissa obtain insight into her purpose—to help others, primarily in some leadership or teaching capacity. Additional inquiry helped Melissa identify her preferred lifestyle. Melissa decided that she wanted a position with regular hours that would give her time to pursue her interests in scuba diving and art as well as allow her time for social activities.

The counselor also helped Melissa realize that staying on a job she had outgrown would be a mistake. Her next move was to set tentative career goals. Melissa decided to target her career search into three general areas: management, self-employment, and training and development.

During the five months that followed, Melissa conducted a thorough job search. She reflects: "These were some of the best months of my life. It was very stimulating. I felt completely in control. I loved setting up my own schedule. I took 'me' on as a new project and worked like a dog!"

Melissa was determined to keep moving and stay in touch with her network of friends and former associates. Good fortune stepped in when a former colleague called to offer her a chance to conduct some workshops in retail management. The $5,500 contract put a little more distance between Melissa and the poorhouse. She used some of that $5,500 as seed money for her job search, investing in a typewriter, an answering service, calling cards, attractive letterhead, and a handsome resume.

Systematically, Melissa explored her network of friends and associates, applying for job after job, until she had sent out more than 50 job inquiries. Some merely involved a letter and a resume. Twenty-one reached the interview stage, and one, a job in the food processing industry, required seven interviews during a single day.

For each management interview, Melissa diligently researched her prospective employer and product. During one interview for the executive directorship of a community welfare agency, Melissa launched a series of tough queries to decide if she and the company were a good career match. Who really held the power in the organization? What kinds of skills did the director need? What was the director's scope of authority? The silence that met her questions was uncomfortable. Her interviewers decided that they would have to postpone the search until they had determined what the job really entailed.

That wasn't Melissa's only fruitless job interview. But then another promising management opportunity, this time with a large flour milling company, slipped past. So Melissa took a cue from a job search book and fired off a letter to the mill's vice-president of public affairs. Instead of the usual "Thanks for your time," it said: "I'm sorry to hear that the position has been filled. I thought I'd be good for it. I also very much appreciate the time you spent talking to me. Because you know so much about the food processing industry, I would like to keep in touch with you from time to time as I continue my search. Would that be okay?" With an approach like that, who could turn her down?

Melissa's time-out period gave her the opportunity to seriously consider an idea that had long intrigued her: going into
business for herself. The possibilities tempted her. Should she
become a free-lance retail consultant? Establish a fashion
boutique? Or buy into a publishing position with a regional
women's fashion magazine? The options were exciting. But
Melissa decided her bottom line, at this point, was a regular
paycheck. She also wanted a more balanced lifestyle than self-
employment could offer. Although these options weren't right
for her now, Melissa promised to reconsider them later on.

Having ruled out going into business for herself, Melissa was
now ready to explore a third possible avenue: training and
development. With a friend's help, Melissa explored the
options by reading relevant books and talking to people
already in this field. She then identified a list of five firms
that seemed compatible with her own personal characteristics. Melissa began a serious, high-gear job search with letters
to the vice-presidents of personnel and phone calls to top
managers. When all five responded that they had no immediate openings, she shifted the nature of her campaign. She
then chose a young, growing, people-oriented, flexible organization that offered her profit sharing and a competitive salary.
Most important, the retail organization didn't yet have a fully
developed training and development program.

Melissa was armed for her attack. First, she made a series of
phone calls to the company's top managers. Finally convincing them that she was serious, she landed an interview with
the vice-president of personnel and the senior vice-president.
It lasted four hours. The company brass were impressed, but
the only job available was a junior position training salesclerks. Melissa persisted. What the company really needed,
she asserted, was a more ambitious training and development
program. A second interview was all it took to convince the
company to hire her as the new director of training and
development, at a higher salary and with six weeks' grace so
she could finish her contract work and take a well-earned
vacation.

How has her new position worked out? "Very well," Melissa
reflects one year later. Although the job hasn't grown quite as
quickly as she hoped, and she doesn't yet have the size of
staff she needs, Melissa is content. "I'm glad I didn't take the
jobs that I thought would be dead ends. I'm glad I avoided
traditional corporations. And I'm glad I took a chance with a

growing, progressive organization because now I can grow with it."

Does she have any regrets? "Absolutely none." In fact, Melissa says, quitting without having another job lined up was lucky. "I might not have conducted such a thorough job search if I hadn't felt so pressured." A good job search, she now knows, is a long process. Melissa was lucky; she found her position in five months. "But, of course," she says wryly, "I had to work like a demon to do it."

Besides the obvious reward of a new position, Melissa's job search had other benefits. One was self-confidence. "I love my work," she says. "I feel good about myself and at the end of the day, I have lots of energy left over." Melissa feels good because she believes she is doing something worthwhile. Her new position is giving her life meaning and purpose. While being 44 seemed like an added pressure at first, her age was no barrier in the end.

Being able to say, with satisfaction, that you risked for a dream is the biggest prize of all.

What Can You Learn from Melissa?

Melissa's experience is a good lesson. It demonstrates that while confidence and willingness to risk can be positive qualities, job searchers also need to protect themselves by reducing some of the risks involved in an occupational change.

Melissa's success was partly due to investing in herself. By realizing that this was the rainy day for which she had been saving, Melissa could allow herself to buy the time she needed.

Taking time out allowed Melissa to learn five important lessons. First, she learned the importance of trusting her instincts. Far from being disastrous, quitting a job before she had another one gave her more time to devote to a job search. Second, she discovered that the most satisfying positions are often ones that allow you to tie together the threads of past experiences and interests. Third, she found that mature age can be an advantage. Having reached the age and level of experience that demanded the opportunity to call her own shots, she discovered that the best job is the one you design. Creating your own job doesn't require that you be self-employed, only that your self be fully employed. Fourth, was the discovery that her options were numerous. Because people become tied to certain jobs and skills, they forget just how vast their actual choices are. Finally, Melissa's job search demonstrates that the tremendous investment of energy that every successful job search demands is what allows people to look back and say, "Win, lose, or draw, I gave it my all." Being able to say, with satisfaction, that you risked for a dream is the biggest prize of all.

Umberto's Story

Success doesn't always come easy. When it does, the experience can be astonishing, invigorating, and a little frightening. Those are the emotions *Umberto*, a former social worker, experienced when he turned into a restaurateur. At 40, this handsome, sensuous, dark-haired entrepreneur with brooding eyes and deep voice has mixed emotions about the success of his Italian restaurant and highly popular cookbook. A cautious risk taker, Umberto is in his fifth job, but his first "real occupational choice." Despite his cautious nature, experience has taught this West Coast entrepreneur that once the first risk is past, the rest follows naturally.

Umberto enjoys talking about career choices because he feels his own risk-taking pattern is fairly typical. "More and more," he explains, hands slicing the air around him, "I see people who, 10 or 15 years ago, would have been expecting to take a long, steady climb up the career ladder to the top of their fields. But they've tumbled off and now they're beginning to rethink what they want, and it's not just to change jobs within their field, but to change occupations completely." Umberto has tried both. For the first 12 years of his professional life, he experimented with moving around in the social work system. Then he made a drastic move that changed not only his career, but his entire life. This is the story of that process.

Like many, Umberto greeted college graduation with uncertainty. The year was 1960. With a B.A. in social sciences, he was not sure what he wanted to do. He took a job as a social worker for a small school division about 100 miles from his home town. The job promised to combine his desire to do socially useful work with his interest in guiding adolescents. Weekly meetings with the school division's psychologist and evening courses and workshops led naturally to a B.S.W. degree. The job was especially gratifying because Umberto liked working with people. "Until then, as an only child, I had led a fairly protected life. The job exposed me to a lot of life that I hadn't seen before and I was forced to do a lot of soul searching to clarify who I was and what I valued. You can't discuss values with kids without looking seriously at your own." For the next few years he worked tirelessly during the days, then, instead of spending time with his new wife, Brenda, he wrote reports endlessly during the evenings. Even in his sleep, Umberto was still writing reports and rehashing problems. Although the job was challenging, it was also frustrating. "You were supposed to help change the students' behavior, but you only saw them once every three weeks."

Five years of frustration were enough. Umberto looked for another job. He found one in the probation system, where, with a smaller workload, he could work with delinquent youths. Now that Umberto had the opportunity to work intensely with his young charges, he felt he could make a real impact. His sense of progress was short-lived. No matter how effective he was, a rigid probation system thwarted his good intentions. Feeling disgruntled, he searched again for a position in the same field.

His third job was the draining task of investigating child neglect and abuse. "What I saw literally made me sick." By December 1974, Umberto had been a social worker for 15 years. "It felt like thirty." His career growth had been agonizing and what he had seen depressed and infuriated him. "I saw people who didn't rock the boat get promoted. Those who did and were their own persons didn't have a chance to advance. I was very good at my job, but there was no incentive to be creative."

Umberto had to maintain some balance in his life. So he took up painting and cooking to relieve his career pressures. But the tragedy of his life didn't fully strike Umberto until he watched his father dying. He recalls, "It was a funny thing.

Here you are, watching a beautiful man with white hair lying in his bed, dying of a heart attack. You hear him ramble and wander, and talk about his life and what he wished he had done. You watch death. Then you say, 'Wait a minute. What's going on with him is going to happen to me. What am I doing between now and my death?' You begin to assess yourself and that's a shock. 'Am I going to do this for the rest of my life? Isn't there another way to earn a living?' That's what you wonder."

Suddenly, Umberto had to do some serious self-evaluation. After a long discussion with his wife, she turned to one of his paintings and said, "Umberto, you're a very creative person, but this job is wiping you out. You're miserable, you have migraines. Please quit." The time had come. With his father's death and Brenda's permission to quit, Umberto's unspoken dreams could surface. Consumed with joy and relief, he burst into tears. "I didn't know what I wanted to do, but I just knew that I had to get out of social work. I saw that I had interests and talents, intelligence, creativity, and energy and that, if I directed them toward the goals I cherished, I could make it." Umberto also realized that he had never really made the choice to be a social worker. Chance and circumstance had led him into an occupation that filled him with misery. He wanted to be able to choose an occupation right for him.

That took time. While his wife encouraged him to quit right away, Umberto was reluctant to leave her carrying the burden of a hefty mortgage. With good management, he was able to accomplish his normal workload in eight hours and devote evenings and a few half-days to exploring his options. Gradually, he discovered what he didn't want. Umberto enjoyed making pastry, but he didn't feel it would be profitable enough to pay the family's bills. And the artist's life was too solitary. Then, at 38, Umberto realized that what he loved most was cooking and entertaining. As a child, he had cooked while his parents worked. Now a grown man, he was still cooking. Maybe this talent could be turned into a profitable venture.

There were other reasons Umberto wanted to succeed on his own. One was his hostility toward rigid authoritarian institutions. He also wanted to rise on his own merits. Excited now, Umberto realized that he didn't want to be a chef, confined to a hot kitchen all day. He wanted to be a manager. Too impatient to return to school for the business and management skills he needed, Umberto took the direct approach. He talked to the manager of a fast food outlet about entrepreneurship. The die was cast when he discovered the outlet's parent company had an excellent training program. Within a day of being accepted, Umberto had quit his job. His co-workers were envious.

Quitting was easier than he had thought. True, his salary would plummet to less than half of what it had been, but his family was prepared to skimp for a while. The next 18 months were among the hardest and happiest of Umberto's life. He quickly advanced to become manager of one of the largest-grossing outlets in the chain.

Soon Umberto began fantasizing about his own place. During the months of training, he had discovered that he really loved the restaurant business, that his counseling skills could be put to good use in dealing with employees and customers, and that he could get the immediate rewards he so desired. This time, quitting was even easier. "Having quit once before, I had finally managed to overcome my fears."

Within a month, Umberto had found the perfect location, a large old house overlooking a river. Raising the money was more difficult; the lowest interest rate he could find was 22 percent. Umberto thought it over carefully, then decided instead to remortgage his home and borrow the money from friends and family. With cash in hand, he then decorated the house and designed the menu, using the motif of a typical northern Italian restaurant. Il Palazzo opened with a staff of 20. In a city noted for sophisticated palates and numerous restaurants, Il Palazzo soon accumulated a dedicated following. As demand for the secrets of his fine cuisine grew, Umberto followed his first success with a guide to Italian cooking. With astonishing presales of 40,000 copies, it, too, was a hit.

Achieving that elusive mix of culinary and financial success was no mean accomplishment. Long before he launched his new venture, Umberto had researched the market and the pros and cons of the restaurant business. He says, "This just felt right. I knew what I was getting into, so I felt ready to take the plunge." Even though, through preparation, he had reduced the risks of failing, this new entrepreneur still experienced the usual anxiety. Today, he says, "I can hardly believe that this is the new me! I did have a difficult time leaving social work. But I remember my father's regrets. I didn't want to have similar ones."

What Can You Learn from Umberto?

Umberto learned to be a risk taker and a Quester by moving carefully at first, researching his options, and taking into account the needs and desires of those close to him. But as he grew more confident, risk taking became easier. Umberto's decision-making style also changed from that of a cautious, play-it-safer to that of an enterprising entrepreneur.

To be truly satisfying, your occupational choice should allow previously disregarded aspects of yourself to finally emerge.

Had Umberto examined his career goals sooner, he may have fulfilled his dream much earlier. His unhappy work history was partly the result of entering an occupation out of expediency rather than conviction. Umberto's desire to make a difference could have been translated into a more suitable position much earlier in his career.

The right pieces to Umberto's puzzle eluded him for a long time. Finally, he found that running a restaurant satisfied his needs for autonomy, for creativity, and for working with people. Umberto learned that he could provide a useful service to many people by offering them superb cuisine and pleasant surroundings. The number of individuals whose lives he enriched was far greater than those he tried to help as a social worker. Most important, he loved doing it!

Umberto's story punctures the fallacy that you can't change the direction of your career in mid-life. To be truly satisfying, your occupational choice should allow previously disregarded aspects of yourself to finally emerge.

Part B: The Process of Risking

In their planned risks, many Questers proceed through a series of stages as they move toward their goals. The stages Questers pass through do not always occur in the precise order outlined, and Questers may pass through some more than once. For instance, many will experience ambivalence (Stage 3) even while they are preparing for risk (Stage 4) and narrowing their options (Stage 5). But if Questers omit one of the stages, they can experience trouble. Moreover, in dealing with different problems, Questers may be at different stages. Because a decision in one life component (occupation, marriage, leisure) affects the processes in another, decisions need to be thought out carefully.

Decisions are based on knowledge about yourself and your environment and are influenced by societal pressures and realities. Most are made with an element of uncertainty and subjective probability, but all involve emotional and intellectual processes. Subconscious and conscious thoughts should be considered in evaluating the information that goes into making a decision. A proper balance of both commitment and tentativeness is crucial in today's work world.

Making decisions is seldom easy. There are no right or wrong decisions because each decision is important for your learning. However, if you make a decision for the right reason, it will probably work out in your favor. No one can tell you if a decision to change jobs is the right move. But to grow and develop to your fullest potential, you have to be willing to evaluate yourself and your current situation and, if you are not growing or satisfied, you should consider making changes. And change involves risk.

By learning how Questers tend to plan for risk, you can alter the direction of your life. Even now, you could be planning the moves you would like to make, rather than waiting until the situation becomes so awful that you feel forced to change or are dismissed. Some of the ways you can reduce risk through planning are described in the remainder of this chapter. Additional factors to consider in making shifts are outlined in chapter 9.

Stage 1: Becoming *Aware* of Negative Feelings

Gloria, petite and 55, is a clinical psychologist in private practice who just completed her Ph.D. Her ambition and ability are inspiring. Obvious intelligence is balanced by a magnetic beauty. Stunning green eyes glitter with excitement and the worldliness of experience. For all of her success, Gloria hasn't had an easy life. Her father died when she was eight. By her early teens, Gloria was burdened with an alcoholic mother. By working part-time, she was able to put herself through an honors program in mathematics. After graduation, she worked in the actuarial department of an insurance company until she and her new husband, Daniel, an up-and-coming lawyer, decided to have a family. Because she had missed out on a happy home life, having one now was important to Gloria. But, once more, she was disappointed. At 39, with four teenagers, she was on her own again. Although Daniel did pay some child support, the money wasn't enough to maintain the standard of living the family was used to, so Gloria returned to school for a year to train as a math teacher.

Being a teacher seemed like a good career choice. She would have contact with people, the salary was good, and the hours and holidays would give her time to be at home with the children. By all external standards, Gloria was successful. After teaching elementary school for four years, she was promoted to principal, where she stayed for five more years. But when the school administration offered her a promotion to a larger school, Gloria turned it down. She reflects, "I was feeling tired and irritable." Frequent outbursts of tears and anger seemed to have no apparent cause. The laughter seemed to have gone from her life. Feeling bored and trapped, Gloria knew she was no longer growing in her job. "I had no intellectual stimulation. I had mastered the job. Even if I had moved on to the other school, it just would have been more of the same." That fall, she fell ill. Bones aching, she huddled in bed. Friends told her to go to the hospital. But Gloria knew it was only the flu. She also knew that what was truly making her ill was that she really didn't know what to do with the rest of her life. She stayed in bed for 10 days. Finally, she asked for a sabbatical. "I needed time to rethink the direction my career was taking."

Gloria's body was giving her messages, but labeling her feelings was hard. Most life changes are heralded in advance by just such physical cues. At first, you ignore them. Eventually, you cannot. You may feel lousy a lot or you may feel that something is wrong with your relationship or that you never laugh anymore. Everyone's body has some physical equivalent for fear, despair, or euphoria—a dull ache in the gut, a feeling of heaviness inside, tears that well up like a flood, a sense of soaring. Sometimes, these feelings are hard to label and distinguish.

Stage 2: *Defining* the Problem

Once Gloria admitted she had a problem, she was able to move into Stage 2: defining the problem. "In thinking about my career, I realized that I went into teaching for the wrong reasons. I made a cold-blooded decision because I needed the money and liked the hours. But I was never really happy in teaching. My subconscious was telling me that I could change and try something that I had wanted to try for a long time." Because Gloria was no longer responsible for her children, taking a risk felt better now.

Gloria had entered the second stage of decision making. This stage is usually a subtle modulation from Stage 1, like a change of key in music. Feelings of discontent are translated into vague impulses that you'd like to chuck the job and start something entirely new. Gloria was aware she couldn't stay in teaching, so she thought of trying her longtime dream, psychology.

Gloria recognized the need to change. Her second stage began with the realization that she wanted to get out of teaching. By listening to and accepting what her body, mind, and spirit were telling her, Gloria identified the feelings behind her dissatisfaction. Her decision to do something about the problem (try psychology) resulted in her leaving a familiar way of life and taking her first step into the unknown. Defining the problem and deciding to make some changes in your life are important preliminary steps in the decision-making process.

Stage 3: Experiencing *Ambivalence*

Gloria's "I will!" was followed by the third stage of the decision-making process, "But can I?" Many experience such conflicting emotions before taking a risk as anxiety asserts itself.

Gloria, for instance, was afraid because she was leaving the security of a monthly paycheck and a pension. As she stepped into an unknown future, she felt conscious of her 49 years. How would she do? She had no job in sight. But she was also excited about testing herself, about trying something new and challenging, about experiencing adventure and change.

Being anxious about risk taking is normal. Many feel apprehensive about losing their known worlds. In Gloria's case, she was trading the horrors of the known for those she couldn't yet imagine. She was giving up a lot.

Stage 4: *Preparing* for Risk

To invite change takes courage and hope; to see it through takes skill.

Preparing for risk also takes resourcefulness and work. Most Questers try to be in charge of change by setting tentative goals, understanding themselves, gathering realistic, up-to-date information about occupational options and related training routes, and preparing contingency plans. To invite change takes courage and hope; to see it through takes skill.

Gloria explored psychology by taking three night school courses while she worked. During this time, she also analyzed her personal characteristics and her suitability to psychology. Then she took a sabbatical to study full-time. This enabled her to further assess her suitability to psychology and initiate some preliminary steps toward achieving her tentative goal. Her contingency plan was to return to teaching, at least for a while.

To make good decisions, you also must control the elements of the risk that are controllable.

Setting Tentative Goals

Questers tend to think carefully about what they want to do. They separate their needs and desires from what society dictates or what friends and family consider best. Most Questers establish tentative short- and medium-term goals. Rather than viewing these goals as a huge, all-encompassing mass (changing a job), they break them down into manageable subgoals (learning more about their needs, interests, and strengths, or reading about the kinds of occupations that fit their personal characteristics). Examined task by task, each step is much more manageable. Breaking down your goal into manageable units makes the formidable possible.

When setting their goals, Questers pay careful attention to their inner voices and dreams. These help Questers identify what's really important to them. Many have learned that disregarding these messages will just lead to more dissatisfaction.

As they gather more information about themselves and their career options, it is natural for Questers to review and revise their goals. Questers' goals give them a sense of direction, but they are not ironclad. Gloria's tentative goal was to leave teaching. Her ideal goal was to be a psychologist. She enrolled in a psychology program, but just in case her dream didn't work out, she retained the option of returning to teaching. Taking courses in psychology gave her time to explore herself and the field to determine if she was suited to her new career choice. Her commitment to leave teaching and enter psychology was flexible enough to allow her to make changes if her plans didn't jell.

Exploring Options

Seeking relevant, up-to-date information is a basic step in illuminating the dark, unknown world one enters when making a major career change. Many Questers use this information as a guide for at least part of the journey. Two kinds of information can be essential to any occupational shift: knowledge about yourself and knowledge about your career options in the current economy. You will also need to know where you can get this information, what books and directories to consult, what personal contacts you will need, and what professional assistance workshops or counseling options are available.

Gloria found out more about herself and her career options from a vocational psychology course. She learned, for example, that she has Social, Investigative, and Artistic interests and that she has strong needs for achievement, altruism, autonomy, creativity, and challenge. Her purpose is to help others, and her skills and strengths include interviewing and diagnosing, advising and teaching, counseling and testing, designing and implementing programs, collaborating and problem-solving, and writing and speaking. All of these traits, coupled with her compassion, ability to inspire, and emotional stability, are compatible with practicing psychology.

Gloria also explored the types of jobs available in psychology as well as the probability of finding a suitable position and the feasibility of establishing a private practice. She consulted directories such as the *Occupational Outlook Handbook* as well as specific books about psychology careers. She interviewed and shadowed psychologists employed in various settings. The information which she acquired helped reduce some of Gloria's anxiety.

Networking

Another way Questers keep abreast of information in various fields is through networking. By attending professional meetings, workshops, and conferences, they develop and maintain contacts with people in occupations of their choice. Gloria joined the American Psychological Association and attended meetings of her local chapter. This enabled her to keep up with recent developments and opportunities in the field as well as meet and maintain contact with future colleagues.

Managing Money

Don't use lack of money as an excuse for not making a career change.

The risks of changing jobs can be reduced if you prepare yourself financially. Melissa's nest egg, for example, enabled her to conduct a full-time job search. Gloria prepared herself financially by taking a sabbatical. That monthly paycheck gave her the opportunity to learn more about herself and the field of psychology, as well as to learn new skills and acquire knowledge. Both women and Umberto learned to live on a considerably lower income so that their savings and money would stretch farther. Some Questers' spouses went back to work full-time to supplement or even bring in all the family's income. One Quester, who went into business for himself, reduced his lifestyle dramatically. He says, "It got to the point where I had to reduce my lifestyle substantially . . . . I was living on rice and watered-down tomato soup."

Some Questers who returned to school were able to obtain financial aid packages from the public or private sector. To help finance their studies or business ventures, many Questers borrowed from friends and relatives. Others approached liberal bank managers with well-researched proposals.

Don't use lack of money as an excuse for not making a career change. Like the Questers, as you work toward your career goal, you will find ways of surviving. But, for a while, you will have to work hard, think creatively, and be willing to forgo some material comforts. Few Questers regret these sacrifices.

Establishing Support

Dispelling misinformation, reducing ignorance, or having financial resources tend to make Questers feel more secure in their decisions. But they don't live by facts and material needs alone. Questers' job shifts are made easier and their anxieties are reduced when they have the support and guidance of others. Whenever you begin any large, new venture, you need to feel that people you are close to care. Many Questers received assistance from partners, family members, friends, and colleagues. Others sought help from spiritual advisers or professional counselors. Not only can caring individuals provide encouragement and empathy, but they can also help you to see your decision more objectively and to analyze it critically.

Gloria received lots of support and encouragement from a friend, Brad. A professor and the director of psychological services for her school division also gave her encouragement to get a Ph.D. Positive feedback from clients and professors gave her a tremendous sense of accomplishment. Even though Gloria's children were not living at home, they often showed support for their busy mother by helping with chores such as grocery shopping and mowing the lawn. Hard work, a sense of humor, and prayer also helped Gloria and many other Questers cope with major changes.

In any major life decision, you can learn to allow yourself breathing or incubating time.

Laying Down Safety Nets

One reason why career changes evoke so much anxiety is that they seem irreversible. But this is not necessarily so, particularly if you think hard and creatively. Many Questers tend to build in fail-safe and retreat positions, contingency plans for an alternative course of action if the present one turns out to be a disaster. Just knowing that other possibilities exist reduces the risk. Identify the worst possible disaster that could occur, then decide what you could do about it. Doing so will not only relieve some of your anxiety, but it will also prepare you for that possible outcome. Gloria's "worst possible disaster" would have been to return to teaching. Having that contingency plan reduced her anxieties and negative fantasies.

In times of acute pressure, Questers have learned not to panic. Deadlines can be moved. Gloria didn't make her decision to leave teaching immediately. She took a year's sabbatical to give herself time to think. A time limit, particularly one imposed by someone else, need not be cast in stone. A prospective employer will wait another day or two while you mull over a job decision. In any major life decision, you can learn to allow yourself breathing or incubating time.

A word of caution: Don't continually extend a self-imposed time frame. There's a difference between giving yourself a buffer to reflect on an offer or decision and procrastinating. Once you commit yourself to realistic goals and set deadlines, put your plan into action.

Stage 5: *Narrowing Options*

Once Questers have assessed their personal characteristics and needs, identified and explored career options, and reduced the risks as much as possible, they begin narrowing their alternatives. Doing so isn't always easy. To facilitate the process, Gloria, like most Questers, used both her intellect and intuition. Although she evaluated the pros and cons of each of her choices mathematically, she learned, that this important technique has its limitations. Incomplete and inaccurate information, human impatience, and the difficulty of calculating the emotional components of hope and fear as well as various unconscious projections complicate the process.

Therefore, in addition to prioritizing her options mathematically by taking into consideration her needs, values, and purpose, Gloria took a week off from her busy schedule to relax in the mountains. During this time she did no conscious thinking about her decision. However, her unconscious was working. While she was taking a walk on the sixth day of her vacation, the answer to her question came to her. She was now convinced that the practice of psychology was right for her.

Using Intuition

By turning away from the muddle of decision making, Questers listen to their subconscious minds. They let go of the intellectual component of the process by letting their decisions incubate. Intuitive insights usually occur when we are in a relaxed state. It is important to first tackle problems consciously by compiling as much information as possible and analyzing the data. The intuitive hunch may then come as a flash of insight when our mind is not focusing on the dilemma. "Sleeping on it" allows the intuitive or incubative process to take over. Many creative people report finding solutions to problems either upon awakening or during a moment of reverie. Almost everyone has had the experience of groping for a name or memory, only to have it swim obligingly to the surface soon after they stop pursuing it.

The incubation period gives the decision time to germinate. Typically, intuitive insights both precede and follow the exhaustive use of analysis and logic. The failure to resolve problems sometimes is due to the inability to put them in perspective. Being overly concerned with certain facets of a problem may cause you to miss others; therefore, you may overlook better solutions. Intuition permits you to delve into the conscious and subconscious storehouse of everything you have ever learned. Tapping into this rich reservoir enables you to perceive the many possible solutions inherent in complex problems. It also helps you clarify what you really care about.

Turning away or letting go may seem like procrastination, but it can be distinguished in two ways. First, rather than feeling guilty about it, you consent to it. Second, rather than a shutdown, it represents an attentive waiting, a poised readiness. Sometimes, you move ahead best by sitting still. It takes time for seeds to germinate. At some points, particularly before moving into action, it is not only permissible, but desirable, to let go so that your deepest convictions can emerge.

Stage 6: Taking *Action*

Questers don't move into action until they have prepared themselves both cognitively and emotionally. But once they decide to take action, they commit themselves to a goal, make plans, and follow through.

Making Plans

After making a choice by committing to a goal, Questers develop tentative plans. Questers realize that they must be flexible in their planning because of the rapid changes occurring around them. They try to make their career choices a reversible process so that they can change direction in midstream if the need arises. Some have learned the hard way that rigid adherence to long-range goals and plans doesn't work in times of change. Questers also ask themselves a number of questions about their personal characteristics and desired goals, for example, "Do I feel good about where I'm heading?" "Are my plans getting me where I want to go?"

Gloria's planning process involved investigating the psychology programs of local schools to determine their suitability for her as well as their reputation in the professional community, applying to the schools of her choice, and preparing a budget.

Taking action also requires acquiring job search or business planning skills. It may necessitate returning to school on a full- or part-time basis for upgrading or retraining.

Going for It

Making a final commitment ends this action stage. Regardless of how well you prepare, acting on any decision always means taking some steps into the unknown. There is always something new to learn about yourself and the situation. But once a commitment to change is made, the rest of the process is always easier. For most Questers, this step, though risky, always brings a heady sense of relief. Finally, you've done all the dreaming, researching, thinking, worrying, and phoning and are ready to act by quitting a job, accepting a position, establishing a business, getting married, or embarking on some other adventure.

In Gloria's case, the action stage began when, after her sabbatical, she was interviewed by the school board about a new principalship. Would she accept it? Gloria decided not to. That first step to act began with an exit. This propelled her to continue with her plans to acquire the Ph.D. so that she could attain her goal of having a psychology practice. Gloria followed through on her plans by completing the Ph.D. coursework and internship. Opening up her office was the next step in her commitment to the practice of psychology.

Stage 7: *Evaluating* the Decision

Gloria was asked to evaluate the gains and losses she experienced from her career move. "There is no way I could go back," she replied. "It would be like dying. I think it's far better to keep trying new things because you're not going to grow if you sit still." As Gloria says, for every risk she took there has been a positive payoff. "And each time I risked, I learned to do it more effectively. I really feel that there isn't much that I can't do at this point in my life. I feel I've walked a million miles, mostly on my own." Like all of us, Gloria has fallen on her face, but she has learned something from every negative experience.

Would she do anything differently? "Not very much," Gloria replies. She has made errors in her practice and has been something of a workaholic. But her only true regret is that she stayed so long stagnating in a job.

Fortunately, Gloria had few doubts about succeeding. "You have to believe that even though all of the odds are against you, you'll make it." Visualizing herself in the situation she wanted to be in helped Gloria to move forward. And, while she doesn't always feel confident, she has learned to put her doubts on the back burner.

Having succeeded at this risk, Gloria has definite plans for her future. She wants to keep working, learning, and growing, though not at the pace she did to attain her Ph.D. and start a practice. Now, she wants to reap the benefits of her hard work, to have more time for herself, her partner, and her family. Gloria feels her age was a definite benefit. She says her accumulated personal and work experiences gave her the confidence and knowledge to make her dream a reality.

Gloria's evaluation of her gains echoes that of most Questers who change jobs. The majority feel that they acquire a considerable amount of personal satisfaction and a sense of inner harmony. They attain greater self-awareness and believe that they gain greater control over their personal and professional destinies. Enhanced job satisfaction and involvement, improved relationships with partners and family members, more leisure time, healthier, more rewarding lifestyles, and more meaningful lives are among the other rewards they mention.

If you have tackled a life challenge carefully and still experienced a poor outcome, you will probably be discouraged. Don't be. It's unrealistic to have perfect results all the time. Learn from your mistakes. You will have many other opportunities. If you are not happy with the consequences of your risk, ask yourself if you were motivated by internal aspirations or the desire to please others, and what you should have done differently. Next time, you will improve your performance.

The fear, excitement, pleasure, and joy of changing jobs rejuvenate most Questers. They tend to learn some pretty important lessons from their career moves. As one says, "Money is far from being the most important thing in life. On the contrary, it can be a trap that becomes a false goal and creates the illusion of security." Growth is a gain, says another Quester. "If you are just living for the next coffee break or the next vacation or raise or retirement or death, you are not really living. You are existing."

Making changes is a necessary part of growing.

Most Questers feel like those you have met. They haven't really tallied up any major deficits from their career moves. Some experienced material losses, such as loss of a steady income, retirement benefits, security, seniority, investments, and health or insurance benefits. But, in the eyes of many Questers, these losses are minor. Though a number, particularly those who became self-employed, took substantial pay cuts to become established, they retrieved those losses. Most felt planned risk taking paid off and will practice the same steps again when they take their next risk. Only about 25 percent said they would do something differently. Among this group, most said they would leave a stagnant job sooner, pursue a work problem with a senior company executive, take more time to explore additional options, leave more gracefully, or seek the aid of a career counselor.

Making changes is a necessary part of growing. But the responsibility for making the alterations to enhance your personal and professional life rests with you. Sometimes this means taking a step out into the unknown and parting with a familiar way of life. And if that's the case muster all the courage you can and think of yourself as a new Quester, because you will become one. Remember, next time it will be even easier.

What's Your Decision-Making Style?

How do you go about making risky decisions? Are you a planned risk taker, like most Questers, balancing the intuitive, emotional self with your cognitive, rational self? Or are you impulsive, agonizing, delaying, and anxious? Or are you intuitive, impulsive, and careless? Although most people are rarely completely consistent in their decision-making styles, most of us can detect some regularity in the way we make important decisions. Think of the important life decisions you have made, for example, about education, marriage, divorce, major residential moves, or career shifts and then answer the following questions. You may not be able to answer some with complete confidence, but give the answer that comes closest to what you believe. This is not a test. It's just an assessment device to help you better understand your own decision-making behavior. For each item, choose one response that best describes how you usually respond to making a big decision.

1. When making a major decision:

    A. I usually plan things. I am thoughtful and organized.

    B. I usually can't make up my mind. Frequently, I'll put things off until tomorrow.

    C. I tend to do what feels right. I usually make up my mind quickly.

2. When making a major decision:

    A. I think of a number of alternatives, but stop after a reasonable search.

    B. I keep producing and going over possible choices.

    C. I make a quick, overall survey of possibilities, hoping something will hit me.

3. When deciding among alternatives:

    A. I take reasoning and feeling into account.

    B. I try to use reasoning almost entirely.

    C. I almost exclusively listen to my feelings.

4. In thinking about consequences:

    A. I tend to think of both the good and bad outcomes.

    B. I tend to focus on the bad things.

    C. I expect things to work out okay.

5. Before making a decision:

    A. I feel a mixture of anxiety and excitement.

    B. I feel mostly anxiety.

    C. I feel mostly excitement.

6. When making major decisions:

    A. I take a fairly long time.

    B. I take a very long time.

    C. I take a little time.

7. Before making a major decision:

    A. I think it out carefully, then decide with as few regrets as possible.

B. I agonize over the alternatives.

C. I make up my mind quickly and stick to it.

8. Once I make a decision:

A. After checking it out, I usually rally behind it.

B. I experience serious doubts and may change my mind.

C. After launching into action, I usually don't think about it.

9. After I have acted on a decision:

A. I tend to think about what I have learned from it.

B. I tend to worry and regret not doing something.

C. I tend to put it out of my mind.

Total Number of Responses

A responses	B responses	C responses

Scoring and Interpretation

If you scored 6 or more A responses, then you, like many Questers, tend to plan your risks, taking both your intuition and reasoning into account. You make decisions fairly slowly and are more concerned with reasonably good outcomes than with fear of failure or the need to make a perfect decision. You usually plan and review, but without worrying a great deal.

If you scored 6 or more B responses, you tend to be an agonizing, delaying, anxious risk taker. You may make big decisions with great effort, indecision, and fear of making mistakes. You may take a great deal of time to ruminate and worry about the decision.

If you scored 6 or more C responses, you are probably an intuitive, impulsive, careless risk taker. You tend to make decisions quickly, with little experience of mixed feelings. You may feel inappropriately optimistic and spend little time in introspection.

Few people are entirely A, B, or C risk takers. Most are mixtures. Because of this, there can be a number of types of risk-taking styles, ranging from cautious to impetuous. The man who is slow to take a career risk may be more impetuous in another area of his life, such as when buying real estate or playing the horses. A woman who operates largely on hunch may, through self-discipline, be able to force herself to spell out the consequences of really major changes before taking action. Some such inconsistencies are both inevitable and healthy. No one is a perfect risk taker any more than he or she is a perfect mate, a perfect manager, or a perfect partner. But you can learn to be a more effective risk taker.

You can learn to think ahead, plan your progress, and negotiate with life as you move toward your goals. Don't be afraid to try. Even if you have setbacks, you win.

Dare to Change

The Questers have shown that you can take the initiative in your own career development during changing times and prevail. Now it's your turn to do something about a dissatisfying career—and life.

As you have seen, transitions and change are normal aspects of personal and career development. If you make voluntary moves, your transitions will be more pleasant than ones made during involuntary moves and you will be more prepared. However, involuntary changes can also have happy endings.

This chapter reviews the decision-making process described in the preceding chapter and elaborates on other important factors to consider when making career decisions and pursuing desired goals. If you are contemplating a career change, coping with losing your job as a result of a layoff or termination, reentering the workforce, considering a return to school for retraining or upgrading, starting your own business, or looking for a job, this chapter will be helpful.

A career change can take months or even years of exhaustive soul searching. Long before you make the shift, you need to know the steps involved in a successful move, how to master the troublesome feelings that accompany taking chances, where possible dangers lie, and how to maximize your gains while minimizing your losses. You will need to understand yourself and your career options, know how to set career goals and where to find advice and assistance on job search and marketing techniques and, if you plan to be self-employed, how to explore business opportunities and plan for success. Creating a life worth living and finding the courage to risk pursuing your dreams aren't always easy. But you, like thousands of others, can do it.

The steps you should take when making career decisions form the acronym ADAPNAE. Keep in mind, however, that you may backtrack several times as you gather more information about yourself and your options. Some people refer to this as a "waffling" process, which may involve redefining goals, looking at alternate ways of attaining them, distancing, reexamining, revising, and reevaluating. Throughout the whole process, remember to take time out to listen to and trust your intuition; then learn to follow its direction.

The seven stages of the decision-making process (ADAPNAE) are:

A Becoming *aware* of negative feelings.

D *Defining* the problem: describing the symptoms and barriers, managing fear, and doing something about the problem.

A Understanding you will experience *ambivalence*: feeling too much or too little anxiety.

P *Preparing* for risk: setting tentative goals, getting to know yourself (identifying your interests, probing your needs, assessing your accomplishments and skills), investigating career options, managing money, establishing support systems, laying down safety nets, and developing positive attitudes and behaviors.

N *Narrowing* your options: using intellect and intuition, modifying career goals, and making a choice.

A Taking *action*: defining job targets, establishing information sources, preparing your resume, marketing yourself, identifying job opportunities and contacting employers, being effective in interviews, making the decision, and going for it.

E *Evaluating* your decision.

The information and techniques provided here are by no means exhaustive. For more in-depth information and assistance on job search or going into business for yourself, investigate other resources or seek professional advice.

Stage 1: Becoming *Aware* of Negative Feelings

Your body and mind may be sending you messages about the state of your job satisfaction. The messages may be physical, such as lingering colds, flu, or headaches. Or they may translate themselves into verbal messages which can no longer be ignored. "I can hardly wait till Friday!" is one message. Counting the minutes till your next holiday is another. In this state, you will be feeling disequilibrium or a loss of balance, the first stage of the decision-making process. Listening to and accepting your feelings is an important part of moving beyond your uneasiness. Admitting that you are unhappy is the first risk in making changes. As you will soon discover, the process of changing isn't nearly as painful as your current state.

It is easy to project the blame for these feelings onto other people or situations. You may shout with frustration that "No one understands me," or "My wife is impossible to live with!" But regardless of where you first pin the source of your discontent, sooner or later you must reckon with the knowledge that you just don't like who you are becoming. The ultimate target of these negative feelings, whether conscious or unconscious, is yourself. How did you become this trapped, stagnant, joyless person?

Listen to and

accept your

feelings.

Perhaps you've been working five to ten or more years in your job and it appears to be going well. You've had steady promotions, good raises, praises from superiors, and admiration from subordinates. Even your parents are proud of you. Then, one day, you get a queasy feeling that something is . . . missing. But what? Like the victim of an accident, you anxiously grope around to feel if your arms and legs are still attached. You run the film of your life in reverse, but still you can't figure out what's wrong. Often, no one single event is responsible. Instead, it's been a gradual process. You may have been seriously ill or your marriage may be falling apart, or you may lack energy and be irritable with your friends. Many of these reactions may be traced to your feelings about your job. The uneasy feelings that many Questers experience are often related to some negative aspects of their work. In many instances, the discontent is intensified by some other traumatic events in their lives and self-evaluation begins.

These feelings may persist for months or years depending on your ability to tolerate them or your masochism. Sooner or later, though, you must verbalize your dissatisfaction by admitting you have a problem. Listen to and accept your feelings. While it is still much too early to speak of "plans" at this point, you will sense that something needs to be done.

Seeking a solution to a problem before it becomes too serious makes good sense. Doing so allows you to use your skills to better advantage and enables you to be prepared if trouble strikes.

Stage 2: *Defining* Your Problem

Clearly defining the problem is the second stage in making decisions. You will need a good written definition of the problem. You must look at the psychological and emotional issues behind your dissatisfaction and clarify what you would like but are afraid to undertake.

At this point in the decision-making process, your goals will be quite fuzzy. They may be wistful, full of yearning without much expectation of gratification, and, yet, they may also contain a kernel of hope. That kernel can blossom into a clearer idea of how you would like things to become. The danger now is that you will abort the fantasies as too distracting or unrealistic. Dismissing these dreams prematurely means ruling out sound possibilities. Be charitable to your brainchild. Ideas and fantasies need care and nourishment. Listen carefully to your hopes and dreams; you may discover that they reflect your deepest needs and give you insight into your "raison d'etre."

Describing the Symptoms

First, describe the symptoms. Ask yourself, "What's making me feel this way?" "What is it about my situation that is unpleasant?" "What is my desired goal?" The discrepancy between these two is what must be overcome. Unfortunately, while you may not like where you are, sometimes it's hard to decide where you want to be.

The Job Satisfaction Questionnaire and The Job Involvement Questionnaire may have helped you identify the sources of your dissatisfaction. Here are some additional questions to consider:

❖ What do I like about my job? What do I dislike?

❖ Why am I in this job? Did I choose it for prestige? To be of service? For security? Power? Money? Independence? Challenge? Personal satisfaction? Other reasons? Do I still have these rewards?

❖ Am I doing my best work? Is my work damaging my self-confidence? My health?

❖ Am I committed to my company? Do I have anything to gain by remaining with the company for the rest of my career? Do I have anything to lose by leaving the company? Does my company really need me? Am I proud of my company? Is there any room in this company for my growth? Where do I want to be next year? In five years? Will my company help me get there?

❖ Are other factors in my life, not job-related, having a detrimental effect on my performance and attitude? Do I have a satisfying and intimate relationship with a partner or spouse? Do I have a partner? If not, would I like one? Do I have satisfying leisure activities? Do I have enough money and time to pursue these? How is my health? Is it affecting my attitudes toward my work and other life components?

❖ Am I a candidate for burnout? (Check your score on The Burnout Questionnaire.) Am I irritable? Impatient? Do I have no time for leisure or family activities? Do I have difficulty sleeping? Do I have little energy? Physical problems? Am I drinking or taking drugs to feel better?

❖ What is my desired career goal? Have I attained it? Have I realized my career dreams? Have I enjoyed success in my career?

❖ Can I achieve my career goal where I am? Why or why not? How can I reach my goals?

❖ Can the bad points about my job be resolved without making a move? Can I restructure my job? Why or why not?

❖ Could I change jobs, yet remain in the same company? If so, what can I do?

❖ Do I want to change employers, occupational fields? Do I want to become self-employed? Take a career pause? Which of these options do I have? How easy or difficult do I feel it would be for me to get another job in the same field? In a different field? Do I want to return to school for upgrading? Retraining?

If your responses to the above questions and the questionnaires in chapter 7 indicate that you are dissatisfied, you may be ready for a job change. If the bad points you listed about your company can be resolved and you are committed to it, work at improving the weak spots and look for advancement within. If, however, you are dissatisfied with your position, the bad points can't be resolved, and you are not committed to the organization, you should move on.

Describing the Barriers

The next step is to describe the barriers blocking you from changing jobs. Examples could be fear or uncertainty about change; fear of losing a secure income, pension, or other benefits; fear that the change will interfere with your relationships, for example, disapproval from partner or children; fear that you will lose power, prestige, or status; fear of having to live up to an image, making a mistake, or being embarrassed; or fear of returning to school for retraining or upgrading. Guilt that change might create family hardships or uncertainty about what to do and where to go for help in beginning your career search may be other blocks.

Every risk involves fear.

Fears often act as barriers to your progress. Growing, which is really just abandoning a comfortable position, usually involves pain. Trying to avoid pain by constructing rigid roles, defenses, viewpoints, or excuses only makes the process more difficult. The first and most important risk you can take is to be honest with yourself. Accept that you are afraid. Like all emotions, fear has a purpose; it alerts you to take action to protect yourself from loss. Every risk involves fear. Lack of fear should signal that you either don't care whether you lose what is at stake or that you don't believe you are in danger.

It is vital that you work through any negative feelings or fears that you have about the decision. Often people hesitate to follow their hearts because they are afraid to fail. Fear will not go away as long as you continue to grow. The only way to conquer fear is to learn to manage it and continue pursuing your goals.

The first step you can take in the management of fear is to identify it. Write down all the fears you think are stopping you from attaining your career goals. Be honest with yourself. These could include fear of failing, fear of losing friends, fear of having too much responsibility, fear of not knowing what to expect, and fear of inability to afford material comforts.

Underlying most fear is lack of trust in your inability to perform or handle situations. You fear because you are not feeling good about yourself. Some fear is good, instinctual. It keeps you alert to danger. But most fear is destructive, a barrier to growth and success.

Fear is the result of conditioning. For example, you learn very early in life to be cautious. Parents warn young children, "Be careful . . . " This conveys messages that the world is dangerous and you won't be able to cope. As long as you continue to grow, you will have fear. Because fear is learned, it can be unlearned. By reprogramming old attitudes and beliefs and learning new ones, you will be able to manage your fear. The following suggestions will help.

Tips for Managing Fear

❖ *Live in the present.* Because most fear centers around the future, don't spend time worrying about what might happen. Instead, deal with the present and do what you can to research and plan for a future major event to minimize setbacks.

❖ *Let go of "attachments."* Fear is an emotion that usually accompanies the process of "letting go." The more attached you are to something, the greater the fear of losing it. If you're attached to a good-paying job, you may be afraid to leave for work that promises more fulfillment. Growth requires letting go of the past, material possessions, and people. Fear is a reassuring signal that you are about to stretch yourself to move forward. Ask yourself, "What do I need to let go of?" "What scares me most about letting go?" "What is the worst thing that can happen if I let go?" "What can I do to minimize this risk?"

❖ *Watch your "self-talk."* Keep a log to track the negatives you say to yourself. Each time you catch yourself saying something that fuels your fear or is negative, say, "Cancel," and replace it with a more positive affirmation or statement.

❖ *Know and accept yourself.* Know your heart, your passion. Fear begins when there is a discrepancy between your actions and your real desires and purpose. When you live in a manner consistent with your calling, you experience harmony and stability. On the other hand, you experience disharmony, indecision, and doubt when you ignore your spiritual ideals. You are a unique person with a special mission that only you can perform. Follow this passion and work at achieving goals and activities that are compatible with it. Believe in yourself and know that you will attain your goals.

❖ *Note your priorities.* What do you really want? What do others think you should have? Replace the "shoulds" with your own values. Shift from a having mode to a being mode. Having is possessing, it can disappear as easily as it came. The being mode is not as transient. In this state, you are centered. Your personal power will assist you in achieving your goals. You feel comfortable with the steps you need to take to achieve your goal. As you turn your priorities around and follow your heart, you'll achieve more. Money and possessions will often be a by-product.

❖ *Take time out for yourself.* Let go of your "busyness." Constant activity alienates you from your real self. Develop your spiritual side. Learn to go within by seeking solitude and quiet times; enjoy nature, meditate, listen to relaxing music, or write in a journal.

❖ *Understand and befriend your fear.* Step back and look at it. Notice that fear usually takes the form of thoughts and feelings in the mind. Don't get sucked into the fear, but calmly watch it. Where do you feel the fear (for example, as butterflies in your stomach, palpitations of your heart, or knocking knees)? How does does the fear look (for, example, what color and shape is it)? What is the fear saying to you? Once you learn what the fear is saying to you, you can talk back to it, for example, by writing in a journal or while relaxing. You will probably be surprised to discover the fear is not as awful as you initially thought. If, however, you learn that it is a monster, you will be more able to deal effectively with it. The unknown is always more frightening than the known.

❖ *Form a support group.* Associate with people who will make you feel wonderful about yourself and encourage and support you in achieving your goals. Pick individuals who are ahead of you in personal growth. See each other regularly to give one another feedback and encouragement.

❖ *Develop the will to risk.* Like any skill, risk taking gets better with practice. Start with small risks in your daily activities. For example, say hello to someone on the street or do something silly. Each day, write down at least five ways that you can stretch your risk taking. Before you go to bed at night, plan the risk you intend to take the following day. Close your eyes and practice it in your mind's eye. Make your visualization as clear as possible. For additional suggestions, refer to Risk in chapter 3.

❖ *Perceive yourself as a powerful person.* You are in control and always have a choice. Not taking action in any situation is exercising choice. Identify the reasons why you are staying. Ask yourself. "Why am I staying in a job I dislike?" "What comfort do I get?" "What image am I holding on to?" When you can identify the reasons that are holding you back, you will be able to move forward.

❖ *See yourself as someone who has choices, takes action, and operates from a position of inner strength.* As your power builds, so will your confidence and your risk-taking ability. Shift your vocabulary from being a victim to someone with power and strength. For example, "I can" instead of "I can't"; "It's a challenging opportunity" instead of "It's a problem"; "I'm responsible" instead of "It's not my fault"; "It's a learning experience" instead of "It's terrible."

❖ *Think positively.* If you want to change your life for the better, start thinking more positively about yourself and the opportunities available to you. Listen to inspirational tapes, read inspirational books, post positive quotes around your home, state and write affirmations, and begin the day with a positive thought.

❖ *Make a no-lose decision.* Before making a decision, affirm that you will win regardless of the outcome. Look forward to the opportunity for learning and growth even if the results turn out differently from those you planned. Believe there is no such thing as the wrong decision if you do it for the right reason. Learn to trust and follow your intuition, the messages you get from your body as well as external cues. Lighten up. Think of yourself as a lifelong student. Each experience is a valuable lesson. After making the decision, accept total responsibility for it and correct any errors.

❖ *Learn patience.* Patience means knowing it will happen and giving it time to happen. It requires trusting that your goal will be achieved if you follow your heart, maintain positive attitudes, and work hard.

❖ *Live a balanced life.* Become involved in a variety of activities. If you create an identity in only one life component such as work, you will feel empty, helpless, and lost if you lose your job. You will also be afraid to take chances thus diminishing your creativity. On the other hand, if you are involved in a variety of activities (for example, a relationship, family, friends, hobbies, spiritual pursuits, community activities), your life will be more complete. You may even enjoy a job which was previously unsatisfying. Moreover, a job loss will not be as devastating because these activities will help satisfy your needs.

Doing Something About the Problem

If you don't recognize the need to change, then maybe you're not yet ready to make the move. In this sense, a major life change such as a job shift is similar to the decision made by alcoholics. Before they can embark on a cure, alcoholics must admit to their problem, alcoholism. Then they must commit themselves to do something about the problem by attending Alcoholics Anonymous.

Similarly, if you really dislike your work, and have identified and dealt with the barriers that are stopping you from making a move, then you must do something about moving on or improving your current situation. After you have worked through these blocks, you are ready to commit yourself to change (or not change). You cannot start a new chapter before you have finished the old one.

To nurture a career, you must take charge of it. Once you are convinced that a job change is in order, go for it. Don't stick with a dissatisfying position any longer. You need to feel in control of your career to take steps to get it moving again. Turn a deaf ear to those cynics who will tell you it is immature to expect your job to be interesting and satisfying. Patience may be a virtue but resignation is not. If you are thinking there must be more to life, start making some of your dreams come true. A useful word of caution, however, is not to change jobs while you are in the midst of other turmoils. Making a career move when you are experiencing the pressures of family or marital problems can be disastrous. Wait until you can concentrate fully on your new position. Here is some additional advice:

❖ *Avoid guilt.* The sense that you have let everyone down can be the most difficult aspect of quitting a job. Don't worry about what your mentor or colleagues may think.

❖ *Avoid idealizing your former position.* Why mourn a job you have outgrown or one that is no longer meeting your needs? Traditional and emerging fields offer many exciting options.

❖ *Don't remain with a job you dislike because of security.* Security during these times of globalization, rolling recessions, mergers, and political changes is wishful thinking. But developing positive attitudes, believing in yourself, working hard, and being willing to risk will enable you to steer your career through these stormy times.

❖ *Realize that change involves trade-offs.* Change may involve some temporary personal or financial sacrifice. But most Questers agree that in the long term, their gains far outweigh their losses. They feel they've gained greater job and life satisfaction, independence, flexibility, and greater control over their personal and professional lives. They say that risking becomes easier each time they gamble.

❖ *Listen to yourself.* When you make a career switch, you will have to overcome the obstacles of others' expectations. Don't base your self-respect on what coworkers, parents, or friends think. Listen to your feelings. They will help you identify what you really want. If you make the move that feels right for you, you will feel better about yourself. This may also bring you closer to your family and friends. Moreover, no one else can define what you consider dangerous. What is a matter of course to one person may be agony to another. The intensity of a personal risk is largely in the eyes of the beholder.

❖ *Don't make excuses.* Be honest. As Mark Twain said, "There are a thousand good excuses, but no good reasons." If your career has been stagnating, deciding to stay can be just as traumatic as making a move. Too often, the refusal to make a decision turns out to be the wrong decision. While circumstances often force people to take lesser jobs, choosing to remain in a position with no hope of advancement or satisfaction is not only self-defeating, it can be enormously risky. True, there must be some balance between reflection and action. But if you are just putting in time, the losses of enthusiasm, self-confidence, and enjoyment may be greater than you realize.

❖ *Don't be afraid to fail.* Failure is a learning experience. Questers eliminate much failure by planning and persisting. But when they do fail, and they do, they say, "I've done my best . . . I'm only human. I forgive myself." Then they take time to figure out what went wrong, modify their plans, and try again.

❖ *Don't be afraid to change.* It is comfortable to live as you always have. But if you persevere, the new behavior will soon become the comfortable way, and you will have eliminated the dissatisfaction.

❖ *Learn to manage fear.* Refer to the suggestions discussed earlier.

Stage 3: Experiencing Ambivalence

The decision to change can provoke mixed feelings. You may be anxious, depressed, guilty, yet excited at the prospect of trying something new. You're not alone. A certain amount of ambivalence is natural. Inner emotional preparation—weighing losses as well as gains, fears as well as hopes—is a necessary prerequisite for successful risk taking. As you let go of old structures, perhaps you will discover that you miss the friendly, familiar babble of the gang at the water cooler. Friends may say you're crazy to change jobs. The fear of failing may seize and shake your convictions. At the same time, you may be exhilarated about the opportunity to test yourself, to enjoy some excitement and adventure.

Ambivalence is the push and pull between the desire to approach and the desire to avoid. One day you may think, "Of course, I can change fields. Lots of people do it. It can't be so difficult." The next day, or even minute, you are convinced that "There are too many unknowns. I'm better off staying put."

Both feelings are valid. Careless risk takers need to think through the difficulties ahead before they take action. Anxious risk takers, on the other hand, need to look for the pluses. Rather than focusing on just one set of possible outcomes, try to keep risk taking in balance by considering all of the pluses and minuses. Fear balanced by excitement and purpose offers the emotional balance that planned risk taking requires.

Don't be overly alarmed by the first few stages of risk taking. They are usually the most frightening. Once in action, you will find the situation less fearful.

Feeling Too Much Anxiety

If the prospect of undertaking a change is so great that your stomach is constantly churning, you can't sleep, you have constant headaches, or you feel you're developing an ulcer, your body, in its wisdom, is telling you to forgo the risk. Don't persist in the face of pervasive anxiety.

Milton, a highly skilled rehabilitation counselor, was approached by a prospective partner to start an executive recruitment agency. For weeks before making the move, he went straight to bed immediately after dinner and pulled the sheets over his head. He tried to make light of it by brushing off his exhaustion as the terror anyone might feel at starting a new venture. But, in his personal and professional life, Milton had undertaken many risks before and had never felt this way. Clearly, his physical response was evoked by something else. He later discovered that the hard-sell, aggressive style required for executive recruiting was not for him. His underlying fears turned out to be prophetic. The difference in basic values and counseling styles between the two partners proved to be such a handicap that within five months both had agreed to disband.

Yvonne had a similar experience. She applied to a school of social work. Soon after being accepted, she developed a chronic headache. It disappeared the day she called the school's director to say she wouldn't be attending. Yvonne's body was correctly telling her that she didn't have the temperament for social work. She felt she would need more autonomy and would get too involved in her clients' problems. Today, Yvonne is a happy and successful free-lance journalist.

The moral seems clear: If your body tells you to "stop," consider rejecting the risk. Doing so may also be a risk—the risk of trusting your deep feelings more than some abstract notion of what ought to be best for you. Lists or inventories may be useful in making risky decisions, but ultimately they won't work unless feelings are also considered. One ulcer can counterbalance a bigger paycheck any day.

Feeling Too Little Anxiety

Little anxiety and few negative feelings about an impending risk can be just as debilitating. What's wrong? Well, first of all, the risk may not really be a risk. Perhaps what you are moving to has many virtues and a highly predictable outcome. Almost no danger is involved. Or maybe the negative aspects of your current situation are so overwhelming that there seems to be no other choice. If everything about your present job is unbearable, then the decision to change may feel like a compulsion rather than a decision. Without a sense of choice, there is little ambivalence. or you may be avoiding, rationalizing, or denying the anxiety you actually do feel.

It is only natural that the prospect of change should toss you back and forth between fear and hope, exhilaration and anxiety, panic and a sense of adventure. These mixed feelings need to surface and be accepted.

The key to avoiding potential potholes is to set tentative career goals before you explore new roads.

Stage 4: Preparing for Risk

It's important to prepare for career change. You will want to set tentative goals, assess your personal characteristics, explore your occupational options, network, figure out how to manage your money, establish support systems, and lay down safety nets. These are the same steps, dealt with in more detail, that you read about in chapter 8.

Setting Tentative Goals

The key to avoiding potential potholes is to set tentative career goals before you explore new roads. Goals force you to focus on what you really want. Only then can you exploit opportunity and luck to

achieve them. So what do you want to do? Where do you want to go professionally? What kind of person do you want to become? As you think over your responses, remember to be open and creative. Years from now, as you review your life, what regrets do you imagine you might have?

Considering what you might do is an important step in increasing your job satisfaction. Explore the whole range of possibilities before you. Fantasize about the ultimate goal, your "star." If you could do anything in the world, what would it be? When you were a child, what did you dream of becoming when you grew up? Dare to admit your fondest fantasy. Identifying this dream or star will help you set goals that are in tune with your inner self, that will help you identify what is really important to you.

Try this Guided Fantasy Exercise to help you clarify your career goals. Close your eyes and imagine yourself working at your ideal occupation and living your ideal lifestyle. Describe your whole day in detail including getting to work, work tasks and surroundings, and evening activities. Pay particular attention to the details of your home and work environments, your duties at work, your leisure activities, and your feelings about your various activities as well as the people you encounter. Then ask yourself what made you excited and happy about your work and other activities? What made you frustrated, resentful, unhappy, or bored? Your positive and negative feelings will help you identify the kind of work and lifestyle you want.

What kind of occupations would enable you to pursue your life purpose? For example, if your purpose is to promote family harmony, you could express your mission by being a social worker, a family living teacher, a writer, a counselor, a psychologist, a religious leader, a mediation lawyer, or a full-time parent. If you are not sure what your purpose is, review your response to the activities described under Purpose in chapter 3 or identify a long-time dream or longing. This will be compatible with your purpose.

Once you know what you want, you will be more willing to take the risks necessary to achieve your goals. So don't underestimate yourself or what you can attain. Also, don't let money, or the lack of it, influence your career goals at this stage.

Write all of your ideas in a notebook. Write down everything you want to do, be, or have. The sky is the limit. Don't be inhibited by seemingly unrealistic objectives. Select three to five of your dreams that are most important, that you are committed to accomplishing within the next year, and the ones you are most excited about. State why you want to achieve these goals, when you expect to realize them, and the benefits of reaching each goal.

As you assess personal characteristics and occupational options, you may want to revise these goals. Career planning is an ongoing process that is constantly subject to review and revision as you learn more about yourself and the world around you. So consider these goals as guideposts that can be rebuilt throughout the planning stage. You, like most Questers, must be able to balance tentativeness with commitment.

Getting to Know Yourself

Selecting a satisfying career and lifestyle requires a very good understanding of yourself. Complete the exercises that follow. They will help you assemble an accurate picture of yourself— your interests, needs, accomplishments, and other personal characteristics. Uncovering a you that you didn't even know existed can be fun and exciting. Because there are no right and wrong answers, here's your chance to be honest about who you really are.

Identifying Your Interests

Interests are simply likes and dislikes, preferences or distastes. You can identify your interests by taking an interest inventory or by analyzing activities you enjoy.

Psychological tests, administered and interpreted by a competent psychologist or counselor, can be useful for some. They can help illuminate potential new directions, reveal valuable insights, and add a sense of certainty about your plans. Many individuals, however, can identify their own interests by completing exercises like those described below.

First, think about your leisure activities, school, and continuing education courses. Remember those that you liked and excelled at. Review job accomplishments you are particularly proud of and review why. Following this, make two lists. One should contain at least a dozen activities you enjoy; the other lists activities you detest. Next to each item, note why each activity is appealing or unappealing. Now classify your interests into patterns. The two exercises below will help you do this.

Activities I enjoy	Activities I do not enjoy
1.	1.
2.	2.
3.	3.
4.	4.
5.	5.
6.	6.
7.	7.
8.	8.
9.	9.
10.	10.

Exercise 1

An easy way to classify interests is to arrange them on the basis of work tasks you enjoy. Most work tasks involve working with data, people, things, and ideas. Read over the descriptions of the four work tasks and rank them in order of preference, one representing your highest preference and four your lowest.

___ Data tasks are impersonal tasks that involve working with people indirectly (for example, with files, accounts, business communications) or that involve formulating and/or following schedules, directions, business operating procedures, etc.

___ Ideas tasks are intrapersonal tasks involving insights, theories, and new ways of expressing something, perhaps with words, paint, equations, or music.

___ People tasks are interpersonal tasks such as caring for, educating, entertaining, serving, persuading, or directing others.

___ Things tasks are nonpersonal tasks involving machines, tools, living things, and materials such as food, wood, or metal.

The tasks usually blend together in varying amounts. Moreover, although any occupation will involve some work with data, ideas, people, and things, only one or two of the work tasks will typically predominate.

Exercise 2

According to the research of John Holland, a vocational psychologist, people can be categorized as one of six personality types: Realistic, Conventional, Enterprising, Social, Artistic, or Investigative. The personality types seek out corresponding occupational environments based on their interests. Because it is unlikely that people fall solely into one of the major personality types, a coding system has been devised to indicate the individual's primary and secondary types. These codes are reflected in three-letter combinations—each letter corresponding to the first letter of one of the six types. For example, a code of ESA would indicate you are most like the Enterprising type, next most like the Social type, and third most like the Artistic type.

Read over the descriptions of the personality types and then rank them according to which types you believe you are. Then translate your three highest types into a three-letter code.

___ *Realistic* (R). You enjoy activities that involve the precise, ordered use of objects, tools, machines, and animals. Examples are agricultural, electrical, manual, physical, or mechanical activities. Characteristic occupations are auto engineer, surveyor, carpenter, typesetter, and fish and game warden.

___ *Conventional* (C). You enjoy activities that involve the precise, ordered use of data, such as keeping records, filing materials, or organizing numerical and statistical data. Characteristic occupations are usually in the clerical, computational, or business fields, such as accountant, credit manager, office worker, library assistant, or data processing clerk.

__ *Enterprising* (E). You enjoy activities that involve interaction with other people to reach organizational goals or for economic gain. Leadership, interpersonal, and persuasive activities dominate your interests. Characteristic occupations are market analyst, lawyer, personnel recruiter, or manager of enterprises such as restaurants or retail outlets.

__ *Social* (S). You enjoy activities that involve interaction with others for enjoyment or to inform, train, develop, care, or educate. Characteristic occupations are claims adjuster, social worker, teacher, minister, interviewer, therapist, or community recreation administrator.

__ *Artistic* (A). You enjoy activities that involve the use of various living and nonliving materials to create art forms and products. Activities and objects related to language, art, music, drama, and writing fascinate you. Characteristic occupations are drama coach, dance teacher, musician, writer, interior decorator, photographer, or artist.

__ *Investigative* (I). You enjoy activities that involve the exploration and examination of physical, biological, and cultural objects to understand and control them. Scientific and mathematical activities are usually found here. Characteristic occupations are economist, internist, chemist, psychologist, actuary, dentist, computer operator, or engineer.

Write your three-letter code here: _____.

Summarizing Your Interests

To summarize your interests, go back over the exercises. Look for patterns. What interests keep appearing? Identify your interests in the categories described above (data, people, things, or ideas or Holland's types). Have you found any surprises in your interest profile or is it much as you expected? Relate your interests to occupations you would like to explore. For example, if you like activities that involve interpersonal tasks (Exercise 1) or if you characterize yourself as a Social type (Exercise 2), you may be satisfied in occupations such as social worker, therapist, or teacher.

The Work Wheel can help you view your interests with occupational options. The body of the Work Wheel shows the locations of 23 job fields (groups of similar occupations) that encompass all 12,741 occupations recognized by the U.S. Department of Labor in the fourth edition of *Dictionary of Occupational Titles* (DOT). Job field names and locations (A to W on the wheel) suggest differences in the work that is done and the people who do it. Although the jobs in a field differ in their wheel locations, most are near the points shown. A job field's location is based on its primary work tasks—working with data, ideas, people, or things. Arrows show that work tasks often heavily involve both people and things (◄●►) or data and ideas ( ). Related Holland types are indicated around the edge of the map.

You can see the relationship between the four work tasks (data, ideas, people, things) and Holland's types, shown on the periphery of the wheel. For example, Enterprising (Business Contact) occupations are located at the upper left. Data work tasks and, to some extent, people work tasks predominate. Investigative (Science) occupations are located at the lower right. Ideas work tasks and, to some extent, things work tasks dominate.

Work Wheel

© 1986 by the American College Testing Program, Iowa City, Iowa.
Adapted and reprinted with permission.

Your interests can be translated into spokes on the wheel. Identify your interests on the wheel and then investigate occupations in the related job fields. For example, if you have an ESC code (spokes 1, 2, 3, 4, 5, 12), you might wish to look into job fields in spokes 1, 2, 3, 4, 5, and 12.

This is a very simple diagram, but it is a start—a way of beginning to look at occupational alternatives. However, it is important to keep in mind that exploring occupational options is much more complicated. A number of other personality and work world factors should be understood and considered when investigating options.

Think about your interests as you go through the rest of the activities in this chapter. Add each like or dislike that comes to mind to the list you created before and then modify your interest profile if necessary.

Probing Your Needs

Needs form the basis of behavior. Because your behavior is composed of actions designed to fulfill or reduce those needs, understanding them can explain a good deal about your internal conflicts, tensions, anxieties, or stresses. Such unpleasant feelings are often the result of unfulfilled needs or, alternatively, a conflict among needs. To be satisfied, you must find outlets that satisfy your needs.

The range of human needs is limited only by the imagination, but some needs contribute more to job satisfaction than others. As you read through the following list of 23 needs that contribute to job satisfaction, check the ones you consider important. Then complete the questions at the end. You will soon see a pattern in your reasons for wanting to work.

___ 1. *Achievement.* You like the challenge of mastering a difficult task. Work gives you a feeling of accomplishment.

___ 2. *Adventure.* You hunger for change, a fast pace, and excitement.

___ 3. *Altruism.* Helping others is important to you.

___ 4. *Associates.* You value contact with fellow workers.

___ 5. *Autonomy.* It is important for you to have control over your work, to work in your own way as quickly or as slowly as you wish, to be free from constraints imposed by others.

___ 6. *Challenge.* You desire work which has an acceptable level of difficulty, responsibility, and complexity, and which provides you with opportunities for mastery and achievement.

___ 7. *Competition.* You enjoy activities in which you can try to outperform others.

___ 8. *Creativity.* You like inventing new things, designing products, or developing ideas.

___ 9. *Economic returns.* You value work that pays well and enables you to buy the things you want.

___ 10. *Aesthetic.* Making beautiful objects and contributing to the beauty of the world are important to you.

___ 11. *Growth.* You enjoy jobs in which you can develop your talents and potential, learn new skills, innovate, and get things done without having to follow too-rigid regulations.

___ 12. *Intellectual stimulation.* The opportunity for independent thinking and to learn how and why things work is valuable to you.

___ 13. *Involvement.* You must be involved in and identify very closely with your job.

___ 14. *Management.* You enjoy planning and laying out work for others.

___ 15. *Power.* Decision-making responsibility over finances, people, and other resources in your field is an important plus.

___ 16. *Prestige.* You like work that gives you standing or recognition in the eyes of others and evokes both self-respect and the respect of others.

__ 17. *Religion.* It is important for you to adhere to a set of religious or moral principles.

__ 18. *Security.* You desire work that will provide you with the certainty of having a job even in hard times.

__ 19. *Supervisory relations.* Working under a supervisor who is fair and with whom you get along is a prime consideration.

__ 20. *Surroundings.* You value work that is carried out under pleasant conditions, not too hot or too cold, too noisy or too dirty.

__ 21. *Variety.* You need work that provides you with an opportunity to do different kinds of tasks.

__ 22. *Way of life.* You like work that allows you to live the way you choose and to be the person you wish to be.

__ 23. *Purpose.* You need work that gives you meaning and satisfaction and helps you express your real self.

Summarizing Your Needs

Once you have checked off the needs that apply to you, look back over the list and pick the top six needs you most desire from a job. Rank these from one (most desired) to six (less desired). Now go back to your scores on The Job Satisfaction Questionnaire and rank the six job facets that you believe are most important to you. Also rank the six facets that you feel are least important to you. Did you rate the needs that are most important to you VS? If not, these facets will represent unfulfilled needs that have probably spurred you on to a career change. Again, rank the six needs you would like most from a job. Then note the six that are least important. Also identify specific life experiences that helped you satisfy these needs. For example, if you have a need for autonomy, list the activities in your life that give you a sense of autonomy such as being in charge of the car pool, supervising five employees, scheduling softball games, or managing a bank. In addition, describe the feelings you experience when you are in control.

Pay attention to your needs because they represent job facets that you consider important.

Assessing Your Accomplishments and Skills

Interests are frequently confused with abilities. While you may enjoy doing those things you do well, the relationship between interests and abilities is not necessarily high. People with high literary interests, for example, are not necessarily capable of producing a novel, poem, or play. They may simply enjoy reading. Prospective employers are interested mainly in what you have accomplished through a lifetime of paid and unpaid experiences—your track record. Evaluating your experiences as objectively as possible will add new dimensions to the complex and emerging picture of you.

First, look at what you have accomplished in job-related or indirectly job-related endeavors. For example, if you have worked as a controller, your job-related accomplishments could include several things: designed a computerized reporting system used by three subsidiary companies; worked closely with outside consultants to rationalize the use of microcomputers within the company; regulated inventory to reduce short-term interest charges incurred by the company; or taught a financial class to graduate students at a local university. Remember how much you enjoyed these activities. Use action words to describe them: designed, researched, trained, supervised, directed, wrote, managed, created, negotiated, prepared, etc. Make the list as long as possible. Ask your partner, close friend, or a colleague to help you identify these accomplishments. Be sure not to neglect the successes of subordinates that were under your direction or supervision. These, too, belong in your list of accomplishments. Think back over your career carefully. What was done better because of you? What would not have been done without you? What do you consider your most important or most satisfying job-related accomplishments?

My Job-Related Accomplishments:

1. _____
   _____
   _____

2. _____
   _____
   _____

3. _____
   _____
   _____

4. _____
   _____
   _____

5. _____
   _____
   _____

6. _____
   _____
   _____

7. _____
   _____
   _____

8. _____
   _____
   _____

9. _____
   _____
   _____

10. _____
    _____
    _____

Next, include those educational accomplishments of which you are most proud. Unless you have only recently graduated, do not include high school accomplishments. List college courses and activities, graduate work, and continuing education. Include both direct and indirect educational accomplishments—those that related directly to your studies and those, such as extracurricular activities, performed while attending school.

My Educational Accomplishments:

1. _____
   _____
   _____

2. _____
   _____
   _____

3. _____
   _____
   _____

4. _____
   _____
   _____

5. _____
   _____
   _____

Also list civic accomplishments. These are achievements directly related to hobbies and civic, charitable, or religious activities. They should relate to, or demonstrate your competence in, some aspect of work. For example, a major contribution to a fund-raising effort can demonstrate organizational or sales ability.

My Civic Accomplishments:

1. _____
   _____
   _____
   _____

2. _____
   _____
   _____
   _____

3. _____
   _____
   _____
   _____

4. _____
   _____
   _____
   _____

5. _____
   _____
   _____

You may also have an untapped talent that can be turned into a new occupation. Ask friends what dormant talents they suspect you possess. You may even want to take a battery of tests from a psychologist or career counselor which can reveal a wide range of possibilities.

My Untapped Talents:

1. _____
   _____
   _____

2. _____
   _____
   _____

3. _____
   _____
   _____

4. _____
   _____
   _____
   _____

5. _____
   _____
   _____
   _____

The next step is to analyze each of the accomplishments you
have listed. Consider them one by one, paying special attention to the skills, knowledge, or personal attributes that
enabled you to achieve them. Think about your personality as
well as the specific skills and abilities you have acquired.
These accomplishments might include the ability to program
a computer, to use insurance actuarial tables, or to interpret
psychological tests. Personality traits might include patience,
willingness to work hard, ability to handle people, or logical
thinking capability.

Finally, list your weaknesses. These often turn out to involve
tasks you dislike doing. For example, you may feel so uncomfortable at meetings that you become inarticulate. Or you may
hate the paperwork that goes with your job so you put it off
and get backlogged.

My Weaknesses:

1. _____
   _____
   _____

2. _____
   _____
   _____

3. _____
   _____
   _____

4. _____
   _____

5. _____
   _____
   _____

Figure out workable strategies to reduce your weaknesses. For instance, to improve your performance at meetings take a speech course or join Toastmasters. To straighten out your paperwork, set aside 30 minutes each day as catch-up time.

Assessing Personal Characteristics

Taking stock of your other personal characteristics is another essential step in the search for self-knowledge. Certain characteristics seem to be essential in almost all kinds of work. Being responsible, efficient, resourceful, flexible, cooperative, objective, and sensible are basic to a professional attitude. They are necessary traits for almost any occupation. On the other hand, some personal characteristics are very important only in specific occupations and may actually be undesirable in others. While being a loner may be fine for a scientist spending long hours on research, it is not particularly suitable for a construction worker who has to perform as part of a team.

To discover your other personal characteristics, make a list of about 10 that best describe you. Use adjectives such as: active, assertive, attractive, calm, careful, competent, confident, curious, discreet, democratic, eager, energetic, enthusiastic, helpful, humorous, loyal, mature, obliging, open-minded, precise, sociable, stable, strong-minded, tolerant, and warm.

Ten Characteristics That Best Describe Me:

1. _____   6. _____

2. _____   7. _____

3. _____   8. _____

4. _____   9. _____

5. _____   10. _____

Identifying Other Strengths

The following exercise will help you pinpoint your many other strengths. First, analyze your successes. Identify at least three successes that, over the past five years, gave you a great deal of satisfaction. They can be drawn from any area of your life (for example, substituted for son's soccer coach and team won, earned 15 credits at your community college). Now (a) identify what gave you positive feelings and (b) list the skills and abilities you used to accomplish these.

Success	What Gave Me the Positive Feeling?	What Skills/Abilities Did I Use?
Example: Substituted for son's soccer coach.	Working with eager boys, helping coach, contributing to team's first win of season.	Organizing, fast thinking, encouraging others, being enthusiastic, working with parents.

Success	What Gave Me the Positive Feeling?	What Skills/Abilities Did I Use?
1. _____	_____	_____
	_____	_____
	_____	_____
	_____	_____
2. _____	_____	_____
	_____	_____
	_____	_____
	_____	_____
3. _____	_____	_____
	_____	_____
	_____	_____
	_____	_____

Next, identify the skills you possess in three categories: personal skills, transferable skills, and professional/job skills.

1. *Personal skills.* Personal skills are personality traits that can be beneficial for some kinds of jobs, but not for others. They

are part of your nature, but they can be developed. For example, flexibility would be beneficial when working with a community recreational program, but detrimental in jobs requiring strict accounting practices. You can learn to become more flexible. Circle the following personal skills that apply to you, and add any other skills you possess but which are not listed.

Adventurous	Ambitious	Analytical	Assertive
Businesslike	Competitive	Confident	Conservative
Cooperative	Courageous	Creative	Curious
Discreet	Efficient	Energetic	Enthusiastic
Formal	Frank	Friendly	Helpful
Honest	Independent	Industrious	Intelligent
Inventive	Kind	Likable	Loyal
Motivated	Patient	Persevering	Poised
Positive	Precise	Quick	Relaxed
Reliable	Sensitive	Sociable	Stable
Tactful	Thorough	Tolerant	Trustworthy
Unassuming	Understanding	Versatile	Warm
_____	_____	_____	_____
_____	_____	_____	_____

Now list five of your best personal skills.

1. _____

2. _____

3. _____

4. _____

5. _____

2. *Transferable skills.* Transferable skills are generic and can be used in a variety of jobs. Once you have learned a transferable skill, you can apply it in different job settings. They can be broken down into three areas: (a) communication skills, (b) organizational skills, and (c) technical/physical skills.

Communication skills can be categorized into writing, helping, and creating categories. Circle the following writing skills that apply to you and add any additional skills that are not listed.

Analyzing	Clerical	Creative Writing	Editing
Foreign Languages	Formatting	Letter Writing	Note Taking
Persuading	Reading	Record Keeping	Report Writing
Researching	Summarizing	Technical Writing	Translating
Typing	_____	_____	_____
_____	_____	_____	_____

Circle the following helping skills that apply to you and add any additional skills that are not listed.

Advising	Arbitrating	Articulating	Coaching
Convincing	Counseling	Empathizing	Interpreting
Mentoring	Motivating	Negotiating	Parenting
Persuading	Public Speaking	Reading	Teaching
Training	Supporting	Understanding	_____
_____	_____	_____	_____
_____	_____	_____	_____

Circle the following creating skills that apply to you and add any additional skills that are not listed.

Acting	Aesthetic Sense	Composing	Cooking
Designing	Drawing	Illustrating	Imagining
Interior Decorating	Inventing	Landscaping	Observing
Painting	Photography	Playing Musical Instruments	Sculpting
Singing	Writing	_____	_____
_____	_____	_____	_____
_____	_____	_____	_____

b. Organizational skills can be categorized into managing and analyzing skills. Circle the following managing skills that apply to you and add any additional skills that are not listed.

Accomplishing	Assertiveness	Classifying	Controlling
Decision Making	Delegating	Detail-Oriented	Effectiveness
Filing	Follow-Through	Organizing	Precision-Oriented
Problem Solving	Scheduling	Supervising	Systematizing
_____	_____	_____	_____
_____	_____	_____	_____

Circle the following analyzing skills that apply to you and add any additional skills that are not listed.

Analyzing	Budgeting	Calculating	Comparing
Counting	Critiquing	Evaluating	Financial Saving
Integrating	Interpreting Statistics	Investigating	Investment Planning
Remembering Numbers	Reviewing	Thinking	_____
_____	_____	_____	_____
_____	_____	_____	_____

c. Technical/physical skills can be categorized into technical and physical areas. Circle the following technical skills that apply to you and add any additional skills that are not listed.

Auto Repair	Blueprint Reading	Building	Cartography
Computer	Construction	Drafting	Graphics
Keypunching	Laboratory	Mechanical Electronics Drawing	Medical Laboratory
Programming	Tool-Oriented	Working with Machinery	

Circle the following physical skills that apply to you and add any additional skills that are not listed.

20/20 Vision	Active	Acute Hearing	Athletic
Assembling	Coordination	Exploration	Eye-Hand Coordination
Finger or Manual Dexterity	Physical Strength	Sensitivity to Touch	Smell, Taste

Now list 10 of your best transferable skills.

1. _____   6. _____

2. _____   7. _____

3. _____   8. _____

4. _____   9. _____

5. _____   10. _____

3. *Professional/job skills.* Professional skills are related to a specific occupation and are usually very generalized (for example, knowing the steps to take when inspecting a building, knowing how to operate a printing press, knowing the names of good customers on a sales route, developing a grade six science program for an IBM computer). You may use generic skills in developing professional skills (for example, a good memory will help you remember customers' names on a sales route).

Now list five professional skills you possess.

1. _____

2. _____

3. _____

4. _____

5. _____

Now, summarize your skills. List 15 of the above skills that you possess and would like to use in a job. Consider those that would give you positive feelings.

1. _____	6. _____	11. _____
2. _____	7. _____	12. _____
3. _____	8. _____	13. _____
4. _____	9. _____	14. _____
5. _____	10. _____	15. _____

Next, investigate prospective jobs where you will be able to use your skills. You will be pleasantly surprised to see that you possess many skills that are required for certain jobs. You may also wish to identify skills you would like to develop further. Indicate plans you have to enhance these skills.

Completing the Picture

Little by little, you've put together a wonderful picture of yourself. Nobody has precisely the same combination of qualities. Look back at how you have evaluated various aspects of yourself. Decide how your interests, needs, accomplishments, and other personal strengths add up. What pattern do they form? Which qualities would you like to use in a job? What would you like to change?

To synthesize this information, complete the following diagram—My Ideal Job. On the diagram, indicate the following: (1) Your purpose or dream; (2) Skills and knowledge you would like to use on your job: (3) Needs and values you would like to have satisfied by your job; (4) Interests you would like reflected by your job; (5) Your desired work environment and locale; (6) Job tasks or duties you would like to perform most of the time; and (7) Amount of responsibility you would like to exercise and your desired salary.

The next step is looking at career options. You may be surprised to discover just how many are available.

Investigating Career Options

As you read and worked through the preceding exercises, you engaged in focused self-exploration and soul searching. Up to now, you have given most of your attention to your private world—what you dream of, need, want, are, and could become. Starting there is appropriate, but stopping there is inadequate. Now it's time to look at reality. Before you decide to change jobs or make other modifications in your life, you should investigate the options you are considering as well as other alternatives.

Before making a career move, determine if other unrelated aspects of your life are having a detrimental effect on your job performance and attitude. Are you missing an enjoyable and intimate relationship with a partner or spouse? Do you have satisfying leisure activities? If not, you may discover that one of the reasons for your dissatisfaction is the gap in other areas of your life. Feeling lonely or having an unhappy marriage can cause anyone's attitude and performance to drop. Maybe this is the time to get involved in a community activity or hobby. Doing so can add new, rewarding dimensions to your life that may indirectly make your job more satisfying.

You may have decided that, at least for a while, you can get what you want by remaining in the same company. As a result, you may want to make some adjustments to your current position or transfer to another type of job. Let's take a look at each of the options.

Living with Your Present Job

A key way to make job changes is to gain the recognition and support of the political powers who affect it. To do so, you must understand your job's political environment and how to handle it effectively. Office politics need not be vicious or self-serving. By playing along, you are being sensitive to how key people react—people in roles that greatly affect your work. How much power you have is determined by both the formal organization (the organizational chart) and the informal organization (the actual relationships that exist among individuals). Understanding the formal relationships is easy, but figuring out the informal relationships that exist in your organization requires you to be more observant. What roles do people really play? Who is involved in outside activities with whom? The combination of key individuals' information sources, pipelines, seniority, personalities, and relationships all decide how much power they have.

As you try to evaluate the politics of your work environment, ask yourself these key questions: What kinds of people are my bosses? What are their backgrounds? What are their goals? How do they live? What are their beliefs? Remember that religious, social, and ethnic backgrounds can be terribly important. After you have identified who holds the power and what kind of people they are, you will have to examine whether you can reasonably expect their support.

To discover how your boss feels about you and how you think he or she would rate your performance, score yourself from A to E (A representing very well and E representing very poor) on the following questions:

___How well do I perform my overall job?

___How well do I know what my boss wants?

___How well do I help him or her achieve his performance goals?

___How well do I help do his or her job effectively?

___ How sensitive am I to my boss's biases?

___ How well do I communicate with him or her?

___ How loyal do I feel toward my boss?

___ How proud is the boss to have me on his or her team?

___ How well do I set priorities and work toward them?

___ How well do I anticipate my supervisor's needs?

___ How motivated am I?

___ How well do I meet deadlines?

___ How well do I communicate?

___ How effective am I in leading and participating in meetings?

The answers should help you identify your strengths and weaknesses, discover ways to do better work, and present a more favorable image. Here are some other things you can do.

First, develop a program to overcome the deficiencies that you noted in this performance rating. Second, make sure that you are devoting enough time to highest-priority projects. If not, plan a work schedule that will get those high-priority items off your desk quickly and efficiently. Third, improve your conduct in meetings. Be prepared, contribute ideas, and, without compromising your values, try not to take controversial stands that will antagonize the most powerful committee members. Fourth, motivate yourself. Maybe you have become complacent about your job. You have nothing to lose by making an intensive effort to improve your performance, but you could have a lot to gain. Most of all, you could considerably improve your management skills. Effective self-improvement can give you tools that will be keys to the rest of your career. These improved skills will come in handy when you do decide to move on.

Having top management on your side can make you considerably more promotable and increase the challenges that come your way. If the physical structure of your company makes this impossible, explore ways to creatively redesign or restructure your job. Faced with similar situations, to get the challenge they crave, some Questers have virtually rewritten their responsibilities. Try to develop your own challenges. Visualize what would happen if another highly motivated person was promoted to your job. How would he or she tackle it? What challenges would another person find in your job? If someone else in your position could contribute more to the company, your lack of challenge may lie in your attitude or performance. Try to be indispensable. If it's not possible to develop challenges on your current job—and sometimes it isn't—then it's time to consider another job or a transfer.

Changing Jobs Within Your Company

Sometimes it's more desirable to change positions within your company than to seek a new job outside of it. Doing so is far less risky than trying to make the transition to a new occupation and a new company. If you know your skills and goals, and can present yourself effectively to the right people, you might be able to move to a different position in the same organization. Determine if there might be another position within the company that could satisfy your needs. The next step is to develop a favorable image with the key person there. At an appropriate time, make your interest known. You may have to be patient, but if you've made a favorable impression, you could be in luck.

You have the best chance of finding a good job in the company if you anticipate, and keep several steps ahead of, any major changes that may occur. Otherwise, you could find yourself competing with many for very few positions. As companies pare down their workforces, it's even more important to be alert to your organization's plans.

Changing Occupational Fields

A change in occupational fields will usually require a lot of exploration. Initially, at least, it will probably also offer lower pay. But even though your success will involve many more unknowns, starting anew needn't mean starting at the bottom. If you have launched a creative assault on the job market, you can usually find new challenges that equal or better the ones you previously enjoyed. Even if you change occupational fields, your past experiences and knowledge will hardly be wasted.

If changing fields is your choice, and it has been successful for a number of Questers, research your options thoroughly. Bear in mind that people in the prospective field may try to dissuade you because you may not have the appropriate background. Before giving up, determine if their warnings are valid. Find out how many of your personal, professional, and transferable skills will fit the occupations in this field.

Going into Business for Yourself

Maybe you have already considered going into business for yourself. The number of self-employed people is increasing steadily. Part of this trend toward self-employment is caused by recessionary dips. As people find themselves unemployed, laid off, or unable to find desirable work elsewhere, many carve out their own niches. Business people who plan well, cut corners, and know how to work hard do very well indeed. Opportunities abound.

When you create a business, you become the employer, controlling your work and lifestyle, and choosing where you live and work. Research on job satisfaction indicates that self-employed people are among the happiest workers. Most self-employed Questers are living proof. Questers who are in business for themselves tend to score very high on The Job Satisfaction Questionnaire and The Job Involvement Questionnaire.

Like many Questers, people who go into business for themselves usually have a strong need for autonomy, possess a broad range of talents, desire variety and flexibility, and are not afraid to take chances. They are able to get along well with others and have the perseverance, self-discipline, energy, and stamina to work long hours to carry them over the rough spots. Money is not their primary motive, although, in the long run, many do well financially. If you have dreamed of being your own boss, don't let the fear of losing a steady paycheck stop you. Economic security is a personal possession. Relegating it to others is a mistake. Consider the hundreds of thousands of people who sweated out years of stagnation in boring jobs only to have inflation make a nightmare out of retirement.

Broadening Your Career Horizons

Regardless of whether you decide to change jobs or stay put, you should expand your thinking about your career. Figure out your options, then pursue them. Researching occupations will not only reduce uncertainty by providing information but will also temper fantasies. Try to explore, in depth, at least ten occupational options in at least three diverse fields.

As you study each occupation, consider the nature of the working conditions, training, and educational requirements, and how you can acquire these. Examine the pay and fringe benefits, avenues for entering, employment outlook, opportunities for advancement, related occupations, and advantages and disadvantages perceived by people in these fields. Compare each to your personal characteristics, aspirations, and desired lifestyle. Following are some resources to use in determining your suitability for an occupation.

Printed materials. Directories, pamphlets, and books contain invaluable information on occupations. The more popular directories, which are availabe in the reference section of your local library, include the *Occupational Outlook Handbook, Dictionary of Occupational Titles, Encyclopedia of Careers and Vocational Guidance, Encyclopedia of Careers and Work Issues,* and *the Career Information Center.* Libraries also have hundreds of books and vertical files that are filled with updated information about specific occupations and educational institutions.

Rehearsing. Besides researching an occupation, why not try it out? Obtain an evening or weekend job, or work as a volunteer or intern during your next vacation. Consider taking a job on probation while you enjoy a year-long sabbatical. "Shadow" someone who's doing the job already. To get a clearer picture of what the work is really like, spend a day or two at his or her side. Try out jobs related to hobbies or launch an interest you can pursue after retirement.

Interviews. Another good way to collect information is to talk to people in the occupation in which you are interested. These could be friends, relatives, partners, contacts you make over the telephone, or colleagues in professional, trade, or business associations. Prepare carefully. Include the following questions: Describe a typical day or week of your work? What do you like most about your position? What do you like least? What kind of challenges or problems do you deal with? What skills do you need in order to get employed in this field or by your organization? What is the future for this field? What are the opportunities for advancement within the organization? Field? What is the average salary range or hourly pay for this type of position? How did you get your position? How does your company compare to other similar firms in the field? Who else would you suggest I speak to about this kind of work? May I tell her that you recommended I speak to her? Ask for referrals and advice. Follow up each meeting with a thank-you note. Informational interviews are valuable for many reasons. A great networking tool, they establish contacts. They can also uncover a prospective employer's needs and lead to a subsequent phone call asking you to fulfill them. A former freelance writer who learned that poor writing costs companies money now conducts writing workshops for executives. Conduct as many informational interviews as possible.

Computer guidance systems. If you'd like assistance with your career choices but are not willing or able to talk to a counselor or psychologist, try one of the occupational information systems available at some career counseling centers.

Getting the Education You Need

Every occupation, including self-employment, requires some education or training, formal or informal. Investigate the length and type of program required, alternative education, or training routes and their suitability. College broadens the mind and teaches much-needed skills, but you can also gain appropriate knowledge from workshops, seminars, night school courses, independent study, correspondence school, on-the-job training, or an apprenticeship. Before deciding to enter a new field, consult with professionals and company executives to learn what kind of skills you need to become employable, where you can get this training, how long it will take, what it will cost, and if financial or other assistance is available.

Don't despair if college is the preferred route. Thousands of adults return to school every year to discover that they are excellent students. Because they often have clearer goals and more experience than they did when they were young, mature adults often earn higher grade point averages than younger students.

If you believe you can't afford a college education, consider that financial aid for adults is available. Corporations will often pay for part or all of your schooling. Up-to-date pamphlets on financial aid are available in most libraries. Colleges and universities that do try to accommodate adults often offer some of the following options.

❖ *Part-time study.* In addition to evening and summer programs, some schools now offer weekend college. Courses are conducted from Friday afternoon through Sunday evening several times a month.

❖ *Experiential learning.* A few colleges and universities will accept some type of credit for work or volunteer experience. Proper documentation (usually in portfolio form with samples) is required to determine the number of credits acceptable. Although it is next to impossible to earn such credit at the graduate level, this can put you several steps ahead in an undergraduate program.

❖ *Exams for credit.* You can be tested on your knowledge and skills in areas where you already have experience by taking an exam. Although most institutions limit the credit you can earn this way, allowance for up to a year's worth of credit is possible.

❖ *Credit through contract.* By devising your own curriculum, you may be able to earn a degree outside the classroom. The usual procedure is to draw up a mutually agreeable learning contract, specifying what will be learned and required to obtain credit.

❖ *Correspondence courses.* In addition to standard correspondence courses, consider radio or television courses and educational cassettes. Some universities are especially set up for "distance education." Find out about these.

Managing Your Money

How you manage your money will be vital to your success. Before changing or quitting jobs or returning to school, determine how long you can live without an income. How much will you need to live on and where will you get it?

If you are employed, financial planning will consist of estimating the expenses involved in a search. More planning is necessary if you are unemployed. You will eliminate a deadline controlled by finances alone if you allow yourself a certain amount of time, for example, six months. A careful review of expenses, financial strengths, and potential income may reveal that you can manage for several months without a salary.

Develop a budget that takes into account your net worth, monthly cash flow, and total job search expenses. To determine your assets, find out exactly what you can expect in pension funds, severance or other payments from your present employer, as well as unemployment benefits. Include income, savings, possible student loans, and assistance from relatives. What will you need to survive each month? (Consider housing, food, school, furniture, clothing, dry cleaning, medical insurance, recreation, car, and miscellaneous expenses.) Add 15 percent as a cushion. Can you lower your standards for a while? Create a survival budget and prepare for the worst by cutting out unnecessary expenses and saving religiously.

Careful planning and the willingness to live on less temporarily will stretch the amount of time you can go without a full-time job. As a result, you will have more time to find that ideal position.

Be open

to support.

Establishing Support Systems

Once you have decided to change jobs, don't try to be a hero and make the change entirely on your own. Be open to support. You'll feel better emotionally, intellectually, and even financially if you have help from close and supportive family or friends.

A reputable professional career counselor or industrial psychologist can also provide support and feedback, help you identify your needs and interests, give you accurate, up-to-date job and labor information, and also offer objective feedback. But a poor one costs time and money and may weaken your self confidence, so stick with an accredited professional. Set up a preliminary meeting to determine what service is provided and at what cost. Ask for references. Free or inexpensive counseling is readily available at colleges, continuing education centers, churches, and some organizations. You may also consider participating in workshops offered by these institutions.

From wherever you seek help, be careful not to be constrained by phrases like "you should" or "you ought to." While you may tolerate such comments from a partner or relative, be wary if a counselor or therapist lays this on you.

In the final analysis, go with your feelings. Even the most talented counselor can't make decisions for you or guarantee that you will find the dream job.

Laying Down Safety Nets

Few decisions are ironclad, but to protect yourself from surprises, build in a fail-safe or retreat position. Constructing a safety net will help reduce anxiety. Review your responses to the questions in the section called Describing the Barriers earlier in this chapter and consider the following: What is frightening about the change? What do you stand to lose? What barriers are preventing you from reaching your goals? What are some steps you can take to overcome them? Which individuals might help you reach them? What are your chances of success? Why? What are some possible positive and negative outcomes? What are the chances that the negative outcomes will occur? How can the odds be reduced? Do the positive outcomes outweigh the negative consequences? Do you still want to achieve your goal?

By preparing for the negative as well as the positive, you are developing a backup plan. Realizing that there are no right or wrong moves can also be helpful. Viewing a career mistake as a detour or growth opportunity may allay your uneasiness. After all, experience is really the best teacher.

Developing Positive Attitudes and Behaviors

Success is 15 percent aptitude and 85 percent attitude. It will be your attitude, not your aptitude, that will determine your success in your new venture. You are the actor and director of your life. You create your own script by the thoughts you think. Your love and respect for yourself, your hate and disgust with yourself, and your fears are perceived by individuals you meet. They then mirror or reflect these thoughts back to you. If you want to change your career and life for the better, it is essential to develop positive attitudes and behaviors. Practice some of the following:

❖ *Use positive statements about such things as being healthy, being in control, or being blessed.* Don't condemn, criticize, or complain. Think of ways to improve the situation. The big rewards are paid for finding the solution, not the difficulty. Avoid phrases such as, "I can't," "I'm too old," "I will never. . . ."

❖ *Think, act, and look, happy and successful.* You will begin to think, feel, and actually become happy and successful.

❖ *Monitor your "self talk."* Each time you catch yourself using a negative phrase, say, "Cancel, cancel," and replace the negative thought or statement with a positive one.

❖ *Read inspirational books and listen to positive message cassettes.*

❖ *Associate with positive, happy, people.* Stay clear of complainers.

❖ *Write down your negative thoughts or feelings.* Indicate why you feel this way. Then burn the paper or tear it and throw it away.

❖ *State and write affirmations that promote positive thinking.*

❖ *Take your mind off your problems.* Get involved in activities that let you focus your attention away from your problems. For example, go to a movie or concert, play a game of tennis, or invite friends over for dinner.

❖ *Greet others with a positive, cheerful statement.* Smile often. It generates enthusiasm, friendliness, and good will.

❖ *Look for and expect good things to happen to you.*

The following analogy, presented by Executive Development Systems Inc., illustrates how positive thinking works: *All the water in the world cannot sink a ship unless it gets inside of it.* Similarly, all the sorrow, fear, anxiety, frustration, jealousy, and worry in the world cannot sink you unless it gets inside your mind! To keep it out, fill your mind so full of happiness, positive and constructive thoughts, desired outcomes, and helpful ideas that there's no room for the negative to seep in.

Stage 5: *Narrowing* Your Options

The key to successful career management is to find a position that is compatible with your personal qualities and goals. To determine this, you will have to establish priorities and evaluate alternatives. The following checklist, which should be completed for each occupation you are considering, will help you narrow your options.

1.	I have the necessary intelligence and skills to do the work.	True	False
2.	The option is compatible with my needs, values, interests, and other personal characteristics.	True	False
3.	I can acquire the necessary knowledge and skills to do a good job.	True	False
4.	The occupation will give me a sense of meaning and purpose.	True	False
5.	I know how people in this occupation (or who are self-employed in this field) live on and off the job. I find this an acceptable lifestyle.	True	False

6. I can afford the training required for the job or I can obtain the necessary finances to go into business for myself.   True   False

7. I can imagine staying in this occupation for at least four years.   True   False

8. My spouse (or close friends) believes I can succeed at this kind of work.   True   False

9. My shortcomings will not be a problem (for example, health, vision, hearing, size, strength, personality traits).   True   False

10. I know where to obtain the necessary training or experience to enter this occupation or to become self-employed.   True   False

11. I have identified all the potential difficulties in preparing for and working in this field.   True   False

12. I know safeguards I can build in to protect myself from the difficulties or problems identified above.   True   False

Using Intellect and Intuition

To narrow your options even further, complete the following exercises which enable you to use both your intellect and intuition. Career options can be prioritized mathematically, for example, to determine the best ones for you. First, make a chart. Draw a series of vertical and horizontal lines so that the paper is composed of squares. At the top of the page, list all the criteria (one in each square) most important in a job. Include needs (income, responsibility, public image, creativity, challenge, achievement, variety, etc.), interests, skills, and the degree of perceived risk. Relocation possibilities, required study, lifestyle, and approval or disapproval of spouse or partner are other considerations to include. Down the left side of the page, list each occupational option. For each option, consider the criteria identified at the top of the page. If an option doesn't satisfy a criterion, place a minus (-) sign in the appropriate column. If the criterion exists, but not as much as desired, record a zero (0). Finally, if the criterion exists to a desired state, record a plus (+) sign. Add the points for each option and place them in a total column at the far right. The occupation with the most pluses will best meet the greatest number of criteria important to you. Study these numbers to determine why this option appears to be superior. If one option is not an obvious choice, review your criteria and make necessary adjustments.

What does your intuition tell you about these options? Listen carefully to your inner voice. Trust it. It instinctively knows what is best for you. If necessary, take time out to reflect on your priorities or try some exercises designed to help you tap into your intuition. Journal writing is one technique that helps a number of individuals sort out their feelings and thoughts.

Drawing or doodling is another technique that some use to help with decision making. You may wish to try it. Write out a question that clearly and simply states what you want to know or answer. Underneath your question, draw whatever comes to your mind or flows through your hands. Continue to draw until you have nothing to add to the picture. Then, keep on using your intuitive skills to interpret the meaning behind the drawing and the symbols within it. Note the sequence of steps. Pay particular attention to the thoughts and feelings you experience as you look at the picture, such as joy and and a sense of direction, or sadness and confusion.

Modifying Career Goals and Making a Choice

Now that you've gained additional insights into yourself and your work options, take a look at the career goals you set earlier. Are they realistic? Sufficiently ambitious? Just right? Are they consistent with the options you rated highest after investigating your personal characteristics and career alternatives? If not, you'll need to make some changes.

You should now be ready to make an occupational choice. Determine your first, second, and third occupational preferences. These may change as you gather additional information or as various circumstances in your environment change.

Attaining Your Goals

❖ *State your goal and deadline in specific terms.* Make sure your goal is consistent with your purpose or dream.

❖ *Verify that your goal will benefit both yourself and others.*

❖ *Write a paragraph indicating why you want to achieve this goal.* Include all the benefits of reaching your goal.

❖ *Identify all the obstacles or barriers that may keep you from reaching your goal.* Write down all the ways you can overcome these barriers.

❖ *Make a list.* Write down all the groups, people, organizations, resources, character traits, education, personal strengths, and tools you have at your disposal for assisting you in overcoming obstacles and reaching your goal.

❖ *Spell out a plan of action.* Create a step-by-step plan, a sequence of events that will lead to your goal. Make the first step something you can do today.

❖ *Solicit the support of a friend or relative.* Meet with him or her often to review your progress. Call on this person when you need a boost.

❖ *Remove all negative mental obstacles such as fear, worry, or anger.* Avoid phrases such as "I can't."

❖ *Think positive.* Use statements such as "I can be what I want to be," "I can overcome difficulties," and "I am proud of myself."

❖ *Set a schedule for completing your goal.* Every day make it a priority to do at least one action item related to achieving your goal. Use a daily organizer to plan activities that will enable you to reach your goal. Ask yourself, "Is what I'm doing or about to do moving me closer to my goal?"

❖ *Continually visualize the outcome you desire.* See yourself reaching your goal. If you find this difficult to do, try making a collage or taking a photograph depicting it. Imagine yourself living your goal today.

❖ *Embrace failure or rejection.* It can be a learning experience to move you toward your goal.

❖ *Keep mind, body, and spirit in peak condition.*

❖ *Review your goal periodically.* Feel free to modify it.

Stage 6: *Acting* on the Decision

Once you have made up your mind, take steps to realize your goal. Action requires developing a step-by-step method of attack. You will need to devise a well thought-out campaign to market yourself for the job, for establishing your own business, or for returning to school. It is helpful to create an action plan that answers the following four questions: Where do I begin? Whom do I need to see? When do I begin? How do I begin?

Because you and the world around you are constantly changing, your plans should be flexible. An exercise that can help you keep your plans open-ended is the Personal Map of the Future. Select three occupational goals and describe, on the map, the steps necessary to take this week, this month, this year, and thereafter to attain your goals. Consider possible barriers that might impede attainment of your goals and what you can do to overcome these.

Keeping possible barriers and safeguards in mind, write down your first-choice plans, indicating date or time limits, people involved, and resources required. Written plans are efficient; the act of recording each step will give you a handy timetable against which to assess your progress. Planning can also give you a greater sense of security and a better chance to control your life. Few people proceed immediately from starting point to goal. Many intermediate steps must be taken along the way. Be as specific as possible about what each step involves before you act on it. You might, for example, decide to go back to school before taking a job. In that case, find out about programs that give credit for experience or by examination. Whatever you finally decide, take time to write down each step. This will keep you motivated and moving.

Once you have made up your mind, act. Regardless of prevailing economic conditions, good jobs are always attainable. So don't use the state of the economy as an excuse.

The following section outlines basic job search skills. If you are interested in acquiring business planning skills, check the resource books in your local library or speak to small business resource consultants in your state or community.

Defining Job Targets

You are now ready to define the targets of your marketing effort. Pursue three or four career options simultaneously. They may be in the same or diverse industries (for example, management in retail, construction, banking, or government) or have similar or entirely different responsibilities (for example, manager employed by large retail chain, proprietor of fashion boutique, trainer in retail, or financial consultant). The intent is to expand your opportunities by selling yourself to several different markets simultaneously. At the same time, you will be capitalizing on your personal, transferable, or professional strengths.

If you have substantial experience in a particular field and wish to remain in it, concentrate your efforts there. Define second and third targets by considering a different type or size of organization or a new geographic location. Different resumes and cover letters are required for each target.

Employers want

people with

specific skills.

All targets must relate to both your immediate and long-range objectives as well as to past accomplishments, needs, and interests. Demonstrate your probable future success by matching accomplishments that best relate to a prospective employer's needs. But be careful not to sell yourself as a generalist. Employers want people with specific skills.

Clearly, to succeed, you must define each target as specifically as possible. Decide on the size and type of company, the geographical region, title, and desired job description. Finally, determine which targets are your first, second, and third choices.

Establishing Information Sources

Throughout the search, you will need substantial information about prospective employers. Many extensive business information sources are available in local libraries and most librarians are very helpful. General directories which contain listings and descriptions of organizations include *Rich's Guide*, *Million Dollar Directory*, *Ward's Business Directory*, and *Moody's Manual*. Magazines and newspapers which will keep you updated on the changing business scene include *The Wall Street Journal*, *Fortune*, *U.S. News and World Report*, *Business Week*, and *Money*. In addition to trade periodicals and professional association publications, check out the local chamber of commerce directory of industrial and business firms, industrial directories published by government departments, and the *Yellow Pages* of your telephone directory.

In addition to these sources, try networking. Keep abreast of new developments and add to your list of colleagues and acquaintances by joining professional, trade, or civic groups and attending professional meetings or workshops. Networking knows no boundaries. Horizontally and vertically, it reaches into all ranks of business. A key to its success is the fact that people like to do business with individuals they know. Networkers tend to nurture each other because they can select associates without guesswork.

Preparing Your Resume

Prepare a resume using one of the many guides available at libraries and bookstores. Consider your resume as a sales tool. Write it in positive language and emphasize your accomplishments. Most of all, phrase it carefully to satisfy the needs of each job target.

Selecting and cultivating references will require care. You want to maintain close contact with these people throughout your campaign. Select business or professional people who have known you well in one or more of your most recent positions and who will talk positively about your abilities. If possible, choose individuals in positions (of equal or superior levels of responsibility) that relate closely to the kind of job you are seeking. If possible, have at least one reference whose position is above or similar to that of the probable caller.

Marketing Yourself

Now that you have done everything possible to make the risk of changing jobs manageable, move into action. Don't just passively answer help-wanted advertisements or send out resumes. Take charge. Once you act, worry and confusion will disappear. Be creative, show initiative, and be positive.

The fear of rejection can be a major obstacle. This can best be overcome by conducting a thorough job search and uncovering several opportunities. Obviously, some will neither want nor need your "product"—the talent and experience pool that you possess. Remember, you want only one job and the market is huge. Regardless of prevailing economic conditions, good positions are always available.

Starting off the right way is crucial. The impressions you make on possible employers in the first few minutes will make or break the sale. To be successful, you will need to develop a positive image—a neat, appropriate appearance and a self-assured demeanor. Ensure that your written and verbal communications are positive, direct, and to the point. Act comfortable with your accomplishments and confident about your future. The key is to stick with it. If you miss one job, tell yourself that a better one exists and you are going to get it. Be confident, persistent, and have faith.

You can develop greater confidence. Start by saying aloud, "I am an intelligent, confident, wonderful person with many skills to offer." Say it regularly, with conviction. Confidence (in your eyes, your words, your gestures, your very being) transmits directly to the people with whom you come in contact. You reflect your thoughts. So if you don't like who you are, change your belief about yourself. Having faith in yourself and your abilities is closely related to confidence. Faith means believing deeply in yourself and in your ability to attain the position that you believe is right for you.

Identifying Job Opportunities and Contacting Employers

You are now ready to begin making initial contact with the job market. Throughout your campaign, the objective is to secure the maximum number of interviews with potentially interested employers. You need to make as many contacts as your information and time will permit.

Every telephone or meeting contact requires a confirming letter. A polite, pleasant, unexpected reminder that you appreciate their assistance and consideration will encourage the recipient to remember you.

Networking is the most recommended way to get a new job.

Networking

Networking is the most recommended way to get a new job. It is essential because it can dramatically increase your contacts and your chances for finding out about unadvertised jobs.

Networking involves establishing and using contacts to assist in your job search by providing useful information. This can include information such as positions available, companies in a hiring mode, or names of other people who can provide similar information. Networking within a specific industry in which you have experience or interests and networking efforts directed to influential people are particularly important.

The greater the number of people in your network, the greater your access to other groups as well as job opportunities. Contacts may include former employers, suppliers, business or professional associates, religious leaders, alumni, insurance agents, bankers, merchants, friends, doctors, relatives, teachers, trade association officers, attorneys, clients or customers, insurance brokers, and members of various civic groups. You can expand your network by dining in restaurants patronized by those in your field or attending seminars, parties, and business meetings. Taking an active role in community affairs, politics, and service clubs, and speaking at seminars and trade associations are other methods of expanding your network. Many professional, alumni, and trade organizations act as intermediaries between job seekers and employers. Professional groups also fund and manage business magazines, journals, newsletters, membership lists, industry directories, trade show catalogues, and other publications. *The Encyclopedia of Associations* is a source for the names and addresses of thousands of these organizations.

When probing someone you don't know well for information, ask broad questions about the industry. In general, such inquiries are less apt to make the person wonder whether you are "fishing" for a position right then and there. Some appropriate questions include: "What are some important long-term trends affecting your industry?"; "What skills and expertise are companies apt to be looking for in new people?"; and "What are some good sources of additional information?"

When your contact is interested enough to concentrate on your career needs, a different set of questions is appropriate. These include: "From what you know of my career, what would you say is the next logical step?"; "Do my qualifications contain any gaps that I should expand on?"; and "Do you know anyone who may be interested in seeing me?"

Because there are many common errors that people make while networking, it is worthwhile to remember the following points:

❖ *Do your homework and be prepared.* Know what you want to say and practice it first. Decide what strengths or achievements you want to stress.

❖ *Talk with people wherever you go.* Religious meetings, professional association meetings, and casual get-togethers are some good examples. Let people know that you are looking for a new opportunity.

❖ *Recognize that networking is part of the "job" of looking for a job.* List the people you might want to see and find a way to get someone to help you to them.

❖ *Remember to keep your interviews brief.* Ask for 10 minute appointments.

❖ *Try to leave every meeting with several new names.* Of course, always remember the names of secretaries.

❖ *Send a handwritten thank-you note after each interview.*

❖ *Exchange business cards with those you meet.* Keep a file of business cards. Follow every lead.

Answering Help-Wanted Advertisements

Help-wanted advertisements are a good source of potential job opportunities, but because of the extent of their use and the volume of replies to them, you must respond to many advertisements to generate any responses. Answer all enticing prospects, even those that are a month old or more, until you accept a new position. Your cover letter should be accomplishment-oriented responding directly to the qualifications stated in the advertisement. Outline your accomplishments in the opening sentence, then go on to explain the reason for writing, referring to the advertisement, and further illuminating your abilities. In the final paragraph, request an interview. If the company name is known, state that you will phone within 10 days. This will ensure that your letter is reviewed and allow you to gather useful information about the job, plan your approach, and assess your chances. Calling will also demonstrate your interest and assertiveness. Begin by introducing yourself and explaining that you want to ensure the letter was received. Ask how many candidates will be interviewed and how and when they will be chosen. Again, request an interview.

Using the Mail Campaign

A direct-mail marketing campaign can be very effective if you can identify the hiring managers of the organizations you contact. This direct contact with executives in a large number of firms may uncover opportunities that are not, and never will be, advertised. The resulting interviews may convince a company to create a new position just to get you into the organization. When a well-qualified candidate appears, most companies would prefer hiring him or her to the expense and time involved in searching for and interviewing applicants. Your job is to find these companies.

The most important task in this type of campaign is to have your letter read by interested personnel who also have the authority to hire. Be sure to match the organization to your job target as closely as possible. Include as many large companies as you can but don't neglect medium-sized or smaller organizations. That right position could be anywhere.

The recipient of your letter should be the individual to whom you would report if hired. The next best choice is the person to whom that individual reports. Organize and word each letter to address the recipient's probable interests. Begin with the single accomplishment most indicative of your competence in that job. The second paragraph will indicate why you are writing and should be a bridge between your opening statement and the remainder of the letter. Show how you might respond to one of the reader's needs or how you could help to solve a problem he or she might have. Introduce a listing of your accomplishments, itemizing four or five that best relate to the target. Organize the following (third) paragraph to outline biographical information. Use the final paragraph to request an interview and indicate whether you expect to be contacted by the company or whether you plan to phone. For particularly interesting companies, you will want to take the initiative.

Most responses will be polite refusals. Don't be discouraged by the volume of rejections. They are normal. Some letters will be positive, either suggesting you call for an interview or asking for additional information. Again, respond promptly and positively. Sooner or later, you'll get an acceptance letter.

Cruising the Information Superhighway

Cruising the information superhighway is the new way to find a job. Currently, this method is primarily used by employers and recruiters in technology-related companies. Such recruiting enables employers to reach large numbers of candidates relatively cheaply. It also reduces the time required to fill positions because candidates can send their resumes with a simple keystroke and employers can respond before the competition has time.

Online positions can be accessed by anyone with a computer and modem—items possessed by a growing number of people throughout the country. The Internet offers several ways to help job seekers find jobs. World Wide Web (WWW) offers pages of job listings, resume banks, and company-sponsored job databases. Some of these services are free; others charge a fee. Job postings—the online equivalent of classified ads—are a good place to start. The most popular places to find these job postings are through Usenet newsgroups.

Newsgroups are free discussion forums that are open to anyone. You can access a newsgroup through a newsgroup reader which also gives you the ability to post (send) a message. Most of the online services provide a newsgroup reader and allow you to search for newsgroups which interest you.

It is difficult to estimate the exact number of newsgroups because the numbers change daily, but it easily exceeds 10,000. This means that a newsgroup exists for almost any interest, from archeology to zoology. But many newsgroups deal with jobs—either actual listings of jobs, discussions on job search techniques, jobs in particular professions, jobs in a specific city or region, and contracts and resume listings. For example, one newsgroup in San Francisco is a discussion group on jobs for users in the Bay Area. Here, Bay Area companies can post job listings and contract openings. Job seekers eager to advertise their availability can post an online version of their resume. Such newsgroups have equivalents regionally and nationally.

Many job seekers report success with online job searches, especially if they are in a computer-related field. A number enjoy searching for a job online. They feel as if they can actually control their careers by seeing what skills are in demand and what new opportunities are emerging. On the other hand, because listings can be numerous, the process of scanning through them to find employment opportunities listed directly by employers may be frustrating to some job seekers. Nevertheless, for those who do find success on the Internet, the results can be impressive. By adding online search to your job seeking strategies, that ideal position may be closer than you think—maybe even just a few strokes away.

Identifying Specific Companies

Many of the suggestions in the next three paragraphs are suitable only for bold people who are stimulated by difficult challenges. Others may find these suggestions inconsistent with their nature.

Of all the organizations you target, one or two will be highly desirable prospective employers. Make these separate targets. First, identify why you want to work for these organizations, then gather more information to develop your case for employment.

To pursue an individual organization or opportunity, you will need two types of information. The first is a general, but complete, history and description of the firm, including the department, division, or subsidiary of interest. The second is information required to develop a thorough, convincing case for your employment. Gather as much information as possible. When this is complete, develop a case for your employment. Concentrate on the contribution you can make. Demonstrate how hiring you will contribute to the company's performance or success. Finally, try to emphasize past accomplishments to show why you are the best-suited person to fulfill this need.

The next step is to contact the person who has direct responsibility for the functions you intend to perform. You will want to convince this person to hire you. Even though the objective may be clear, the purpose of this meeting is to exchange information. Concentrate on the organization's needs, how to answer them, and the expected results. The intent is to stimulate your contact's curiosity. Bring a list of questions, be alert and sensitive to the other person's responses, and write a follow-up letter. Thank your contact for his or her interest, then, in subsequent interviews, continue to expand the case that you are the best candidate to produce the projected results. Gradually become more assertive until you receive a job offer or, at an appropriate time, can request employment and initiate negotiations yourself. Continue to pursue your interest until you have reached a successful conclusion or investigated every possible approach. Only then, give up the search.

Extending Your Network

What other job search avenues should be explored? Try executive recruiting firms, college placement offices, trade and professional associations, accounting firms, and chambers of commerce. Executive recruiters, who conduct employee searches at a company's expense, are only too glad to steal qualified people from competitors or to hear from you. Although most are looking for specialized talent, all have high-level contacts with many organizations. If you are conducting a national search for a position at the level of district manager, general manager, or higher with a company employing more than 500 people, register with executive recruiters. Refer to your phone book or consult the American Management Association for guidance. For a campaign covering a large geographical area, investigate the placement office at your alma mater. For a local campaign, register with all nearby universities and colleges. Trade and professional associations may also provide placement services. Investigate them all.

Being Effective in Interviews

Now that a wide audience of potential employers is aware of you, expect interested ones to begin phoning. The calls will be of three types: a simple request for an interview, a request for additional information, or a conversation that can range from several questions to a complete interview. Whatever the purpose, be sure to get the caller's complete and correct name and title. Be prepared to discuss your background and experience, to state the contribution you expect to make, and to explain why you are making a change. By concentrating on the most important aspects of the job and relating your accomplishments to the problems requiring immediate attention, you will be stimulating the caller's interest and preparing for the subsequent interview. If, by the end of the conversation, the caller has not suggested an interview, you should do so. If the caller does not wish to set up an interview until a later date, indicate that you will follow up the conversation with another call to arrange an interview time.

Succeeding in the Initial Interview

The initial interview usually determines if you receive a job offer.

The initial interview usually determines if you receive a job offer. Whether you are interviewed by one person or a selection board, this may be the only opportunity to sell yourself to the prospective employer. It may also be your only opportunity to gather sufficient information to properly evaluate an offer. The key to a successful interview is preparation. Research the company. Prepare questions to ask and review those that may be asked of you. Then plan how to manage and structure the interview to your advantage.

The first objective of any interview is to convince an employer that you can make a contribution and are the best candidate for the position. And because both you and the organization are selling and evaluating, you will want to use the interview to gather enough information about the company and its members to evaluate the job in relation to your own abilities, objectives, and other personal characteristics.

Regardless of what might be appropriate dress once you are on the job, you will also want to attend an interview wearing conservative attire. Practice good posture. Look the interviewer in the eye as you negotiate the choppy waters of interviewing etiquette. And remember to take along a note pad, copies of your resume, a written list of questions, and an outline of the information you have gathered about the organization, including any correspondence. Once in the interview, guide the questions and discussion in a manner that satisfies your objectives. Be alert and sensitive to the reactions and feelings of the interviewer. Avoid persisting with questions he or she cannot answer or seems to find disconcerting. If you feel unsure, practice with a friend first.

Most questions you will be asked will concern the relationship between your personal characteristics and accomplishments and the prospective position. You will be asked to describe yourself, your background, likes and dislikes, and motivation. If you consider a question too personal, say so. Otherwise, try to be as open and honest as possible.

Typical Interview Questions

Tell me about yourself.

What are some of your most significant accomplishments?

Were there any unusual difficulties you had to overcome?

What did you particularly like about the last job you had? What did you like least? Why are you leaving your position?

How did you go about making important decisions? What types of decisions are easiest for you to make? What kinds of decisions are most difficult?

How do you think your subordinates would describe you as a delegator? Why do you think you are an effective supervisor?

Describe one or two innovations of which you are particularly proud.

What are your greatest strengths?
Weaknesses?

Can you work under pressure?

Why aren't you earning more money at
this stage of your career?

Do you think you are overqualified for this
position?

How do you feel about reporting to a younger person?

Where do you see yourself five years from now? Ten
years?

Why do you want to work for this company?
How can you make a contribution? What
changes would you make if you came on board?

Why have you had so many jobs?

Why should we hire you?

The questions you ask can be even more important than your
answers to the ones asked of you. By asking the right questions, you demonstrate your knowledge and the contributions
you can make. Your questions can also guide the discussion
into areas where you can comment on accomplishments.
Finally, by asking questions, you will get the information you
need to evaluate the company and the job. Sample questions
are: "What is the first problem that needs the attention of the
person you hire?"; "How has this position been performed in
the past?"; "Why is it vacant now?"; "What is the scope of
the authority I would have?"; and "How would you define
your management philosophy?" Sprinkle these questions
throughout the interview. Intersperse them among the interviewers. But be sure they relate to the company and the
position. Be positive and direct. Once the interview is fin-

ished, you should have sold yourself and now must take the time to evaluate the opportunity.

According to employers, some common errors candidates frequently make during interviews include the following: not asking what qualities the ideal candidate should possess; failing to give specific examples of relevant skills and experience; not sitting still but moving one's foot or fiddling in the chair; not listening to the job description provided by the interviewer, resulting in questions that have already been answered; dressing inappropriately; using jargon or unrelated acronyms; not having a clear career focus; complaining about prior employers; failing to make eye contact; and lacking excitement when discussing the future.

Getting Additional Information

Before you accept any position, get the facts. Going blindly into a job can prove disastrous. Ask tough questions. They could strengthen your position as a knowledgeable and thoughtful employee. Find out what happened to the last person in the job. Why did he or she leave? Why hasn't the company found a candidate from within? The interviewer's reactions are as important as the questions. A defensive, hostile, or evasive response may signal a real problem. Also be aware of your gut reaction to the people and the work environment.

Follow up by meeting prospective peers and top brass. Ask them about their jobs, the company, and its problems. Find out how they spend their time. Discover if there may be problems in working with the immediate supervisor or subordinates. Chemistry between coworkers is a crucial element in any job. If you don't like the people, the duties will be irrelevant. Try to determine the nuances of the decision-making process, the pecking order, the philosophy of the top brass, and whether night or weekend work is expected. If you don't understand how an organization works, you'll be frustrated. For example, do your superiors go by the book or are they entrepreneurs who believe rules are made to be broken? How do they feel about professional women? Many questions need to be asked before the big picture falls into place.

Most important of all is to "know thyself." Many factors are involved in job happiness. If the job requires a move across the country or from suburb to city, to a new industry, or a differen-sized company, make sure you can adapt. Inquire about salary increases, stock options, company benefits, pension plans, vacations, sabbaticals, club memberships, opportunities for promotion, and relocation expenses. Once you and the employer have reached agreement on all aspects of the offer, get it confirmed in writing.

Depending on how far along you are in your job search campaign, the time during which you can appropriately consider an offer will vary from a few days to a month. In most cases, you should limit this time to three weeks. Your objective is only to gain sufficient time to expedite and evaluate additional offers. You can do this by immediately advising other prospective employers of your deadline. Do this only if you are definitely interested in the first offer. If the other organization is not ready to make a decision, you may be turned down prematurely.

Making the Decision

How can you decide whether a decision is right for you? Each job offer needs to be thoroughly evaluated, both individually and in comparison to others. Never accept an offer on the spot. Making a commitment is the single most difficult act in risking. It is the moment when you declare your intentions. Even if you have received only one offer, evaluate it carefully. You have three options: to accept, to delay and recontact other prospective employers, or to reject it and return to your job search campaign with new and expanded effort. The best way to reach a decision is to use both your intellect and intuition.

If a decision doesn't feel right, don't force it. The appropriate decision will come forward at the right time through the surfacing of knowledge already stored in your subconscious. This filtering process can help you decide what's important and comfortable. If your intuition is sending you alarm signals, buy time. Extend your deadline. A prospective employer will usually wait two or three days while you mull over a job decision. Give yourself time for reflection so that you can better understand what is happening in your life.

Recognizing Pitfalls

Certain traps need to be avoided when you make such important decisions. Any one or combination of these hazards can wreck your career or at least put it in a holding pattern.

Typical Pitfalls

Taking a job you don't enjoy because you want to be employed.

Working for someone you don't respect and admire.

Producing or selling goods or services you don't believe in.

Failing to follow a course of continuous education.

Failing to be loyal to your organization.

Relying on long experience with one company for security.

Refusing to consider out-of-town openings when you change jobs.

Accepting a promotion to a job you don't find attractive just for money or prestige.

Failing to take a cut in salary when it could further your career.

Getting too much unsalable experience—sticking to a specialized field without evaluating whether jobs in this area are in demand.

Resigning in a snit.

Rushing into a job without evaluating it carefully.

Taking a job that has poor chemistry.

Staying in a job or taking a job because of security.

Going for It

If your intellectual and emotional preparation are sound, if you have done whatever you can to manage the risk and protect against disaster, and if the decision still feels right, get going. No matter how elaborate the preparation, the next stage always demands a leap into the unknown. In addition to situational unknowns, you will have to face the unknowns deep within yourself. All rational planning leads, if only momentarily, to an act of faith. This moment of free-fall may disrupt your sense of orientation. But because it usually brings with it a heady sense of relief, this minute may also feel like the least risky step in the whole process. One study, in fact showed that skydivers felt less afraid when they were actually about to hurl themselves into space than when they were on the ground deciding whether or not to go up for a jump. You will probably discover the same applies to you.

A dream begins to become a reality only at the moment of action.

A dream begins to become a reality only at the moment of action. A race doesn't begin until one leaves the starting blocks. From that point on, competence, commitment, and determination will decide your future. Decide now that you will succeed and become a Quester. If you want to, choose to, and take the right steps, you will become one. Don't give in to thoughts of failure. Setbacks are just opportunities to learn. They are but detours on the road to your goals.

Confirming your Acceptance

After you have accepted an offer and established a starting date, confirm this acceptance in writing. Also write to each of the other firms that made offers. Thank them for their consideration and advise them that you have accepted another position. This polite follow-up will help should a desirable position become available in the future.

If you have decided to go into business for yourself, you will have much much more to do. You must go through various steps such as writing a proposal, obtaining financing, deciding on your business type and location, finding a lawyer and an accountant, purchasing equipment and supplies, determining marketing techniques, and hiring personnel needed to get a business on its feet. Take your time. You'll want to start it off right.

Resigning from Your Present Job

Before moving to a new position or starting a new business, it will, of course, be necessary to resign from your current job. The starting date of your new job or business should permit sufficient time for an orderly completion or transfer of unfinished tasks. Maintain good relations with your former employer and avoid harming the morale of colleagues. You may require their help in the future.

Stage 7: *Evaluating* Your Decision

The good feelings that result from taking a risk (even if the results don't turn out as hoped) can be incredible. First, there's the gain of seeing yourself as a survivor, as someone who can accomplish something. Mastery, or the sense of accomplishment and achievement that comes from seeing that you can control a difficult situation, is an important gain. When you test yourself by risking, you are forcing yourself to grow by calling on skills, talents, and perceptions that have never been used before.

The urge to risk reflects the need for achievement. Correctly approached, taking risks can enhance that sense of accomplishment so intimately connected with self-confidence. Many people say that even when things didn't work out, they were nevertheless pleased with themselves for venturing, for asserting themselves, for testing their mettle, and for not stagnating.

A second related good feeling comes from learning more about yourself, whether you succeed or fail. The lessons you learn from your setbacks are sometimes the most precious.

Risking gives you an opportunity to explore your needs and values, your coping skills, and your bottom line.

When you've worked hard at making a decision, it's not only satisfying, but necessary, to evaluate it. Doing so can help you learn to become more effective in making future decisions. Ask yourself the following questions:

Do I feel good about making the move? Did I attain the job satisfiers that are most important to me? Are my needs being met? Am I using my skills and abilities? Is my level of job satisfaction, as measured by The Job Satisfaction Questionnaire, any higher?

What other gains did I derive from the move? What did I lose?

What contributed to my success? To my failure?

If I were to do it all over again, what would I do differently? Could I have achieved the same results with less work?

Who was most helpful? How can I strengthen that relationship? Who let me down? Does he or she know?

What pleasant, unexpected surprises did I encounter from my move?

How do feel about the degree of success or failure I have achieved? If my efforts are only partially successful or a complete disaster, can I think of any way this can be turned to my advantage? What did I learn from the experience? Would I do the same thing over again?

How do I feel about myself as a consequence of taking the risk?

Evaluation is a continuous process. Assess yourself, your needs, goals, and job satisfaction periodically to determine if your developing personality fits your position and lifestyle. When you feel your job or some other component of your life needs modifying, make the necessary changes to bring them into harmony with your personality. Nothing remains static. To continue to grow and develop, you must constantly modify who you are. Why wait for a crisis to clear your vision? Don't miss out on the joys of living. Achieve the well-being that comes from living your life to your fullest each and every day.

If after three, six, or twelve months, you find you are not reaching your goals, don't hesitate to seek help. Many people have difficulty translating ideas into action, but with the help of a competent professional, they can accomplish this. Do what you must to complete the task. Accept the possibility that you may have made an error. Mistakes do happen. Learn from them. Next time, you will emerge stronger.

Keep Going

As you grow and develop your potential, the rewards will be

As you grow and develop your potential, the rewards will be enormous.

enormous. Along with the satisfaction that results from using the full range of your abilities comes independence, self-confidence, maturity, purpose, greater flexibility, and the power to affect change. You will become stronger and wiser, but don't stop here. Most important risks merely open the door to greater risks. If you take the right chances, those that encourage growth and fulfillment, you will find that you will want to take additional risks. Each time you gamble, risking becomes a little easier.

There really is no substitute for risk as a way to grow. Knowing that you have honestly faced the painful struggle and accepted the trade-offs and losses involved, yet proceeded in spite of them, is extremely gratifying. To have a satisfying life, you will need to risk again and again

Life is a challenge,
meet it.

Life is an opportunity,
take it.

Life is an adventure,
dare it.

until you have created the best possible life for yourself, a life where you feel comfortable being yourself, without apology or pretense. A life where you can have choices in an uncertain job market.

About the Author

Dr. Carole Kanchier is a psychologist, counselor, instructor, trainer, researcher, and author with more than 20 years of experience in the fields of career, adult, and transpersonal psychology; education; and management for consulting. Uniquely qualified to write *Dare to Change Your Job and Your Life*, Carole has researched (voluntarily and involuntarily) career transition and has personally experienced several job and locale changes. She regularly counsels individuals experienc-
ing transition; writes about transitions for business, lay, and professional journals; and conducts workshops on transition and empowerment topics.

As principal of Questers, Carole provides counseling and consulting services to individuals and organiza-
tions. She has taught at numerous North American colleges and universities including the University of Calgary, the University of Alberta, and the University of California, Santa Cruz and Berke-
ley. Dr. Kanchier has chaired the Career Change and Retire-
ment Committee, National Career Development Association; serves on the executive board, LifePlan Center in San Francisco; and is an adult education faculty member at the Univer-
sity of California, Santa Cruz.

What Others Are Saying about *Dare to Change Your Job and Your Life*

"*Dare to Change* . . . is chock-full of information, suggestions, guidelines, and case histories that will help you control your own life and career."
—S. Norman Feingold, Ed.D., President, National Career and Counseling Services, Washington, D.C.

"*Dare to Change* . . . a change from the typical, popular career books . . . . It offers a holistic approach to contemporary career development . . . . It dares you to take a look at your life to see if it's as gratifying as it can be."
—Beverly Carlozzi, *New York Personnel Management Association, Inc., Bulletin*

"*Dare to Change* . . . provides some excellent examples of adult decision making . . . also provides concrete evidence that adulthood is not a plateau."
—Helen M. Madill, Ph.D., *Canadian Journal of Occupational Therapy*

"*Dare to Change* . . . a 'must' read if you are at a career crossroad or contemplating serious changes in your business or personal life."
—Les Hewitt, President, Achievers of Canada

"*Dare to Change* . . . an exception to career books . . . offers unique ways to both view career development and make applications to career counseling."
—Thomas Bachhuber, Ph.D., Editor, *Career Waves*

"*Dare to Change* . . . provides numerous examples of what can be done to develop interesting and challenging careers . . . lots of good new ideas by a skilled career writer."
—Bob Calvert, Editor, *Career Opportunities News*

More Good Books from JIST Works, Inc.

The Very Quick Job Search
Get a Better Job in Less Time

By J. Michael Farr

The techniques in this book are proven to cut your job search time in half! It was selected as one of the top job search books ever and a "must have" by career counselors. Features a thorough career planning section, information on hundreds of jobs, and current labor market trends you need to know.

ISBN 1-56370-181-2

$14.95

Order Code J1812

The Quick Resume & Cover Letter Book
Write and Use an Effective Resume in Only One Day

By J. Michael Farr

This books looks great, is very easy to use, and provides solid advice on both creating and more importantly, *using* a resume in an effective job search. With many worksheets and examples, its extensive content and many sample resumes make it a good reference book.

ISBN 1-56370-141-3

$9.95

Order Code RCLQG

The Quick Interview & Salary Negotiation Book
Dramatically Improve Your Interviewing Skills in Just a Few Hours!

By J. Michael Farr

Employer surveys indicate that more than 80 percent of applicants do not present themselves well in interviews. This book explains how to dramatically improve interview skills within a few hours. It includes special sections on advanced interviewing and career planning advice.

ISBN 1-56370-162-6

$12.95

Order Code J1626

*Look for these and other fine books from JIST Works at your full-service bookstore,
or contact us for additional information.*

More Good Books from JIST Works, Inc.

Helping Your Child Choose a Career

By Luther B. Otto, Ph.D.

This valuable book shows parents how to help their children select and begin successful careers. The author presents essential and realistic information in a friendly and easy-to-read style. He helps parents understand and plan how to assist their teenagers in the career selection process.

ISBN 1-56370-184-7

$14.95

Order Code J1847

Career Satisfaction & Success
How to Know and Manage Your Strengths

By Bernard Haldane, Ph.D.

Bernard Haldane founded a chain of executive search firms with offices throughout the country and is regarded as one of the founders of the modern career counseling movement. This major revision presents advice to achieve your full potential in your career and your life.

ISBN 1-56370-200-2

$14.95

Order Code J2002

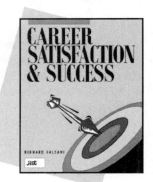

The PIE Method for Career Success
A Unique Way to Find Your Ideal Job

By Daniel Porot

Porot's method combines elements of Pleasure, Information, and Employment into a uniquely useful and motivating career planning and job search approach. The previous edition of this book sold more than 90,000 copies and this new revision presents Porot's new concepts in a graphic and memorable way.

ISBN 1-56370-182-0

$14.95

Order Code J1820

Look for these and other fine books from JIST Works at your full-service bookstore,
or contact us for additional information.

More Good Books from JIST Works, Inc.

Ready, Set, Organize!
Get Your Stuff Together

By Pipi Campbell Peterson

Readers are shown how to use eight simple time management steps and master the organizational skills needed to manage all aspects of their lives. A progress bar in each chapter makes it easy to monitor progress. Also includes a daily planner and section for recording personal and family information.

ISBN 1-57112-072-6

$12.95

Order Code P0726

Franchise Opportunities Handbook, 23rd Edition
A Complete Guide for People Who Want to Start Their Own Business

By United States Department of Commerce and LaVerne Ludden Ed.D.

This book can help readers decide whether franchising is a feasible career path for them. This handbook details information on more than 1,500 franchise opportunities and provides information on basic business planning, how to evaluate and select a franchise, and what franchising is all about.

ISBN 1-57112-073-4

$16.95

Order Code P0734

We've Got to Start Meeting Like This!
A Guide to Successful Business Meeting Management

By Roger K. Mosvick and Robert B. Nelson

This dynamic book demonstrates how to have fewer meetings and get better results. It explains how meeting management practices and attitudes have changed and which are the most appropriate and effective meeting formats to obtain timely, high-quality group decisions.

ISBN 1-57112-069-6

$14.95

Order Code P0696

Look for these and other fine books from JIST Works at your full-service bookstore, or contact us for additional information.